LEADERSHIP AND THE RISE OF GREAT POWERS

The Princeton-China Series

Daniel A. Bell, series editor

The Princeton-China Series aims to publish the works of contemporary Chinese scholars in the humanities, social sciences, and related fields. The goal is to bring the work of these important thinkers to a wider audience, foster an understanding of China on its own terms, and create new opportunities for cultural cross-pollination.

The Constitution of Ancient China by Su Li, edited by Zhang Yongle and Daniel A. Bell, translated by Edmund Ryden

Traditional Chinese Architecture by Fu Xinian, edited by Nancy Steinhardt, translated by Alexandra Harrer

Confucian Perfectionism: A Political Philosophy for Modern Times by Joseph Chan

A Confucian Constitutional Order: How China's Ancient Past Can Shape Its Political Future by Jiang Qing, edited by Daniel A. Bell and Ruiping Fan, translated by Edmund Ryden

Ancient Chinese Thought, Modern Chinese Power by Yan Xuetong, edited by Daniel A. Bell and Sun Zhe, translated by Edmund Ryden

Leadership and the Rise of Great Powers

Yan Xuetong

PRINCETON UNIVERSITY PRESS

PRINCETON AND OXFORD

Published by Princeton University Press
41 William Street, Princeton, New Jersey 08540
6 Oxford Street, Woodstock, Oxfordshire OX20 1TR

press.princeton.edu

Library of Congress Control Number: 2018958065
ISBN 9780691190082

British Library Cataloging-in-Publication Data is available

Editorial: Eric Crahan and Pamela Weidman
Production Editorial: Mark Bellis
Jacket Design: Carmina Alvarez
Production: Jacqueline Poirier
Publicity: Tayler Lord and Caroline Priday
Copyeditor: Kathleen Kageff

The research conducted for this book was funded by the Chinese Fund
for Humanities and Social Sciences

This book has been composed in Adobe Text Pro and Gotham

Printed on acid-free paper. ∞

Printed in the United States of America

10 9 8 7 6 5 4 3 2 1

To my wife, Peizhi

CONTENTS

List of Tables and Figures   xi

Preface   xiii

1   Morality, Power, and Authority   1

The Role of Morality in Realism Theory   3

Levels and Components of Morality   7

Differences between Power, Capability, and Authority   11

Influence of Morality and Strategic Credibility   19

Summary   23

2   Leadership and Strategic Preferences   25

The Role and Types of Leadership   26

Leaderships of a Rising State and Strategic Preferences   33

Strategic Credibility and International Leadership   40

The Principle of Humane Authority   48

Summary   51

3   Corollaries of International Change   54

State Leadership and Change of Power Configuration   55

State Capability, Leadership, and Strategy Preference   61

International Leadership and Norm Change   67

Changes in International Order and Systems   71

Summary   78

4   Power Redistribution and World Center   81

Leadership and Bipolarization   82

Bipolar Configuration Not Equal to Cold War   87

Conditions for Forming a World Center   93

Summary   102

5   Leadership and International Norms   104

Early Studies of Leadership and Norm Change   105

Types of Leadership and Types of Norms   107

Change in the Type of International Norms   116

Summary   123

6   International Mainstream Values   126

Value Challenge and Competition   127

Devaluation of Strategic Credibility   136

Beyond Liberalism   145

Summary   153

7   Transformation of the International System   155

Component Change versus System Change   156

Conditions for System Transformation   162

Political Leadership and System Transformation   165

Summary   171

8   Historical Cases of System Transformation   173

Ancient Chinese Cases   174

Cases in Modern History   181

Summary   188

9 Conclusion   190

Theory Summarization   190

A New Bipolar World   197

Appendix: Ancient Chinese Figures   207

Notes   215

Selected Bibliography   241

Index   253

TABLES AND FIGURES

Tables

2.1 Types of State Leadership   30

2.2 Types of International Leadership   43

5.1 Types of International Norms   109

7.1 The Components of Interstate Systems
Academically Defined   159

Figures

3.1 Joint impacts of capability and leadership on
strategy preferences   62

3.2 Components of international order and
international system   76

3.3 Types of rising states' leadership and changes in
international systems   78

4.1 GDP of China and the United States 2005–16 (US$)   83

5.1 Types of international leadership and formation of
international norms   111

5.2 Mechanisms through which states change
international norms   113

7.1 New types of international leadership and
transformations of international systems   167

PREFACE

This book originates in research, carried out in 2005, into ancient Chinese thought on interstate relations. In the years since then, this research has produced various papers and books that include *Ancient Chinese Thought, Modern Chinese Power*. Based on previous achievements, *Leadership and the Rise of Great Powers* takes the big step of formulating a systematic theory explaining the mechanism for a rising state to replace the leadership of a dominant state in an independent international system, including both the modern global system and geographically separated ancient interstate systems.

There are abundant works on the transition of international power that generally ascribe such transition either to a combination of various elements or to the decline of the dominant state.[1] None, however, can explain why a given rising state is able to perform better than the dominant state in related domains, or why other rising states cannot match its achievements during the same historical epoch. The dramatic decline of America's soft power in 2017 during Donald Trump's first six months in office underscored the limits of existing theories of international relations.

China's rise and America's relative decline after the financial crisis of 2008 engendered an academic puzzle for students of international relations; namely, why was China successful in reducing its disparity in capability with the United States during the early twenty-first century? Theoretically, China should not have been able to do so without matching or surpassing the United States in some way. Institutionalist theories attribute modernization, industrialization, or rapid growth in national capability to either government institutions or political systems. According to these theories, China's absence of elective democracy and strict separation of institutional power suggest that both the Chinese government and its political system are backward, and thereby inferior to the American system characterized by such features. In light of institutionalism's inadequate explanation for recent trends, therefore, this book instead tries to crack the puzzle by exploring the significance of varying types of political leadership.

Borrowing ideas from ancient Chinese philosophies, this book attributes international power transition to the greater capability to reform on the part of the leadership of a rising state than that of the dominant state. At the domestic level, national leaderships are categorized as inactive, conservative, proactive, or aggressive, while international leaderships are grouped under the headings of humane authority, hegemony, anemocracy, or tyranny. The advantage of treating the type of political leadership as an independent variable is that we can use the same variable to explain the decline of the dominant state, the success of a given rising state, and the failure of other rising states during the same historical period. National leadership is a key factor in shaping a country's foreign policies, political principles, official ideologies, and political institutions, while different types of leaderships have corresponding attitudes toward reform and strategic preferences. Therefore, the different leadership types of the dominant state and of rising states could reshape the international configuration, order, norms, world center, or even the international system as a whole.

The structure of this book is as follows: Chapter 1 discusses the definitions of major concepts used to establish the theory of moral realism. Chapter 2 categorizes political leadership as respectively domestic and international leadership and meanwhile explores the connections between types of leadership and strategic preferences. Based on realist assumptions, chapter 3 deduces four corollaries from the changes in foreign strategies, in international configuration, in international norms, and in the world order, as well as their impacts on international systems. Chapter 4 focuses on changes in international configuration and shifts of the world center. Chapter

5 discusses the relationship between the type of international leadership and type of norm, and also the approaches through which leading powers establish or reform international norms. Chapter 6 takes up the issue of challenges to liberalism and the possible formation of new international mainstream values. Chapter 7 addresses the transformation of the international system by distinguishing component changes from the system change. Chapter 8 uses both ancient interstate history and modern international history to illustrate the relationship between changes in the leadership of dominant states and transformations of the international system. The conclusion presented in chapter 9 gives a bird's-eye view of the logics of the theory constructed in this book.

I am indebted to many individuals for their contributions to this book. Jin, my daughter, shared with me her knowledge of biology and psychology, so precluding any lay misunderstanding of the differences between inherited and socialized human behaviors. She also provided language help in writing the first draft. Dr. Zhao Yujia undertook meticulous proofreading of the manuscript. Her hard work made possible its submission on schedule to Princeton University Press. I am deeply appreciative of Pamela Lord's help in copyediting the entire manuscript and so enhancing its fluency. Professor Kai He gave me his generous help on linguistic matters. I am grateful also to the two anonymous Princeton University Press reviewers for their comments and suggestions on developing the moral realist theory and their helpful advice during the book's final revisions. I also owe thanks to James Anthony, one of my international students, for his help improving some paragraphs. I also thank Eric Crahan, my editor at Princeton University Press, and Kathleen Kageff, my copy editor.

My warm thanks also to Zhang Feng, Sun Xuefeng, Zhou Fangyin, Xu Jin, Yang Qianru, Liu Feng, Gao Cheng, Song Wei, Zhao Kejin, Xing Yue, Qi Haixia, Ma Yanbing, Nie Wenjun, Cao Wei, Yin Jiwu, Yang Yuan, Chen Yudan, Chen Zheng, and Wang Peng. All offered their comments on this research, either privately or at the seminar on December 20, 2015. My students at Tsinghua University provided a steady source of feedback as the book evolved. From 2011 to 2017, I had the luxury of teaching a course that was based on the research carried out for this project, so allowing me to try out my ideas before an attentive and challenging audience. I would like also to express both my gratitude and my apologies to people I have failed to mention by name owing to lapses of memory.

My greatest debt of gratitude is to my wife, Peizhi, to whom this book is dedicated. Her unwavering support for my academic career over the last thirty-six years remains constant. She not only takes care of all the housework but also shares with me her thinking about my writing. Her timely critiques have enabled me to retract many flawed ideas.

Finally, my thanks to the Chinese Fund for Humanities and Social Sciences for its financial support for this book.

Yan Xuetong
Tsinghua
May 2018

1

Morality, Power, and Authority

为政以德, 譬如北辰, 居其所而众星共之。
(He who exercises governance through virtue
will be like the North Star keeping its position
surrounded other stars.)

CONFUCIUS

The shift of the world center is an enduring topic in the theoretical study of international relations (IR). Spain, Portugal, the Netherlands, France, the United Kingdom, and the United States were successively the world's dominant states after the formation of a global system of states in the sixteenth century. Along with the changes of dominant state came occasional shifts of the world power center from one region to another. Scholars of IR have long sought to trace and explain how various great powers have risen and fallen relative to one another over the past five centuries.

There have been many explanations for the rise and fall of leading powers. The most well-known research on this issue is arguably that of Paul Kennedy, who attributes the decline of a hegemon to imperial overstretch, which in turn leads to a shift of the world center. Imperial overstretch occurred when the global obligations as defined by policy makers far exceeded the hegemon's defensive capability.[1] Robert Gilpin, on the other hand, cites economic inadequacy as the cause of hegemonic decline. That is to say, the economic costs of maintaining a dominant power's international status quo outstripped its financial capability.[2] However, Richard Ned Lebow has raised an altogether different explanation, ascribing the decline of hegemonic powers to their hubris, contending that "behavior at odds with the accepted morality of the age undermines the standing, influence and even the hegemony of great powers."[3]

Like the above studies, most theoretical research has focused on answering one question, "Why does a hegemon decline?," while taking little account of the other component of the issue, "How does another state rise?" It seems logical to assert that for the global center to shift, not only must the existing hegemon fall, but a new global power must rise. Yet attempts to answer this question wholly ignore the reasons for such a rise and its mechanism. Thus, the focus of this book is on offering explanations for the rising state component of the conundrum from the perspective of moral realism.[4] This book wishes to raise a potential mechanism through which a rising state is able to replace the dominant state in a given interstate system. The theory created in this book suggests that when a rising state's political leadership surpasses that of the dominant state, the power disparity between the two states reverses, rendering the rising state the new dominant state. In other words, when the rising state's leadership is more capable and efficient than that of the dominant state and that of other contemporary major states, international influence is redistributed in a way that allows the rising state to eclipse the dominant state. To systematically explore the relationship between political leadership and redistribution of international power, the first chapter will clarify the concepts of morality, power, capability, and authority, because these are the resources of political leadership. Based on the distinctions between these concepts, we will analyze the influence of morality on power, capability, and authority.

THE ROLE OF MORALITY IN REALISM THEORY

As Jannika Brostrom has observed, each IR school responds differently to the task of pinpointing where morality belongs in theory building. Constructivists generally understand morality as part of the normative agenda of a political entity that is often linked to identity and ideas. Thus, they suggest that norms and interests are mutually constitutive as well as intersubjective. Liberalist IR scholars characterize moral forces as the ends in themselves and require a deontological methodology to explain policy learning and epistemic community building. The English school is divided on this issue between solidarists and pluralists. Although both take a normative approach to the study of morality, they have different views as to the function of norms. Solidarists regard the norm as an independent variable, while pluralists deem it the product of an anarchical system.[5] Different from previous schools, realism approaches morality from an instrumental perspective. This standpoint, however, is often misunderstood.

Misunderstandings of IR Realism

Since Hans J. Morgenthau modernized the classical realist theory of international relations, many scholars have mistakenly assumed that realism denies any moral influence on the conduct of states. For example, Kenneth W. Thompson and W. David Clinton observed, "It has proved particularly thorny in the realist tradition, not least because that tradition has so often been misunderstood as denying any connection between moral principles and the practical responsibilities of statecraft. At no realist has the charge been leveled more often than Morgenthau."[6] However, as Brostrom has noted, the classical realist works of Hans Morgenthau, Reinhold Niebuhr, and George Kennan all stress the relationship between morality and power.[7] After a close scrutiny of classical realist writings, Lebow argues that " 'classical' realism, as presented by Thucydides, Carl Von Clausewitz and Hans J. Morgenthau, was very much concerned with questions of justice."[8]

Here we review Morgenthau's *Politics among Nations: The Struggle for Power and Peace* to see how he discusses the function and effect of morality in international affairs. He says, "A discussion of international morality must guard against the two extremes of either overrating the influence of ethics upon international politics or underestimating it by denying that statesmen and diplomats are moved by anything but considerations of material power."[9] Among his six principles of political realism, principles 4 and 5 are about morality. The fourth principle demonstrates that political realism admits the great importance of moral political actions by asserting, "Realism maintains that universal moral principles cannot be applied to the actions of states in their abstract universal formulation, but that they must be filtered through the concrete circumstances of time and place. The individual may say for himself: '*Fiat justitia, pereat mundus* (Let justice be done, even if the world perish),' but the state has no right to say so in the name of those who are in its care."[10] The fifth principle reiterates this point, stating that "political realism refuses to identify the moral aspirations of a particular nation with the moral laws that govern the universe."[11]

It is clear from the above citation that classical realism neither denies the role of morality nor ignores its effect on state capability or power. What scholars must avoid is conflating the morality of a single nation with international morality. Morgenthau opposed the waging of war based on a state's particular moral values. Nor did he support attempts to export political values to the world as a whole through the vehicle of war. It was from that perspective that he opposed America's initiation of war for the sake of human rights.[12] This idea has a strong impact on my theory, which defines the morality of political leadership at the universal level rather than at the national level.

To make matters worse, the doctrine of realism is misunderstood not only by idealists, legalists, moralists, liberalists, and constructivists, but also by certain realist theorists. For the sake of developing a scientific rather than a normative theory, Kenneth Waltz expunged morality from his theory in *Theory of International Politics*. After his reformulation of realism, many realists followed suit in constructing

IR theories. John Mearsheimer, a leading offensive realist scholar, argues against the incorporation of morality into theoretical models, saying, "It should be emphasized that many realists have strong moral preferences and are driven by deep moral convictions. Realism is not a normative theory, however, and it provides no criteria for moral judgment. Instead, realism merely seeks to explain how the world works."[13] During our dialogue in 2013 he insisted, "It is critically important that a real realist resists the seductions of any unrealistic consciences and never over-expand into other unfamiliar realms."[14] However, not all realist theorists agree to the expulsion of morality from realist theory. For example, Edward Hallett Carr, an early classical IR realist, said, "If, however, it is utopian to ignore the element of power, it is an unreal kind of realism which ignores the element of morality in any world order."[15] This sentiment is echoed by Mark R. Amstutz, who, after careful study of realist theories, said, "However, most realists do not deny morality. Indeed, they assume with Aristotle that politics is rooted in ethics."[16] Gilpin, moreover, said, "I would argue that a moral commitment lies at the heart of realism."[17]

Mearsheimer's rejection of incorporating morality into realism theory stems from Morgenthau's claim that "moral principles cannot be applied to actions," while ignoring the caveat "in their abstract universal formulation."[18] In this context, Morgenthau has claimed that applying moral principles to action can avoid dangerous pitfalls if "filtered through the concrete circumstance of time and place."[19] Moral realism's proposal of comparing state action to universally accepted moral codes works off of such a "filter."

Since nothing in the world is immutable, universal morality also changes through the course of history. Therefore, the analyses in this book will be conducted according to the moral standards of the relevant historical period in a given international system. The analyses will focus on how the moral actions of states affect policy choices by examining the following relationships: the impact of moral actions on national capability; the varying degrees of adherence by types of state leadership to moral standards; and the impact of types of international leadership on international norms.

Instrumental Morality in Moral Realism

The theory created in this book follows in the footsteps of classical realism in that it analyzes states' moral behavior from the perspectives of international power, national capability, and national interest. Classical realist Carr asserts, "Just as within the state every government, though it needs power as a basis of its authority, also needs the moral basis of the consent of the governed, so an international order cannot be based on power alone, for the simple reason that mankind will in the long run always revolt against naked power."[20] Similarly, moral realism regards morality as of equal importance to policy making as power, capability, and interest. There are two ways to study national interests within realist theories: logical deductive and empirical inductive.[21] Because this research aims at establishing a new realist theory, issues and instances related to national interests in this book fall under the former category.

When speaking about morality many theorists take a value-based approach, but moral realism adopts an instrumentally based approach. For example, Brostrom defines moral realism as a way of understanding a calculation of national interest that imbues concerns about morality.[22] He says that "it is in fact possible to treat morality as instrumental. This means that it can be seen as part of the rational decision-making process in a state's foreign policy, with the potential to produce specific outcomes."[23] Lebow has a similar view, contending that "ethics are not only instrumentally important, but it is impossible to formulate interests intelligently outside of some language of justice."[24] I would go a step further by saying that the benefits of adopting a moral foreign policy stem from strategy preferences rather than calculations of national interest. Moral realism's emphasis on strategic preferences is rooted in the common agreement among realists that national interests are determined objectively and defined by a state's material capability. Therefore, the role of morality is to influence policy makers' concerns about how national interests should be achieved rather than what national interests ought to be. In a concrete situation policy makers sometimes have to decide which interest should take priority. The core of policy making, therefore, lies in making strategic decisions on how to achieve interest maximization. However, whether an interest is major or minor is determined by objective reality rather than by morality. As such, I would define moral realism as the approach to understanding a major power's behavior when morality is a contributing factor to its leadership's strategic preferences. Certain realist theories ignore the impact of a national leader's moral concerns on decision making—an approach that is at odds with moral realism.

LEVELS AND COMPONENTS OF MORALITY

To avoid any semantic disputes, it would be best first of all to define morality, as IR scholars all too often debate concepts according to different understandings of the same word. Furthermore, lay understandings of what morality means will further confuse matters. Before addressing the logic of moral realist theory, therefore, it is necessary to clarify the levels and components of morality as applicable to IR theories.

Governmental Morality as the Standard

Discussions in this book of a state's morality are not structured on any arbitrary set of standards, but rather on the actions that the state undertakes irrespective of the individual policy maker's motivations or personal beliefs. When the state's actions accord with universally accepted codes it is deemed moral, and when the reverse is true, it is deemed immoral. Thus, determining whether or not the action of a state is moral entails an assessment of that action according to universally accepted codes. This assessment does not require any subjective perception but depends on giving yes or no answers to questions that determine whether the action under scrutiny is moral or not. If there are more "yes" than "no" answers, then the action is moral; if "no" is the predominant answer, then the action is not moral.

Judging whether or not the act of a policy maker is moral means first of all determining which set of codes is applicable to that action.

This is decided by the status of the person committing the act. As such, the morality judgment is made on one of the three levels: personal, governmental, and international.[25] For example, an everyday citizen is expected to provide for his or her dependents' health care. Although it would be commendable if this person were to go beyond his or her personal responsibility and help others in this respect, no one would accuse this person of immoral behavior if he or she did not endeavor to provide for the health care of people other than his or her family members. This is because the acts of an individual citizen are judged according to morals at the personal level. However, it is not acceptable for the leader of a state to consider solely his or her family's welfare, as that leader is expected to enact policies that will provide health care coverage for all citizens of the state. Yet, at the same time, no one expects a state leader to be concerned about the health care issues of other nations. The reason for these two differing expectations is that a state leader is judged at the governmental level. The third level would apply, for instance, to the leader of the World Health Organization. Tasked with providing health care for people across the globe, the international leader is expected to implement health care policies that are beneficial to all people, regardless of national borders or the interests of individual countries. This leader's actions, therefore, are judged according to morals at the international level.

To avoid dissension, therefore, and because moral realism is a theory that specifically addresses international relations, discussions in this book of "morality" refer solely to governmental morality, whereby leaders' actions will be judged according to the accepted codes of conduct pertaining to national interests and national capability. There has been a widely accepted distinction in the Western world, in both ancient and modern times, between public and private morality. Niebuhr distinguished between the moral behavior of individuals versus social groups in his observation that personal morality is sublimated, along with the individual ego, into the group, which then re-expresses this egoism at a higher level.[26] Such conflating of public and private morals can lead to dissension over which codes of morality apply. This difference is illustrated by the debate over President Clinton's impeachment. Some people thought Clinton's private behavior did not constitute grounds for impeachment; others disagreed. Different levels of moral code are at the root of disagreement in that discussion.

When talking about "governmental morality," we are referring to what Max Weber called the "ethic of responsibility," which requires, "one . . . to give an account of foreseeable results of one's action."[27] Nannerl Keohane says that "the 'ethic of responsibility' is a form of consequentialist morality as distinct from the Kantian deontological approach."[28] In this book, governmental morality addresses such concepts as the responsibility to protect national interests, the duty to practice international norms, and strategic credibility with regard to allies. The government's responsibility to the country it represents and the people it governs is the core of governmental morality. For instance, many Americans criticize Donald Trump's foreign policies as "less than out of a sense of moral responsibility," because these policies create a global leadership vacuum for China to fill, undermine American strategic relations with traditional allies, unite American competitors and adversaries, and drive major powers to sell some of their stock in Washington.[29]

Universality of Governmental Morality

In addition to the morality level, it is also necessary to clarify the components universally applicable to the morality under discussion. The components of morality can be categorized as national and universal codes. Differing from national morality (such as American, Chinese, or Japanese political culture), universal morality (such as patriotism, obligation, or justice) is accepted by all members, even adversaries, of a given international system. Therefore, we will use universal codes to judge the morality of a state's leadership. Governmental morality thus refers to those universal moral codes.

The existence of universally accepted moral codes may, at a glance, seem to disregard cultural differences and so evoke worries about imperialist tendencies. However, our growing understanding of the biological basis of psychology and sociology makes more and more apparent that human behavior is as much determined by will as it is by nature. Research shows that different cultures actually share certain similar moral foundations. Jesse Graham and colleagues, a group of cultural psychologists, offered an evolutionary explanation of why moral judgments are often so similar across cultures. Their model, the Moral Foundations Theory, proposes that the ever-popular tabula rasa hypothesis—that humans are born as a blank state—is wrong. Our evolutionary history has shaped the human propensity to place value on five ethical foundations, and it is on these five basic building blocks that each tribe/culture developed a moral narrative. These five foundations are care/harm, fairness/cheating, loyalty/betrayal, authority/subversion, and sanctity/degradation.[30] All humans, irrespective of cultural backgrounds, universally revere the first component of the dyad and despise the second. Individuals who do not possess these moral foundations, aka sociopaths, are rejected by the social group.[31] In short, humans are evolutionarily predisposed to morals and to being moral, and the moral foundation is the same across the species.

Because international morality is still formed by humans, we can find the same foundations underlying universally accepted codes of conduct. For example, the Geneva Conventions address the concept of care/harm in international disputes (i.e., war); the WTO addresses concepts of fairness/cheating on the subject of international trade; strategic alliances such as NATO are built on the foundation of loyalty/betrayal; the hierarchical structure of the UN submits to the concepts of authority/subversion; and international environmental efforts, such as the Paris Climate Accord, apply the concept of sanctity/degradation to planetary health. It is because morality is built on shared moral foundations that we are able to agree to these international moral codes. While the specifics may constantly change, the underlying values do not. This book considers these universal moral foundations "universal morality."

Qualitative differences, however, exist among universally accepted codes of governmental morality with regard to adherence. Some codes, such as maintaining good terms with one's allies, showing diplomatic courtesy to state leaders, ensuring the personal safety of diplomatic envoys, and paying off foreign debts, constitute basic morality and are easy for states to follow and practice. But the higher demands of altruistic actions, such as providing continuous foreign aid, are much harder to fulfill. As most states generally practice the moral codes that are easier to keep to rather than the more difficult ones, the former have wider impact on state behavior. Therefore, as realists, we judge the morality of political leadership according to the easily executed, universal governmental morals, as opposed to the more demanding ones.

DIFFERENCES BETWEEN POWER, CAPABILITY, AND AUTHORITY

In English-language IR writings, the term "power" can simultaneously refer to social influence, material capability, and political authority, even though the functions of these three elements differ significantly. This is because the English language defines "power" in a multitude of ways, including control, authority, ability, capability, might, and influence.[32] The interchangeability between power, capability, and authority, therefore, makes it difficult for people to understand the functions of the three resources of leadership capability. It consequently becomes impossible to understand the influence that morality has on each of them.

Differences between Power and Capability

The phrase "balance of power" is a typical example of the simultaneous reference to influence and capability. Although frequently used, there is no consensus among IR scholars as to whether it refers to a balance of political influence or of physical capability. Morgenthau recognized this problem and employed two differing expressions— power and elements of power (referring to capability)—to differentiate the two meanings of power as it is used in *Politics among Nations*. This differentiation, however, is still not clear, because the phrase "elements of power" may also refer to "elements of capability." Frankly, the term "power" remains vague in Morgenthau's book, wherein it alternately means influence and capability, or in some cases carries both meanings. Noting that "the concept of power is one of the most troublesome in the field of international relations," Gilpin defines power as the capability of states yet still cannot avoid using "power" in reference to influence when he says, "In time, the differential growth in power of the various states in the system causes a fundamental redistribution of power in the system."[33] The vague usage of "power" has loitered in IR theories for decades. As late as 2007, William Wohlforth's writing still concerned the "problem with conflating power-as-resources with power-as-influence."[34]

This vagueness amounts to a theoretical shortcoming in Morgenthau's discourse. When defining national interests by power, he fails to distinguish whether power is a type of national interest or its foundation. In other words, if power refers to influence on other states, then it is a type of national interest; if it refers to capability, then it is the foundation of national interest.[35] Since Morgenthau did not rigorously distinguish between the nature of power and of capability, therefore, he was unable to demonstrate clearly the relationship between morality and power.

To avoid any confusion of logic in theory building stemming from unclear semantics as regards the "meaning of power," this book makes a rigorous distinction between power and capability. When discussing power, we refer only to influence, such as police power. When discussing capability, we refer to strength, as in the competitiveness of athletes. This differentiation between power and capability allows us to avoid the circular logic that defines national interest by power while simultaneously regarding power as a national interest. When we define power as influence, we consider power a factor of national interest, and usually the most important one. National interests are usually categorized under the domains of politics, security, economy, and culture. Power is often viewed as a factor of political interest, such as the veto power of permanent members of the UN Security Council. When capability is defined as strength, it serves as the basis for defining national interests, including power. The extent of a state's power in the domain of each national interest is determined by the capability of the related component. Therefore, when analyzing a country's holistic strategic interests, we should do so according to its comprehensive capability (CC).

A state's comprehensive capability includes both material and nonmaterial resources, especially that of political capability. Like national interests, comprehensive capability is divided into four domains: politics, military, economy, and culture. In this model, political capability functions as an operational element, and the other three (military, economy, and culture) are resource elements. In other words, political capability exerts a multiplicative effect on the sum of the other three elements. Should political capability decrease to zero, then the effect of the other three is reduced to nothing. Mathematically, this can be expressed as: $CC = (M+E+C) \cdot P$, where M is military, E is economy, C is culture, and P is political capability. Political capability is mainly determined by the efficiency of state leadership, which is mainly determined by two factors: the political direction of reform and the extent of its execution. When the direction of reform is correct, a larger extent of reform leads to an increase in P, and when the direction is wrong, the effect is reversed.[36] Reform is both a descriptive term and a prescriptive one; it embraces a moral dimension and is antithetical to retrogression. On this account, reform refers to changes in a positive direction, while changes in a bad direction constitute retrogression.

In this formula, "political capability" is different from the "soft power" as coined by Nye. Nye's "soft power" rests on three basic resources: culture, political value, and foreign policies.[37] These three resources engender the attractiveness of a country's government model, which influences other countries' actions without the use of hard power. However, a country's attractiveness is based on the deeds of that country's leadership rather than on its culture and political value. Therefore, I would argue that political leadership, rather than political value, is the core element of soft power. As such, I would combine political value and culture into one variable, and put foreign policies into the variable called "political capability." This is because foreign policy is decided by political leadership, while political value informs, but does not determine, the policy making of the leadership. This argument can explain why US soft power declined so dramatically after the Trump administration had been in office for only half a year, even though American culture and political values remained the same. Nye may also have realized that the two concepts of "hard power" and "soft power" alone do not adequately explain the efficiency of leadership, and consequently he coined the term "smart power." He said, "In practice, effective leadership requires a mixture of soft and hard power skills that I call smart power."[38] Because foreign policy making is the main skill of operating resources of soft and hard powers, Nye actually treats foreign policy as both smart power and a resource of soft power, namely, picking out a resource of soft power as smart power. The concept of smart power confuses the relations between different types of state capability rather than clarifies them. In fact, if we accept the concept of "smart power," it implies that the attractiveness of "soft power" depends on leadership's manipulation of soft power, rather than on culture or political values.

The practical reason for the theoretical distinction between power and capability is that by defining national interests according to a state's capability we can avoid misjudgments that lead to catastrophic policies. The comprehensive capability of states can be categorized into four international status groups: dominant, rising, regional, and small states. A dominant state's main interest is to maintain its position in the world, while that of a rising state is to gain more international power. A regional or subregional state's main strategic interest is to maintain dominance in its own region rather than gain world supremacy. Survival is the main strategic interest of a small state. Post–Cold War history illustrates how changes in the capability of the United States, Russia, and China redefined their main strategic interests.

When, after the Cold War, the United States became the sole world superpower, it targeted global dominance as its priority interest. Russia, as successor to the collapsed Soviet Union, did not possess Soviet capability and consequently did not contend for global hegemony, as had its predecessor, instead establishing itself as a regional power in the Eurasian neighborhood. As a rising state, China became the second-largest world economy in 2010, and this changed China's main strategic interest from economic prosperity to national rejuvenation in 2012.[39]

Accepting that national strategic interests are defined by comprehensive capability sets the objective boundaries of national interests. Clearly defined boundaries can help statesmen and scholars to avoid unrealistic ambitions, and allow them to agree on a common standard. Take the George W. Bush administration as an example. In response to 9/11, having set absolute security as the target of its national interest, it attempted to eradicate terrorism. But as this goal was far beyond the capability of American national capability, the Bush administration's counterterrorism campaign failed. In fact, terrorism now seems to have become as commonplace as burglary or theft, with no foreseeable solution in the future. This is because the United States may have the capability to reduce external terrorist threats to the American homeland, but it lacks the capability to eliminate terrorists from the world entirely. By overreaching its capability, therefore, America's war on terror not only failed to achieve its goals but also undermined the country's national capability.

Similarly, underestimating the capability of opposing countries can lead to an underestimation of the bottom line of their national interests, which also results in failed policies. The Sino-Japanese dispute over the Diaoyu/Senkaku Islands in 2012 is a typical example. In 2012, the naval might of China was approximately equal to Japan's; therefore, it would have been beneficial for both sides to maintain the status quo of the islands and shelve the disputes.[40] Nevertheless, having underestimated Chinese naval capability, the Japanese government ignored China's determination to protect its sovereignty over the islands. On September 11, 2012, the Japanese government nationalized its control over the islands.[41] Japan's nationalization of these islands was unacceptable to China, and it accordingly reciprocated Japan's hard-line position on this issue by announcing its territorial sea baseline and air defense identification zone, as well as official maritime and air navigations.[42] Because Japan misidentified its own interests over the Diaoyu/Senkaku Islands by considering its ambitions rather than its military capability, the country made an erroneous decision that resulted in a long-lasting confrontation between Japan and China.

Differences between Power and Authority

In English-language writings, "power" and "authority" are often used indiscriminately. Even scholars who are aware of the semantic distinction between these two concepts still regard them as being the same in nature. For instance, David Lake says, "Authority is, simply stated, rightful rule. That is, an authoritative ruler has the right to command subordinates to perform certain actions and, because the commands are rightful, the ruled have a duty to comply. In this way, authority is a type of power over others."[43] Therefore, many people regard obtaining power as equal to gaining authority. In the Chinese language, the two concepts, wherein *quanli* (权力, power) means legitimate coercive rights or duty while *quanwei* (权威, authority) means prestige or popular trust, are quite removed from each other. This book will use the Chinese connotation of these two terms in explaining the role and types of political leadership.

Both power and authority are resources that a leadership can wield to influence others, but they function through different means. Power enforces behavior through coercion, while authority entices others to follow an idea based on trust in it. One daily life example that highlights the difference is the way in which police officers and medical practitioners change people's behavior. The former represents power, the latter authority. Motorists obey police officers because police power forces them to; patients take advice from physicians because of trust in their medical knowledge as proven by their credentials. These principles also apply to international leadership. For instance, the United States possesses the dominating power as the "World's Police Force" based on its unmatched military force since the end of the Cold War. The EU, meanwhile, provides authoritative leadership in dealing with climate change, based on its higher achievements in reducing carbon dioxide emissions in the 2010s than other international actors.

When discussing leadership authority, Max Weber's definition springs to the mind of many scholars, but the concept of authority in this book is not the same as Weber's. Weber categorizes authority into three types: rational, traditional, and charismatic.[44] In regard to the basis of charismatic leadership, he says that "it is the charismatically qualified leader such as who is obeyed by virtue of personal trust in him."[45] That means men do not obey him by tradition or status, but because they believe in him. According to Weber, rational and traditional authorities rest on status and tradition respectively, rather than on others' confidence in the leadership. Yet both status and tradition are actually defined by power. In this book, the concept of authority bears similarity to Weber's charismatic authority, but not to the other two types, because it is defined by followers' confidence in the qualities of a leadership.

When we define the source of power as force and the source of authority as the confidence of its followers, we may argue that authority can increase one's power naturally, but that power cannot automatically improve one's authority. Therefore, it is possible for a leading state to increase its international power by promoting its material capability, but such promoted material capability cannot automatically establish the international authority of that state when other states do not accept its leadership. The improvement of a leading state's international authority entails winning more external support, which automatically increases that state's international influence, or international power.

We can expand on this point from the perspective of strategic credibility. Strategic credibility is an important part of international authority and is gained through moral actions. An important element of strategic credibility is honoring commitments to other countries, especially allies. Protecting allies and punishing countries that disturb international order are regarded as moral actions of leading states. Therefore, a leading state's strategic credibility implies consistency between its promises and its actions. Its allies will follow its leadership willingly when they trust its promises, and its enemies will be cautious to challenge it when they believe that it will determinatively maintain international order. Therefore, a leading state that has improved its strategic credibility enjoys international authority and stands the best chance of winning diplomatic conflicts. Such victories mean more international support, and more international power. For the same reason, those with poor strategic credibility will often suffer diplomatic defeats. For example, in March 2018, the UK blamed Russia for the poisoning of a former spy and his daughter in Salisbury, England, and expelled twenty-three Russian diplomats in retaliation. This policy gained support from more than twenty countries, including eighteen EU states, the United States, and Canada, through their collective expulsion of Russian diplomats.[46] This collective effort represents a significant diplomatic victory for the UK and defeat for Russia. The UK later stated that there was no substantive evidence to prove Russia's alleged murder attempt, and the two victims recovered after treatment in hospital.[47] However, these facts illustrate how much Russia suffered from its poor strategic credibility.

The difference between authority and power implies that one leading state could enjoy higher international authority than another, even when both wield the same level of international power. In some cases, a state's international authority may decline even as its international power increases. For example, the United States continuously improved its international power as the sole superpower after the Cold War until the financial crisis of 2008. Yet its international authority suffered a dramatic decline after its launch of the war in Iraq in 2003 without UN authorization. In particular, the disproving of America's sorry excuse that Saddam Hussein possessed weapons of mass destruction irreparably damaged America's strategic credibility.[48]

The decline of American international authority started with George W. Bush rather than Trump. The 2008 financial crisis exposed Wall Street's fraud to the world. The Standard and Poor's Financial Services LLC accordingly reduced the United States' credit rating from AAA to AA+ in 2011.[49] In the same year, President Obama abandoned Mohammed Hosni Mubarak, former president of Egypt and long-term ally of America, in the Middle East amid the Arab Spring revolutionary wave.[50] As Herb Keinon, an

American-born Israeli journalist, said, "All of these treacheries largely repudiated America's reputation among its allies, and even staggered Israel's belief in Washington's strategic credit."[51] This series of actions has led to the situation wherein America's international authority in the twenty-first century is much lower than it was in the 1990s.

These cases do not signify that America is the only leading state to adopt irresponsible foreign policy. In fact, all major powers, including China, Russia, France, the UK, Germany, and India, have undertaken actions since the end of World War II that have undermined their international credibility. Some may have records even more notorious than that of the United States. Here I merely argue that immoral actions will reduce a major power's international authority, regardless of how powerful the state may be.

INFLUENCE OF MORALITY AND STRATEGIC CREDIBILITY

The previous discussion analyzed the differences between capability, power, and authority—the three resources of leadership. Owing to their special characters, morality shapes them through different approaches. The lowest level of international morality is strategic credibility; thus, high strategic credibility becomes a precondition for a leading state to establish international authority. A strong power without basic strategic credit cannot hope to establish its authority in an international community.

Influence of Morality through Different Approaches

Morality can directly affect the power of states, because moral actions increase the legitimacy of a state's leadership, thereby giving that state more influence. Morality also can affect a state's capability but may achieve this effect only indirectly. That is to say, a state's morality first trickles down to other factors through its influence, which then changes other actors' support for or opposition to it, so culminating in changes to that state's capability. Morality has direct influence on a state's power, but the direction of that influence depends on whether or not that state's actions are consistent with universally accepted moral codes.

Palestine can be used to illustrate the phenomenon whereby moral actions increase a state's power but not its capability. Palestine's protest against Israel's settlement policy of occupying Palestinian territory was in line with international moral codes of conduct. Accordingly, Palestine received both sympathy and political support from the international community, as seen from the seventy-seven UN resolutions from 1955 to 2013 that condemned Israel.[52] Palestine's moral actions, therefore, enhanced the legitimacy of its claim of sovereignty but nevertheless failed to increase Palestine's capability to the extent needed to protect its territorial sovereignty. Consequently, Palestine remains vulnerable to Israeli encroachments on its borders.

Japan, by contrast, can be used as an example of how immoral actions decrease a state's power but not its capability. In 2013, Shinzo Abe, the Japanese prime minister, made formal visits to the Yasukuni Shrine, where World War II Class-A war criminals are enshrined. His actions, which go against international moral codes and are thus considered immoral, provoked international wrath—from China, South Korea, and even America and Europe.[53] However, although the Abe government's immoral actions considerably damaged Japan's international image, causing a reduction in Japanese international political power, Japanese capability remained constant. Moreover, its defense expenditure increased by 3 percent in the year 2013.[54]

The influence of morality on a state's capability varies according to whether such influence gained or undermined it. Adherence to international moral codes enhances the legitimacy of a leading state's mobilization of support both at home and abroad. This raises the state's international power, which then transforms into its material capability. This is particularly visible in the creation of alliance networks. For instance, the United States formed a strong multinational force to save Kuwait from Saddam Hussein's annexation and punished the aggressor in January 1991.[55] America's decision conformed to the principles of territorial integrity backed by the UN

Charter and was considered moral by international standards. As a result, the United States gained thirty-four nations as allies, which increased its material capability in the Gulf War.

By contrast, the Saddam Hussein government of Iraq violated international law, an act that was considered immoral by international standards. It consequently lost the support of the general public both at home and abroad, and the military disparity between Iraq and the United States considerably broadened. This case signifies that even if immoral actions do not undermine a state's absolute capability, they may considerably weaken its relative capability.

Although authority and power are two different matters, morality has direct influence on both. The direction of morality's influence on a leading state's authority is also determined according to whether or not that state's actions are consistent with universally accepted moral codes. Moral actions improve its authority, and immoral actions undermine it. The international power of a leading state will increase according to the moral foundation on which it lays to build up its authority. History shows that leading states that have established a high authority have a greater chance of maintaining international leadership than those with lesser authority. On the current decline of America's international leadership, Steven Metz, a professor from the US Army War College, says, "It is difficult to defeat the US, but it is possible to thwart it by seizing the ethical high ground and manipulating the fault lines in the American political system. . . . Perhaps the biggest lesson of all, though, is that moral ambiguity hinders, even paralyzes the United States."[56]

Strategic Credibility and Leading by Example

Strategic credibility is the lowest level of international morality, and a prerequisite to a leading power's establishment of international authority. Levels of morality are mainly decided by the cost of observing it. Low-level moral codes, such as not lying, not deceiving, and not stealing, can be observed at low cost or no cost, while high-level moral codes, such as charity, altruism, and helpfulness, require a high cost of personal interests. Because observance of low-level moral codes is less costly, doing so becomes easier and more popular than adhering to high-level moral codes. Therefore, it is possible to trust those who do not practice high-level moral codes, but impossible to trust those who do not observe codes of a low level. Strategic credibility is a moral code on the same low level as not lying; hence no country without it can obtain other states' trust. It has therefore become the precondition whereby a leading state can establish authority in an international community.

Strategic credibility is a universally accepted moral code among states, crossing the boundaries of civilization, culture, politics, and governments. In the same way as a credible person is considered moral by other people, a credible state is also considered moral by other states. The strategic credibility of a leading state signifies to other members of a given international community a reliable leadership. Through credible behaviors, a leading state earns the strategic confidence of others in it, so lending it greater international authority and ultimately greater power. On the importance to a leading state of strategic credibility, Nye says, "Soft power depends on credibility, and when governments are perceived as manipulative and information is seen as propaganda, credibility is destroyed."[57]

The level of a leading state's strategic credibility relates positively to its international status and the durability of its leadership. History shows that a lack of strategic credibility is generally at the root of short-lived interstate leadership. Noting this phenomenon, Xunzi said, "Accordingly, one who uses the state to establish justice will be a sage king; one who establishes trust will be a hegemon; and one who establishes a record of expediency and opportunism will perish."[58] Xunzi's statement implies that international authority cannot be forced on other states but rather requires other states' voluntary acceptance.

The example a leading state sets is instrumental to other states' voluntary acceptance of its leadership. In Chinese traditional culture, *yishen zuoze* (以身作则, leading by example), rather than giving orders, is a main facet of leadership doctrine and relates to Confucius's argument "It is known that people proactively come to learn rites from masters, but it is never heard that masters proactively go to educate others about rites" (*Li wen lai xue, bu wen wang jiao,* 礼闻来学, 不闻往教).[59] In other words, when people seek to learn from someone, it is because they regard him or her as an example. Some of the early American political thinkers also advocated expounding moral principles through example. For instance, John Quincy Adams argued that "it was not for the United States to impose its own principles of government upon the rest of mankind, but, rather, to attract the rest of mankind through the example of the United States," while Thomas Paine said that "those universal principles the United States had put into practice should not be exported by fire and sword, but presented to the rest of the world through successful example."[60]

These American thinkers' cognizance of the risk of war in trying to spread morality by force was at the root of their opposition to that kind of foreign policy. However, this thought holds little sway in modern American IR studies. Since Woodrow Wilson, more and more American thinkers have sought to make the world safe for democracy by transforming it according to the will of the United States. This ideology, known as the Wilsonian conception of democracy and human rights, has had a strong impact on American foreign policy since World War I.[61] After World War II, America became fixated on waging war in the name of democracy. The United States' persistent and prolonged practice of warring against nondemocratic countries has caused certain American IR scholars to conflate the implementation of universal morality with the export of democracy by force.[62] This has contributed to diminished consideration of the distinction between international authority and international power.

SUMMARY

Realism has long been misunderstood as an IR theory that ignores the role of morality in international politics. In fact, classical realism theorists never ignored the functions of morality in their studies on international relations. Resuming classical realism's concern about morality, this book attributes the success of a rising state to its political leadership that adopts foreign policy according to universal moral codes. There are three levels of morality judgment: individual, governmental, and international. Governmental morality refers to a government's responsibility to the interests of the people it rules. Therefore, it is a public rather than a private morality, as well as a universal rather than a national morality.

This book defines capability as strength and power as influence. This distinction lays a foundation for modeling political leadership as an operational factor that determines the growth or decline of a state's comprehensive capability. The military, the economy, and the culture function as the resource elements of comprehensive capability, which changes according to the efficiency of political leadership—an operational capability. The efficiency of operational capability is mainly determined by the direction and execution of political reforms initiated by the government. Reform politically embraces a moral dimension and is antithetical to retrogression. This implies that the political leadership of a state that is able to implement more and deeper reforms improves that state's comprehensive capability faster than does the political leadership of other states.

The distinction between power and authority helps our understanding of the durability of an international leadership. Power is based on brute force, and authority is based on others' trust. Both are the resources of a leadership, but the latter entails voluntary acceptance of that leadership, which the former cannot achieve. It is possible for a leading state to improve its international power by improving its international authority, but not necessarily the other way round. That is why a leadership with high authority lasts longer than one of low or zero authority. Strategic credibility is the lowest level of international morality, and thus the prerequisite to establishing international authority.

2

Leadership and Strategic Preferences

王霸、安存、危殆、灭亡，制与在我，亡乎人。
Domination, or safety, or peril, or destruction,
all is determined by the Leader.)
XUNZI

The central question that this book wishes to address is how a rising state, one that has significantly less material capability than the dominant state, is able to surpass that state and become the new world leader. As the study of international relations has been deeply affected by the behaviorism revolution over the past fifty years, the type of political leadership as an independent variable has been ignored in many realist IR theories for quite some time.[1] This is why many realist theories have not been able to offer an explanation for the fast-paced narrowing of the disparity in capability between China and the United States in the early twenty-first century, or for the rapid decline of America's international leadership in the first six months of Donald Trump's administration. The theory developed in this book incorporates political leadership as the key variable in the formula for national capability that provides an explanation of how a rising state is able to surpass the dominant state despite having less material capability.

Ancient Chinese political thinkers shared the view that power shifts between states result from changes in the rulers of major states. They hence treated types of rulers as an independent variable in their analysis. However, this approach is not uniquely Chinese. In fact, we can find similar analyses in both ancient and modern Western political writings.[2] The mission of this chapter is not to emphasize the importance of political leadership, but to characterize the types of political leadership that are concerned with governmental morality, and to study the influences that different types of leadership impose on perceptions of the strategic preferences through which to achieve national interests.

THE ROLE AND TYPES OF LEADERSHIP

In the 1980s, Robert H. Jackson and Carl G. Rosberg studied the relationship between types of leadership and their impact on African politics. They said, "In the provision or the destruction of such 'political goods' as peace, order, stability, and non-material security, the actions of Africa's rulers and other leaders have been more important than anything else."[3] This emphasis on the importance of leadership is applicable beyond just African or developing countries; the same could be said of every country. The types of national leadership and international leadership categorized in this book are thus designed not only for China but for all modern leading powers.

The Role of Political Leadership

As stated in the first chapter, this book defines political capability as the operational variable of comprehensive capability, and political leadership as the core component of political capability. Therefore, political leadership is treated as a dynamic factor in decision making. When the capability of a state remains the same, it is still possible for the type of leadership of that state to change and formulate different foreign strategies. For instance, China's comprehensive capability remained the same in 2013, but the newly elected government changed China's foreign strategy from keeping a low profile to striving for achievements. This was because the new Chinese leader had faith in power, while the previous leaders from Deng Xiaoping onward set greater store by wealth.[4] This concurs with Margaret Hermann and Joe Hagan's observation: "Leaders define states' international and domestic constraints. Based on their perceptions and interpretations, they build expectations, plan strategies, and urge actions on their government. . . . Such perceptions help frame government orientations to international affairs."[5]

The author regards decision making as a collective action rather than the result of a single leader's individual decision; therefore, political leadership in this book refers to the leading group of policy makers rather than a single supreme leader. Although there are differences between individual top leaders as regards policy making, all decisions are still made by a committee, even under a dictatorship. For instance, the leaderships headed by Franklin Roosevelt, Joseph Stalin, and Adolf Hitler are strikingly different types, whose members had different ideologies. Nevertheless, the strategic decisions these leading bodies made during World War II were all based on consultations among the members of each one of those leading bodies.

A leading body does not denote the supreme leader him- or herself but consists of the top leader, close assistants, and the relations between them. Noting this, Xunzi says, "If the ruler follows the example of sage kings and associates with men advocating governance of sage kings, he will be a sage king. If he follows the example of hegemony and associates with men advocating hegemony, he will be a hegemonic ruler."[6] Morris Fiorina and Kenneth Shepsle regard leadership as "a term we apply to one part of a web of mutually dependent anticipations, expectations, and choices. . . . One cannot have leaders without followers."[7] I believe that the supreme leader and his or her aides naturally coalesce, because like attracting like is a common phenomenon in both Chinese and Anglophone societies. There are similar colloquialisms in the two cultures that reflect this phenomenon. The Chinese have the expression *ren yi qun fen, wu yi lei ju* (人以群分, 物以类聚, human beings are grouped by types and animals by species); the English version is "birds of a feather flock together."

In this book, political leadership is categorized according to its concrete policies rather than the supreme leader's personality or the beliefs of any individual. Alexander Hamilton says that "the true test of a good government is its aptitude and tendency to produce a good administration."[8] The categorization is made from the aspect of foreign policy making since the purpose of this book is to create an IR theory. It is commonplace that members of a decision-making body are not always able to agree with one another. If they do not reach consensus on a specific issue, the problem might be postponed until a decision either is forced or can be reconstituted. As Margaret G. Hermann and Joe D. Hagan have observed, scholars have found that excessive group cohesion can produce "groupthink," and premature closure around the options preferred by the more powerful policy makers.[9] Nannerl Keohane noted that "the distinctiveness of leadership is the persistent asymmetry of the top leader and his/her followers, so that leaders affect or shape the behavior of followers to a greater degree than followers affect or shape the behavior of their leaders."[10] This situation is especially obvious during an international crisis, when the authority for a final decision tends to be concentrated in the top leader, who bears ultimate responsibility for maintaining the government in power. Since the leading body's policies are usually in alignment with those of the supreme leader, the supreme leader can be used as a proxy when conducting qualitative analyses.

Types of State Leadership

International and domestic systems are different in nature; the former is anarchical and the latter hierarchical. Therefore, the two different systems of state leadership and international leadership are differently legitimized and performed. A state leadership is politically legitimized by law, tradition, or religion, while an international leadership rests on material capability and the support of other countries. A government can implement plans through directives at home but internationally must negotiate with other countries, even when they are allies, and obtain their agreement on a strategic plan it has formulated. For instance, China issued its global "One Belt One Road" (OBOR) plan in 2013.[11] Cognizant of the crucial differences between domestic and international leaderships, the country refers to the plan as the "OBOR strategy" at home but calls it the "OBOR initiative" in international situations.[12] Owing to their different natures, this book categorizes state leadership and international leadership according to different variables.

Leadership can be categorized into different types according to various criteria. Since this research studies the political leadership of great powers at both the domestic and international levels, it uses political criteria to categorize it. In general, political leadership refers to a leading body that has the capability to enlist the support of other individuals, teams, or organizations in the accomplishment of a common task. According to this definition, the criteria for categorizing political leadership should focus on capability to enlist social support. Because the basic characters of domestic society and interstate society are respectively hierarchical and anarchical, the logic with regard to winning domestic support is different from that applicable to obtaining international support. Therefore, the criteria in this book for categorizing state leadership of great powers, from the aspect of foreign policy, is the leading body's sense of national responsibility and capacity to carry out its duty, while the criteria for classifying interstate leadership is the leading state's responsibility to maintain interstate order and strategic credibility in a given international system.

State leadership is hence categorized into four types: inactive, conservative, proactive, and aggressive, based on two interacting independent variables: (1) a leading body's attitude toward its state's international status quo, and (2) a leading body's responsibility toward the possible result of its policies. Both of these independent

TABLE 2.1: TYPES OF STATE LEADERSHIP

Attitude toward State's Status Quo	Leadership Responsibility	
	Responsible	*Irresponsible*
Maintain status quo	Conservative	Inactive
Change status quo	Proactive	Aggressive

variables are binary. The attitude toward the international status quo could be classified as "maintain" or "change," and leadership responsibility as "responsible" or "irresponsible." Table 2.1 demonstrates the classifications based on these two variables.

In table 2.1, the difference between maintaining and changing the status quo is that neither conservative nor inactive leaderships have any motivation to enhance the international power of their states, while proactive and aggressive leaderships have a strong desire to increase their countries' international power. The difference between responsible and irresponsible leaderships is that conservative and proactive leaderships are capable of acknowledging their mistakes in the face of failure and display a willingness to change the direction of their policies accordingly. By contrast, inactive and aggressive leaderships are not willing to acknowledge their mistakes, even if their policies cause disasters, and will continue with the original policies despite all criticisms. Following on from the above classifications, we can use the next four categories of leadership as references for the corresponding political philosophies.

(1) *Inactive leadership—Daoism*: a state leadership that subscribes to the philosophy of governance by noninterference: *wu wei er zhi* (无为而治, laissez-faire). Such a leadership believes that to maintain current international status, the best strategy is to take no action. Daoism is a well-known laissez-faire philosophy that many people adopt in their way of life.[13] Decision makers do not need to be learned in or to have read Daoist philosophy to adopt a laissez-faire style of leadership, just as there are many foreign policy makers that subscribe to realism even though they have no knowledge about IR realist theories. This type of leadership prefers to avoid

controversy at home and often seeks to accommodate the domestic opposition by granting concessions on foreign policy, an approach that is unresponsive to international pressures but that entails little risk.[14]

(2) *Conservative leadership—economic determinism*: a state leadership that advocates maintaining the international status quo, and that adopts strategies that maintain the achievements of their predecessors. This type of leadership views economy as the foundation of a state's comprehensive capability. This is also a belief shared by both Marxism and liberalism, although the two schools of thought may have conflicting perceptions in other aspects. When policy makers have no intention of improving their country's international status, and believe in economic determinism, they consider enlarging economic benefits as the best strategy for maintaining the status quo achieved by their predecessors. This type of state leadership is more popular than the other three types. Many policy makers in the latter years of a dynasty are of this type, because they have no ambition to attain international power any greater than what their predecessors achieved.

(3) *Proactive leadership—political determinism*: a state leadership that advocates improving a country's international status by carrying out appropriate reforms. This type of leadership subscribes to political determinism and believes that political talents are the decisive factor. It attributes the rise and fall of a state solely to the capability of that state's leadership, taking no account of other factors. Such a state leadership has rarely existed in any country's history. Among the few great leaders in Chinese history, the rule of Li Shimin, Emperor Taizong of the Tang Dynasty, represents this type of leadership. During his reign (626–49 CE), he and his ministers established the highest interstate status quo in Chinese history, known as the Governance of Zhenguan. *Zhenguan Zhengyao* is a collection of Emperor Taizong's quotations and conversations, wherein Li Shimin acknowledged the mistakes he had made, including erroneous martial decisions, four of them in writing, on forty-four occasions before his ministers and other subordinates during the first eighteen years of his rule.[15]

(4) *Aggressive leadership—social Darwinism*: a state leadership with the ambition to increase its country's international status through military means. This type of leadership subscribes to social Darwinism and believes in the efficacy of violent force, including military aggression. The leadership of many state founders was of this type. They include Ying Zheng, the first ruler of the Qin Empire (221–207 BCE); Genghis Khan, the first ruler of the Mongol Empire (1206–59); and Nurhachi, the first ruler of the Later Jin, which became the Qing Empire (1636–1912). Their successful establishment of an empire through wars led them to believe that winning more wars was the only way to enlarge their countries' interstate power.

In times of peace, this type of leadership may bring disaster to its people and undermine the country's international status. For instance, the leadership headed by Mao Zedong during the Cultural Revolution (1966–76) was calamitous for the Chinese people and dramatically undermined China's international status.[16] Mao perceived the world as a place for struggles among people that would be reshaped to adapt to the primacy of human beings. Kerry Brown, a British China watcher, believes that Trump emulates Mao Zedong's style of political leadership. He says, "The real heir to the spirit of Maoist politics sits these days not in Beijing, but several time zones away, in Washington. Trump's tendency to speak directly to the public through Twitter and his own personal voice has eerie parallels with the way that Mao often subverted his own propagandists and state media, reaching above their heads to the people, whom Mao always claimed to stand with."[17] Philip Gordon, an American diplomat, described what Trump's administration had inflicted on the United States in the first few months after taking office as the unleashing of a barrage of attacks on the underpinnings of democratic governance, threatening checks and balances, civil liberties, civil rights, and long-established norms at home while continuing to challenge accepted international norms, and breaking with diplomatic traditions abroad.[18] It is widely agreed that Trump's leadership undermined American democracy.[19]

LEADERSHIPS OF A RISING STATE AND STRATEGIC PREFERENCES

As the theory in this book is designed mainly to explain why a rising state can replace the dominant state, the following examples will focus solely on the strategic preferences of rising states with different leaderships. By focusing on rising states, we can control the variable of states' comprehensive capability, thus making it easier to illustrate how different types of state leadership determine strategic preferences.

Inactive Leadership—Avoiding Conflicts

Inactive leadership of a rising state tends to avoid the dilemma of being a rising power. Sun Xuefeng notes the dilemma and defines it as "the rising state's dilemma" where a rising state strategically confronts growing international pressure or negative responses from another state that result from the rapid growth of its capability and influence.[20] Avoiding danger and difficulties is instinctive to all animals, including human beings. Xunzi says: "To be fond of what is beneficial and to hate what is harmful—these are the characteristics man is born possessing."[21] Therefore, it is natural for political leaders to avoid the pressure and problems that accompany the rise of their state. For example: on the one hand, it is almost impossible for China to peacefully unite with Taiwan; but on the other, there would be a danger of war between China and the United States if China were to unite with Taiwan through military force. Faced with this dilemma, inactive leaders would change the policy of uniting with Taiwan to one of maintaining peace and pursuing benefits across the Taiwan Strait.[22] This policy avoids the danger of war against the United States, the military patron of Taiwan.

In the case of power transition, the inactive leadership of a rising state is often unable to withstand the dramatically increasing external pressure emanating mainly from structural conflicts between the rising state and the dominant state. By lowering its strategic goals the rising state can substantially reduce tensions between it and the dominant state. In most cases, the inactive leadership of a rising state will likely reject the goal of becoming a rising state, and certainly make no move to formulate a strategy through which to rise. In 2004, for example, the Chinese government formally banned the term *jueqi* (崛起 rise) from official documents. The inactive approach has two obvious advantages: first, this strategy entails a lesser degree of statecraft; second, it is demonstrably effective by virtue of the resultant rapid reduction of discord with the dominant state. In China, most of those in favor of avoiding conflicts with the United States follow Laozi's philosophy of governing by noninterference as expounded in his masterpiece the *Tao Te Ching*.[23]

Conservative Leadership—Imposing Economic Impacts

The conservative leadership of a rising state tends to adopt foreign strategies that exert economic or trade impacts on other countries. Following the doctrine of economic determinism, they define economy as the foundation of a state's comprehensive capability, and economic interest as its primary national interest. Acting in the belief that the rising state's dilemma is rooted in economic conflicts between rising states and other states, this type of leadership opts to reduce international pressure by expanding economic relations with the states with whom it experiences conflict. In the mid-1990s, the strategy of *yi jing cu zheng* (以经促政, improving political relations through economic cooperation) became the most popular strategy among China's policy makers and scholars of economic determinism.[24]

Although the strategy of imposing economic impacts cannot reduce external pressure as effectively as would directly avoiding conflicts, and consequently the risk of war, it can nevertheless temporarily ease tensions between a rising state and the dominant state. Such efficacy serves as evidence of the conservative leadership's wisdom, and of the correctness of the strategy of imposing economic impacts. However, one should not be misled into thinking that this exercise of economic determinism is solely motivated by economic cooperation, and never with the intent to impose economic sanctions. The conservative leadership of a rising state will also use economic sanctions to wield economic power over weaker states, and subsequently improve relations with them by lifting such sanctions. In fact, the effectiveness of this type of strategy is often limited to the domain of economics.

Proactive Leadership—Enlarging International Support

The proactive leadership of a rising state tends to favor strategies that enlarge international support for its cause. Leadership thus implies a symbiotic relationship between leader and followers. According to this logic, the more followers a leading state has, the more powerful its leadership is. For millennia, making alliances has been the most popular and effective strategy for leading states to gain international support. Nevertheless, the leading state must undertake certain risks of war, and also the costs of protecting allies in maintaining the alliance. Proactive leadership commits to undertaking those risks and costs for the sake of improving its international power. Such a strategy, however, will inevitably intensify the structural conflicts between the rising state and the dominant state, as the latter will necessarily attempt to contain the former. Faced with such conflicts, the proactive leadership of a rising state will seek allies, especially from among surrounding countries, to obtain the political and military support necessary to counter the dominant state's suppression.

By making alliances with neighbors who are enemies of the dominant state, however, a rising state runs the risk of war with the dominant state; therefore, this strategy is often employed by governments capable of providing strong leadership through proactive thinking. China became a rising state during the early twenty-first century, yet none of its policy makers have displayed a willingness to adopt the alliance strategy. It is mainly because the government insisted on the nonalignment principle that the strategy of making military alliances has been demonized in China in the post–Cold

War period as a "Cold War mentality."[25] Nowadays, only a few Chinese scholars advocate resuming the alliance strategy. They point out that China lacks staunch strategic supporters in the international arena and believe that no other strategy is more effective for gaining China international support than making alliances.[26] Their argument is that China cannot achieve the goal of national rejuvenation without substantial international support.[27]

Aggressive Leadership—Military Expansion

The aggressive leadership of a rising state espouses military expansion. Because forcefully obtaining benefits is a strategy favorable to the strong in competition against the weak, such leadership of rising states often adopt the opportunistic policy of initiating military attacks against lesser states, including the allies of the dominant state. This strategy, however, may trigger a major war resulting from the escalation of military clashes between the rising state and an ally of the dominant state.

As the military expansion strategy carries a high risk of failure, aggressive policy makers are often immune to the instinctive human fear of war. China has not been involved in a war for nearly thirty years, since 1989. This would not imply that no aggressive leadership has been established in contemporary China because ultraleftism is shaping such a leadership. Certain Chinese military officers are advocating the adoption of a military expansion strategy to achieve China's national rejuvenation, arguing that military expansion and invoking the aggressive wars that the Western powers historically waged is the only feasible approach to seizing international dominant power.[28]

The above analysis matches four ideal types of strategic preferences (avoiding conflicts, imposing economic impacts, enlarging international support, and military expansion) with four ideal types of leadership (inactive, conservative, proactive, and aggressive) of rising states. Since the types of state leadership are categorized according to their responsibility to their national status, the categorization of strategic preferences is decided by the relative efficiency of different strategies for improving national status. In fact, the state leaderships and strategic preferences of most rising states consist in hybrids of any two types mentioned above. By using these ideal types of leadership it is possible to predict the strategic preferences of different rising states as well as those of the different leaderships of a given rising state.

Changes in Leadership Type

It is important to note that the type of leadership of any state is susceptible to change, one that may occur without any significant change in the resource elements of a state's capability. There are often two mechanisms through which a change in leadership type can happen: regime change and self-transformation of leadership.

Regime change refers to the change in a state's supreme leader and is often accompanied by the establishment of a new leading body. The Chinese nationalist government was replaced by the Chinese Communist Party in 1949. This constitutes the most popular type of regime change. The change of US president from a Democrat to a Republican is another type of regime change. Both types may cause a change in leadership type. For instance, the type of US leadership changed from conservative to proactive when Bill Clinton replaced George H. W. Bush as American president in 1993. When George W. Bush took over the presidency from Clinton in 2001, the US leadership type changed from proactive to aggressive. When Obama entered the White House in 2009, the leadership type changed from aggressive to conservative. When Trump took office in the White House, he established an aggressive economic political leadership—a hybrid of the conservative and aggressive types.

Self-transformation of leadership refers to the change in the type of leadership when headed by the same supreme leader. When the supreme leader stays in power for only a short period of time, there is little likelihood that the state leadership he represents will undergo a change in type. However, the leadership type may change in the latter part of his rule, when his power is either consolidated or undermined, owing to his having been in power for an extended period. Political leaders who have been in power a long time often become more impulsive, less risk aware, and less adept at seeing things from any point of view other than their own. Modern research by psychologists and neuroscientists has shown that power can adversely affect the brain. Based on a study of US presidents and UK prime ministers over the course of a century, neurologists David Owen and Jonathan Davidson concluded: "Hubris syndrome is a disorder of the possession of power, particularly power which has been associated with overwhelming success, held for a period of years and with minimal constraint on the leader."[29] After years of lab and field experiments, Dacher Keltner and colleagues, a group of psychologists, found that "the excesses of powerful leaders—their propensity for disinhibited behavior and stereotypic, error-prone social perceptions—are certain to feed into the processes that lead to changes in leadership."[30] Jeremy Hogeveen and colleagues, a group of neuroscientists, strongly suggest that power is negatively related to motor resonance, and that the powerful tend to be disinclined to gain a deep understanding of the less powerful.[31]

Yet we have observed many political leaders who have undergone substantial changes in their political perspectives in the latter part of their political careers. Former Egyptian president Anwar el-Sadat was an anti-Semite yet at the age of sixty-two took the lead among Arab states to establish diplomatic relations with Israel. Former Israeli prime minister Yitzhak Rabin fought in many wars against Arab countries and the Palestine Liberation Army, yet in the year he turned seventy-one he pursued the Oslo Accords with Palestine. Former American president Richard Nixon was a strong anticommunist ideologue yet at the age of fifty-eight decided to initiate US relations with China while it was under the rule of Mao Zedong. The most recent example is Vladimir Putin, who served as Russian president from 2000 to 2008, as premier from 2008 to 2012, and as president again since 2012. During his eighteen-year rule, Putin has gradually consolidated his personal power in Russia to an unchallengeable extent. The national leadership represented by him thus changed from proactive, in his first term of presidency, to aggressive in his current term.

Identifying the leadership type of a rising state can help us to predict the strategic preference of that state, but not to forecast whether that strategic preference wins the competition between the rising state and the dominant state. The result of this strategic competition is dependent on the respective strategies of both sides, rather than on the decision of just one side. In most cases it is the outcome of interaction between multiple decisions. Guanzi says, "When your own state is well governed and your neighbors are badly ruled, these two conditions are the basis for you to establish a hegemon or a sage king."[32] This means that the correctness of one player's strategic decision will not necessarily secure the result of a game with two players. Williamson Murray defines strategy as "a process, a constant adaptation to shifting conditions and circumstances in a world where chance, uncertainty, and ambiguity dominate."[33] Based on the insightful ideas of Guanzi and Murray, I would argue that, out of all four strategic preferences, the proactive strategy stands the best chance of leading to the successful rise of a state, but there is no guarantee.

When a dominant state and a rising state are both governed by the same type of leadership, the former, owing to its advantageous capability of resources, will have a better chance than the latter of winning the competition between them. When the leaderships of both are the proactive type, the dominant state will have a better chance of consolidating or even improving its international dominance, while the rising state will have fewer opportunities to achieve its goal. Obtaining international power is different from obtaining the reign over a government. Xunzi says, "A state, being a small thing, can be obtained by villains through dishonest ways and held by them for a while. The all under heaven is a great entity, so it is impossible for villains to obtain it through dishonest ways and hold it."[34] Inspired by Xunzi's statement, the author suggests that the result of the strategic competition between a rising state and a dominant state is mainly decided by the disparity between them of the leadership capability necessary to win international support. In other words, the side that wins the most international support will win the competition.

STRATEGIC CREDIBILITY AND INTERNATIONAL LEADERSHIP

This book defines the core morality of a leading state as responsible and benevolent governance at the domestic level, and high strategic credibility at the international level. The type of international leadership provided by a leading state is determined according to whether or not the leadership values its international strategic credibility. Thus, international leadership can be categorized into four types: humane authority, hegemony, anemocracy, and tyranny. The four types of international leadership have different preferences as regards exercising their leadership in an international system.

International Strategic Credibility

Unlike state leadership, which is based on political power, international leadership mainly rests on national capability and strategic credibility. National capability is the instrument through which an actor exercises international leadership, and strategic credibility legitimizes an actor, so enabling him to attract international followers. Therefore, high international strategic credibility helps a strong state to provide gladly received international leadership. According to the distinction made in chapter 1 between power and authority, the authority of an international leadership is established on the basis of its high strategic credibility rather than on its national capability. Therefore, a leading state can enjoy high international authority only by retaining high strategic credibility.

International strategic credibility consists in both the legitimacy of international leadership and the political capability of that leadership. High international credibility usually leads to greater political capability. As the operational element of comprehensive capability, political capability can multiplicatively increase the effect of a leading state's resource capability. High credibility, therefore, can dramatically improve a rising state's comprehensive capability. This logic makes it possible for a rising state with high strategic credibility to reduce its disparity in comprehensive capability with the dominant state, even when its resource components of capability are by far the lesser of the two. The same logic can also be applied to a dominant state that tries to increase its superiority over a rising state by improving its strategic credibility.

The mechanism through which to convert international strategic credibility into improved comprehensive capability is reliance on the support of allies. By improving its strategic credibility, a leading state is able to gain more allies and wider international support. Having more allies avails a leading state more material resources through which to handle international difficulties; it also carries the bonus benefit of reducing the availability of international resources to rivals. This process will gradually change the disparity in comprehensive capability between the rising state and the dominant state. When the coalitions headed by the rising state overwhelm those led by the dominant state in terms of capability, the dominant state will have no other choice but to relinquish its pole position to the rising state. Conversely, the dominant state is able to constrain the rising state from expanding international support by making more allies, thereby consolidating the alliance it heads. This is why the number of allies is often used as a key index of international strategic credibility and political popularity. Providing security protection for other states, especially neighbors, through alliances is the main approach whereby a leading state establishes international strategic credibility.

After the Cold War, the Clinton administration improved America's strategic credibility by making more allies, mainly through expanding NATO.[35] The strategy of enlarging alliances helped the United States both to contain Russia and to effectively constrain China from gaining the international power commensurate with its quickly growing economic capability. Concurrently, although China became the second-largest world economy in 2010, it still has been insisting on a nonalignment principle and has been reluctant to provide security protection for other countries, including its neighbors. China's nonalignment policy undermines its international credibility and was a favorable factor in Obama's strategy of rebalancing toward the Asia-Pacific.

Trump's presidency is an example of how an international leadership is undermined by ignoring the value of alliance. Six months into

Trump's leadership, the United States had not experienced any change in resource capability; however, its international leadership had dramatically diminished. Western countries are no longer comfortable with looking to the United States as leader of the free world. During the NATO summit in May 2017, President Trump complained that European members of NATO had not contributed their "fair share" of resources toward their defense. In private meetings, NATO leaders expressed dismay at Trump's behavior and bearing, to the extent that the ultracautious German chancellor Angela Merkel declared in a major speech shortly after Trump's departure that Europeans could no longer completely rely on the United States.[36] "We Europeans truly have to take our fate into our own hands," Merkel said, adding, "We have to fight for our own destiny."[37]

Types of International Leadership

At the end of World War II, the international leaders dominating the world stage were Joseph Stalin, Winston Churchill, Charles De Gaulle, and Harry Truman, all of whom, on reflection, seem to have been larger than life. In the twenty-first century, international leaders are said to be limited because their key systematic constraints are no longer security issues but economic and environmental ones. In fact, this is not true. International leadership is still the key factor of international order. International leaders are called on to decide how to frame what is happening in the international arena through their involvement in establishing regional and global regimes, as well as in defining the rules and norms that will guide the international system into the future.

International leadership requires international followers; that is to say, there can be no leadership if there are no followers. However, other states do not follow different leaderships for the same reasons. Therefore, the type of international leadership is closely related to the level of authority that particular leadership carries. Since strategic credibility and a consistent principle of actions are the necessary conditions for establishing international authority, we can categorize

TABLE 2.2: TYPES OF INTERNATIONAL LEADERSHIP

	Strategic Credibility	
Principle of Actions	*Trustworthy*	*Untrustworthy*
Consistent	Humane authority	Tyranny
Double standard	Hegemony	Anemocracy

international leadership according to these two variables. The strategic credibility variable has two values: trustworthy and untrustworthy; the two values of the action principle variable are: consistent and double standard. Thus, we have four types of international leadership: humane authority, hegemony, anemocracy, and tyranny (see table 2.2). This categorization is inspired by the three types of rulers as classified by Xunzi. He says, "Accordingly, one who uses the state to establish justice will be a sage king; one who establishes trust will be a hegemon; and one who performs political deception will perish."[38] He defines the different approaches of the three types of rulers to governing a society as: "a sage king who tries to win men; a hegemon to acquire allies; a tyrant to capture land."[39] The four types of categorization here actually add anemocracy, between hegemony and tyranny, as a new type of international leadership.

Humane authority leadership. When an international leadership is trustworthy and its policies are consistent, it is categorized as a humane authority. Such an international leadership adopts foreign policies in accordance with international norms and is strategically trustworthy. In an international system, a leading state is deemed a humane authority by others if it practices moral principles; that is to say, it maintains high strategic credibility and pursues international order in the following three ways: (1) by setting itself as a good example to other states through actions in accordance with international norms; (2) by promoting beneficial international norms through rewarding the states that obey these norms; and (3) by punishing the states that violate international norms.[40] Guanzi makes a distinction between humane authority and hegemony, saying "One able to enrich the state is a hegemon, while one able to rectify wrong states is a sage king."[41] Since the leadership of a humane authority is able to rectify those states that disturb the international order, the order based on its leadership can durably be maintained. The Western Zhou Dynasty in the ancient Chinese interstate system is generally acknowledged as a model of humane authority that exercised enduring and stable maintenance of a relatively peaceful interstate order.

Humane authority constitutes a high moral standard of international leadership. Therefore, there have been few such leaderships throughout history. In modern history, Franklin D. Roosevelt's administration may serve as a representative of this type. Under his leadership, American troops liberated many countries occupied by Nazi Germany and militarist Japan during World War II. Such actions were known as *xing mie guo, ji jue shi* (兴灭国, 继绝世, the revival of states that had been extinguished and restoration of families whose line of succession had been broken) and accorded with the Confucian standard of humane authority leadership.[42] Roosevelt's administration, as a humane authority leadership, made a great contribution to the establishment of the United Nations. Unfortunately, President Roosevelt passed away before the UN's establishment on October 24, 1945, leaving no hope of carrying on that type of international leadership after World War II. Postwar history could otherwise have been much different.

Hegemonic leadership. When an international leadership is trustworthy but follows a double standard, it is classified as hegemonic. Such a leadership applies a double standard to policy making, insofar as it is helpful to its allies and, therefore, trusted, because it makes good on its pledges to them, but is meanwhile ruthless toward its rivals, who, therefore, would never expect the hegemonic state to follow international norms. With regard to strategic credibility and moral actions, the hegemonic leadership is no match for that of humane authority but is much better than an anemocracy or a tyranny. The hegemonic leadership will maintain its strategic credibility within an alliance while adopting the law of the jungle as the principle for dealing with nonallies. This contributes to maintaining the solidarity and stability of the alliance headed by a hegemonic state but undermines the stability of the international system as a whole. Thus, the international order dominated by a hegemonic state is relatively peaceful compared to one dominated by an anemocracy or tyranny, but far less peaceful than one led by a state of humane authority.[43] The State of Qi was a hegemon in the Spring and Autumn period and in 651 BCE organized the then largest alliance (of seven states) in the ancient Chinese interstate system. Under the rule of the Duke Huan, the State of Qi demonstrated the actions and strategies espoused by a hegemonic leadership.[44] The US and Soviet governments during the Cold War are usually regarded as modern representatives of hegemonic leadership.

Adhering to the content of international treaties that a leading state has signed is regarded as a moral action, and the leadership it offers is usually deemed a reliable and humane authority. In contrast, pursuing a double standard when practicing international norms is criticized as immoral, and the actor is treated as an unreliable state. The double-standard principle of a leading power is often viewed as hypocrisy. In fact there are nuances between hypocrisy and the double standard. The former implies that actors know that their behavior is immoral. As La Rochefoucauld says, "Hypocrisy is the homage vice pays to virtue."[45] The latter, however, often implies that actors believe it legitimate to pursue a double-standard principle without any feeling of guilt. For instance, Western states believed it moral after the Cold War to support secessionism in authoritarian regimes but not in democratic countries.

Anemocratic leadership. The leadership of a leading state that both is untrustworthy and follows a double standard is classified as an anemocracy. This type of leadership is irresponsible and adopts foreign policies simply because they accord with those chosen by other major states. This implies a leadership that bullies states weaker than itself, bows to those that are stronger or tougher, and is hence strategically untrustworthy. An anemocracy will not take responsibility for maintaining international norms, and its actions are often contradictory and confused. As its inconsistent policies make it unpredictable, the anemocracy has zero credit among its allies. The unreliable character of such leadership inclines other members of that interstate system to rely on their own military force to survive. As a consequence, military solutions become the popular outcomes of conflicts between states.

In Chinese history, King You, who reigned during the Zhou Dynasty during 781–771 BCE, typifies an anemocratic leadership. For the sake of entertaining Bao Si, his favorite concubine, he lit a beacon to trick his allies into sending troops to save him. After being so duped, none of his allies sent troops to help him when foreign powers really did invade his state.[46] As there can be no order in an interstate system under this type of leadership, an anemocracy is doomed to destruction. Some American scholars view Donald Trump's administration as this type of leadership. Soon after Trump's announcement of the United States' withdrawal from the 2015 Paris climate agreement, Nobel laureate Joseph E. Stiglitz published an article titled "Trump's Rogue America."[47] Pulitzer Prize–winning journalist Thomas L. Friedman went so far as to call Trump a Chinese "agent,"[48] and John Ikenberry, a professor from Princeton University, said, "the world's most powerful state has begun to sabotage the order it created. A hostile revisionist power has indeed arrived on the scene, but it sits in the Oval Office, the beating heart of the free world."[49]

Tyrannical leadership. When a leadership is untrustworthy but consistent, it is classified as a tyranny. Jackson and Rosberg say, "In a tyranny, not only legal but also all moral constraints on the exercise of power are absent, with the consequence that power is exercised in a completely arbitrary fashion according to the impulses of the ruler and his agents."[50] A tyrannical leadership always adopts foreign policies that are consistent with the principle of realpolitik, thus neither ally nor rival is willing to trust it. An obvious difference between the leaderships of an anemocracy and of a tyranny is that the former fears the strong or tough but the latter does not. A leading state is classified as a tyranny if its leadership is based on others' fear, and it has no strategic credit with respect to adhering to international norms. The immoral actions of a tyranny undermine the moral principles that other states practice while strengthening the law of the jungle in anarchical systems. When a tyrannical state is the dominant power, it takes the lead in undermining international moral codes, which inevitably tempts other states to imitate its actions. Thus, moral norms perish rather than expand, and the interstate society led by a tyrannical state is consequently often at war.[51]

Take the Qin Dynasty as an example: it was the first Chinese empire, and infamous for its brutal reign. It created an interstate order through its leadership in 221 BCE that lasted only fourteen years. Over the next two millennia, this has been the case most often cited by Chinese historians as illustrating how material capability alone is insufficient to maintain interstate order. In modern history, the German Nazi government headed by Adolf Hitler and the Japanese militarist government during World War II are generally regarded as representatives of tyrannical leadership.

Although there are four categories each of state leadership and of international leadership, they do not have a one-to-one correspondence, because the two systems of leadership are qualitatively different. State leadership undertakes responsibility only for its own country, and is thus concerned solely with its country's interests. International leadership undertakes responsibility for both its own country and the order of the international system. Because of this fundamental difference, a leading power may have different strategic preferences at the domestic and international levels respectively. It would be a misconception to believe that a state leadership that can expand the comprehensive capability of its own country is necessarily a good one for the international community. Theoretically speaking, inactive and aggressive leaderships place less value on strategic credibility than conservative and proactive leaderships do, but that does not guarantee that the latter are humane authority leaderships. To be a humane authority, the international leadership must push for international strategic credibility as an international norm. Doing so requires the leadership to use international strategic credibility as an instrument to enhance the international authority of its own state.

THE PRINCIPLE OF HUMANE AUTHORITY

In the previous section we discussed the correlation between types of international leadership and the influence of their foreign policy on international order. Among the four types of international leadership, humane authority and hegemony, rather than anemocracy and tyranny, have the ability to maintain a relatively stable international order. Nevertheless, *wangdao* (王道, the principle of humane authority) and *badao* (霸道, the principle of hegemony) are quite different with respect to the ways they provide international leadership. This section will clarify the differences between these two principles of international leadership, and discuss the means through which the principle of humane authority can find application in shaping the present international order. The most important precondition for implementing the humane authority principle lies in the consistency between the leading power's domestic ideology and the ideology it advocates internationally.

The Different Principles of Hegemony and Humane Authority

As far back as antiquity, whenever China rose to a leading position in East Asia, a debate arose among high-ranking officials in the royal court and ordinary scholars too about the contrasting ruling principles of humane authority and hegemony. Starting out from the belief that humans are self-interested, the principle of humane authority encourages China's rulers to adopt a benevolent foreign policy toward their weaker neighbors in the expectation that recipients of said benevolence will express gratitude for the benefits provided by following such leadership.[52] In contrast, the principle of hegemonic rule advocates that China's leaders adopt a deterrent strategy toward its neighbors. Based on the belief that human beings place greater value on what they might lose than what they stand to gain, the principle of hegemony argues that China's neighbors will value more what they stand to lose by challenging China's leadership than what they might gain from following said leadership.[53] Although both principles maintain that the only method of preserving interstate order is through the establishment of a hierarchical system based on a leading state's superior capability, humane authority tends toward use of the carrot while hegemony advocates the stick in this regard.

Because "hegemony" has negative connotations in modern times, its supporters have tried to find a more palatable descriptor for the concept. Chinese disciples have replaced the principle of hegemony with *xiong cai da lue* (雄才大略, great talent and bold vision), while American adherents have coined the phrase "benevolent hegemon" to distinguish American hegemony from its historical counterparts.[54] However, neither *xiong cai da lue* nor "benevolent hegemon" adequately expresses the different tenets that link hegemony with a better type of international leadership; consequently both are no more than sugar coatings for the hegemonic principle.

Rather than contrive more palatable terms for the hegemonic principle, ancient Chinese thinkers distinguished the types of interstate leadership according to their ruling principles. For instance, Guanzi categorized interstate leadership according to descending levels of good governance: huang (皇, the grand ruler), di (帝, emperor), wang (王, humane authority), and ba (霸, hegemon).[55] Guanzi proposed that a humane authority understands morality while a hegemon knows how to win wars.[56] Xunzi proposed that the difference between humane authority and hegemony does not lie in power, but in morality. He distinguished the two in light of the former's ability to win the voluntary subordination of others through moral actions, and the latter's to build alliances through establishment of strategic credibility.[57] Mencius made a similar distinction, holding that humane authority practices benevolence through morality while a hegemon feigns benevolence while relying on might.[58] Mencius may have been the first of the philosophers to characterize hegemony in a negative light, but his definition of hegemony is nonetheless closest to the connotation of a "benevolent hegemon."

Possibility of Humane Authority Leadership

It is true to say that the principle of humane authority has only a slight chance of becoming the doctrine of the new international leadership at the present time; the contemporary world is after all quite different in many aspects than the ancient Chinese interstate system. Nevertheless, the rise of China affords the possibility that the values of humane authority will be transposed to the present day according to the needs of future world leadership.

The advantages of Chinese traditional values constitute the favorable conditions under which new international leading powers may adopt the principle of humane authority, but they are not in themselves sufficient. The principle of humane authority also traditionally requires consistency between a ruler's internal governance and his or her conduct of foreign affairs, known as *neisheng waiwang* (内圣外王, domestic governance follows the principle of the sage, and foreign policies follow the principle of humane authority).[59] With respect to modern politics, *neisheng waiwang* calls for both domestic and foreign policies to be rooted in humane values. For this reason, the important precondition for the elevation of humane authority is that of the consistency of values espoused by leading states at home and abroad. For instance, liberalism has become the contemporary mainstream value since the end of the Cold War most closely associated with the domestic policies of the American government. This argument does not deny the important influence of European governments but rather emphasizes the crucial role of the leading state's domestic policies in maintaining the dominant position of liberalism. This argument is further supported by the fact that liberalism's global influence declined rapidly after the American government began advocating anti-establishmentarianism at home in 2017.[60]

Although China stands poised to be the most powerful rising state in the coming decade, that the world might witness its full embrace of the principle of humane authority as a new type of international leadership in the foreseeable future is less possible,

owing in part to the current Chinese government's pursuit of different values at home and abroad. However, differing from their parents' political mentality, Chinese millennials are politically open and
individualistic because of their modern educational background and
international experience and have learned about both traditional
Chinese culture and modern science in their primary education.
Unlike their parents, who during childhood were subjected to mistaken concepts about the rest of the world, this younger generation
studied foreign languages as children and also learned about different cultures. Therefore, it would not be difficult for leaders from this
generation to understand the logic whereby a leading state has a
greater chance of maintaining a long-term dominant status through
adoption of the principle of humane authority. As the relationship
between leading and lesser states in any international system is
asymmetric, as regards both capability and interdependency, the
principle of humane authority will enable lesser states to realize the
benefits of aligning with the leading state through trading off asym-
metrical wants for lasting security.[61] Thus, under such a model, international support for a new type of leading state will see greater
stability and longevity.

SUMMARY

Different types of political leadership tend to adopt different strategies even if the state's capability and external environment remain
the same. Therefore, the political leadership of a leading state is integral to changes in that state's comprehensive capability, international power, and international authority. State leadership is based
on a hierarchical power structure; thus, policy makers are able to
carry out their decisions through institutionalized forces. By contrast, international leadership is executed in an anarchical system;
thus, leading powers must implement their strategies through cooperation or coercion between independent states. Therefore, state
leadership and international leadership are categorized into different typologies. State leadership is classified into four types: inactive,

conservative, proactive, and aggressive. International leadership is also categorized under four types: humane authority, hegemony, anemocracy, and tyranny.

Because inactive, conservative, proactive, and aggressive leaderships believe in Daoism, economic determinism, political determinism, and social Darwinism respectively, their strategic preferences vary accordingly. When dealing with the rising state's dilemma, the four types of leadership of a rising state are most likely to opt for the strategies of avoiding conflicts, imposing economic impacts, enlarging international support, and military expansion respectively. The four types of international leadership usually adopt different foreign strategies to maintain the order of an international system. A humane authority adopts policies according to international moral codes, a hegemony practices the principle of double standards, an anemocracy behaves irresponsibly, and a tyranny acts according to the realpolitik principle.

These four categories each of state leadership and of international leadership, however, do not correspond with each other. The leadership of a leading state that is able to improve its national capability does not necessarily provide a benevolent international leadership or create a stable order of the international system. It is also true to say that a government that undermines its international status is not necessarily a tyrannical international leadership. In this book, the categories of both state leadership and international leadership are ideal types. By drawing comparisons between these ideal types of leadership, we can identify the dominant character of a given leadership and predict its strategic preference with regard to foreign policy making, and its attitude toward international norms. In real life, most state or international leaderships are hybrids of two types; thus, analyses of foreign policies should use the ideal leadership types as references rather than being constrained by categories.

In the era of globalization, the principle of humane authority maintains certain advantages with respect to becoming the doctrine of international leadership. Distinct from both traditional hegemony and American benevolent hegemony, it will embrace certain humanitarian values into its core values, so enabling its leadership to become favorable to the majority of UN members. Its moral principles can intensify its followers' confidence in a leadership of humane authority. However, to achieve universal adoption, humane authority requires consistency between a leading state's domestic ideology and the political values it pursues abroad. Unfortunately, the present Chinese government is conflicted in this regard, and thus the Chinese leadership of the next generation bears moral realist expectations.

3

Corollaries of International Change

满招损，谦受益，时乃天道。

(He who is proud shall fall, he who is humble shall prosper, such is the Way of the world.)

YU THE GREAT

Based on the definitions in chapter 1 of morality, capability, power, and authority, and the roles of leadership types as discussed in chapter 2, this chapter will expound a new theory about changes in international configurations, norms, orders, and systems. As a branch of IR realism, this theory follows fundamental realist assumptions, paramount among which is that the nature of interstate relations has not changed fundamentally throughout human history. Morgenthau says, "Human nature, in which the laws of politics have their roots, has not changed since the classical philosophies of China, India, and Greece endeavored to discover these laws."[1] Thus, if Guanzi, prime minster of Qi, a hegemon in the seventh century BCE, were placed in our midst today he would have no problem understanding the power struggles of our age. In this chapter, the four corollaries derived from these assumptions are shown to be mutually related and contain logically deduced conclusions. The following discussions will deal with the detailed relationships among the variables of political leadership, international configurations, foreign strategies, international norms, international orders, and international systems.

STATE LEADERSHIP AND CHANGE OF
POWER CONFIGURATION

History has witnessed several instances where a rising state has dramatically reduced its disparity in capability with a dominant state that is more advanced in almost all visible domains, including political institutions, ideology, technology, education, economy, and military, than the rising state. This phenomenon provides the impetus for this section to attribute the power transition from a dominant state to a rising state to improvements in the rising state's leadership, and to the decline in leadership of the dominant state. Therefore, the logic of the first corollary is that different types of state leadership result in the uneven growth of the capability of major powers, which, if it continues over decades, will lead to a change in the entire international configuration.

Corollary 1: Improvements and Declines of State Leadership
Lead to Changes in Relative Capability between States
and Eventually the Entire International Configuration

Realism assumes that differential growth of capability between states is a law of nature. In this world, natural growth is uneven—there are innumerable variables having impact on individuals' growth, many of which defy equal influence, such that identical growth is a statistical improbability. Even identical twins develop unique fingerprints. The law of differential growth also governs states' capability. Along with the differential growth of each state's capability, the capability structure between them gradually changes in favor of those that grow the fastest and hence leads to power redistribution and sometimes the shift of world power from dominant states to rising states. Based on this assumption, we can discuss corollary 1 in two aspects; the first, how does leadership influence the growth of capability? And the second, what impact do leadership types have on changes in power distribution?

(1) State Leadership Determines the Growth or Decline of That State's Capability

In chapter 1, we created the formula for national comprehensive capability: $CC = (M+E+C) \cdot P$. In breaking down the political capability in this formula, we focus on conscious human activity, that is, political leadership, because it is the operator of military, economic, and cultural resources that can play a role in international politics only when exploited by the governing body of a state. As an operational element, political leadership plays the essential role in improving, maintaining, or undermining state capability. An efficient political leadership is able not only to accelerate the growth of economic, military, and cultural resources, but also to enlarge the utility of these resources. In addition, an efficient leadership is able to win both domestic and foreign support, which improves a state's capability and international power.

Following the above logic, we can develop an explanation of the mechanism behind the law of differential growth of state capability. As state leadership is the foundation on which resource elements can be transferred to its capability, the different efficiency of each state's leadership results in differential growths between states in two aspects. First, the differing efficiencies of state leadership cause the resource elements to increase at different rates. Second, these differing efficiencies cause the same amounts of resource elements to enact different capabilities. As Guanzi said, "If a state is huge but the achievements of its government are insignificant, the state will become insignificant. If a state is small but the achievements of its government are significant, the state will become significant."[2]

Both the collapse of the Soviet Union in 1991 and the escalating decline of the United States in 2017 support the idea that state leadership is more important than the resource elements of a state's comprehensive capability. Taking the first example, when the Soviet government announced its demise at the end of 1991 it still had a much stronger military, economy, and cultural capacity than most countries. Its collapse was the result of the reduction to zero of the efficiency of state leadership, whereby the capabilities of all resource elements ceased to have any effect. As to the second example, the present US government is unable to mobilize either domestic or international support for its policies. The decline of its leading capability thus undermines the effect of America's comprehensive capability, including its international influence. "According to a new Pew Research Center survey spanning thirty-seven nations in 2017, a median of just 22 percent has confidence in President Trump to do the right thing when it comes to international affairs. This stands in contrast to the final years of Barack Obama's presidency, when a median of 64 percent expressed confidence in Trump's predecessor to direct America's role in the world."[3] A Gallup poll produced similar results. Only 30 percent of people interviewed in 134 countries in late 2017 approved of American leadership under Trump, a drop of nearly twenty percentage points since Obama's final year.[4]

(2) Different Leaderships between Dominant and Rising States Determine Changes in the International Configuration

The international configuration refers to the power structure, which is decided by both the major states' relative capabilities and their strategic relations with each other. In theoretical IR studies, the three ideal shapes of international configuration are unipolar, bipolar, and multipolar. In the real world, there are many hybrids between any two of these three ideal shapes. Because an international configuration is composed of both the capability structure of powerful states and the strategic relations between them, changes in international configurations are due not only to the rise and fall in capability of powerful states, but also to the influence of fluctuations in their alliance numbers.[5]

For example, the transformation of the international configuration from bipolar during the Cold War to unipolar in the post–Cold War era was driven by (1) the enlarged disparity in capability between Russia and the United States (change in states' capability) and

(2) the disintegration of the Warsaw Pact whereby Russia lost its allies (decrease in the number of alliances). With regard to the terms of leadership of their respective alliances, the United States performed much better than the Soviet Union during the Cold War. The Soviet Union's leadership of the Warsaw Pact was brutal, its having used military invasion to change its allies' governments on several occasions. This eroded the durability and reliability of the loyalty to the Soviet Union of its allies. Meanwhile, the United States did not abuse its leadership of the North Atlantic Treaty Organization (NATO), and nor did it use military force against its allies. This helped to consolidate NATO as a collective power. After the Cold War, the United States remained as the sole superpower, and the Soviet Union ceased to exist. The bipolar configuration was thus transformed into a unipolar one.

The cases of the Warsaw Pact and NATO demonstrate how the international leadership of superpowers can have different effects. Leading states with high strategic credit are able to establish and expand unbreakable alliances, while the opposite is true for states without high credibility. Xi Que, a minister of the Jin State during the Spring-Autumn period, once remarked on the relationship between the strategic credit of a leading state and the reliability of the alliance it headed. He said: "How can a ruler demonstrate his authority if he does not suppress mutinying states? How can a ruler demonstrate his benevolence if he does not show mercy to those coming over to pledge allegiance? How can a ruler prove his morality without demonstration of his authority and benevolence? Without morality, how can he be the head of an alliance?"[6]

State Capability and International Status

The capability structure of leading states constitutes the core of the international configuration. That means the international configuration will generally remain unchanged when leading states cannot dramatically change the disparity in capability between them. In most cases, changes in the capability structure of leading states are accompanied by changes in strategic relations between major powers. For instance, the bipolar configuration of the Cold War could not be changed as long as the Soviet Union did not collapse, and the unipolar configuration of the post–Cold War world would endure as long as China did not dramatically reduce its disparity in capability with the United States. Since change in power distribution mainly results from the increase or decrease in major powers' capability, it is necessary to establish a capability category before we are able to judge whether or not a configuration changes.

We can categorize states into four classes according to their capability. They are dominant states, rising states, regional states, and small states. The growth or decline in capability of dominant and rising states has an impact on changes in the international configuration of an independent international system, while that of regional and small states does not. The following categories enable assessment of a state's comprehensive capability according to its international status, and the identification of its strategic interests according to its capability. The traits of each category are as follows:

(1) *Dominant states*: These are countries that have a dominant influence within any independent international system that is not necessarily a global one. In ancient times, there were several independent interstate systems before the global international system was formed in around 1500 CE.[7] In this book, leading powers in ancient compartmentalized systems and modern worldwide systems are treated equally as dominant states. For example, during the Spring and Autumn period in ancient China, five hegemons—the State of Qi, the State of Jin, the State of Chu, the State of Wu, and the State of Yue—established themselves in succession, and each gained the dominant position in that system during different periods.[8] Thus, they are all defined as dominant states, equivalent to ancient empires, such as the Roman Empire, the Ottoman Empire, the Tang Empire, and the Mongol Empire, and modern superpowers, such as France and the UK in eighteenth century and the Soviet Union and the United States during the Cold War.

(2) *Rising states*: These are countries whose comprehensive capability grows to an extent that narrows their disparity in capability with the dominant state, enabling them to seize some of its power.

The United States was a rising state in the 1870s, the Soviet Union in the 1950s, and Japan in 1980s. After the financial crises of 2008, China became a typical rising state. The capability of a rising state may surpass that of the dominant state, so making it the superpower; the United States is a case in point. It may also become a superpower but not surpass the dominant state, as with the Soviet Union. Such a state may also narrow its disparity in capability with the dominant state but not reach the level of a superpower, as was the case of Japan during the Cold War. China has dramatically reduced its disparity in comprehensive capability with the United States in the first seventeen years of the twenty-first century. Since 2017, however, America's strategic mistakes have played a far more important role in reducing this disparity in capability than China's growth could.

(3) *Regional states*: These countries are dominant in geographic regional or subregional affairs; although uncontested in subsections of independent international systems, they are nevertheless still under the influence of dominant states at the level of the entire system. Today, Russia, Japan, Germany, France, the UK, Brazil, and Australia belong to the category of regional powers, while India, South Africa, Saudi Arabia, and Indonesia are subregional powers. Modern regional states are different from those ancient dominant states in separate independent interstate systems, even though their influence is in similar geographic areas. Unlike their early predecessors, modern regional states do not wield influence within the system to which they belong as a whole. Take for example India, which is a subregional state in South Asia in the present global international system, while the Mughal Empire (1526–1857) was a dominant state in that region and constituted an independent interstate system that had little contact with the rest of the world during that period. Another example is the UK's Brexit referendum in 2016, which resulted in the UK leaving the European Union. Although this sent shock waves through European politics, it had negligible impact on non-European states.[9]

(4) *Small states*: These are countries that are too weak to exert any leading influence at the regional or subregional level of either system.

It is important to note that all the above definitions are based on comparisons of the relative capability of states in the same international system or in the same region or subregion. For example, Canada and Australia are fairly equal in terms of absolute capability, but the former lacks regional influence compared with the latter because of the countries' different geopolitical status. Therefore, Canada is classified as a small state because it is a weak neighbor of the United States, a superpower, while Australia is classified as a regional power in Oceania, because its capability is much larger than that of all the other countries in the Oceania region.

Based on the above definitions of state capability, both dominant and rising states compete for the configuration most favorable to themselves in an independent international system; regional powers keep a watchful eye on changes in the power configuration in their particular region; and small states give no thought to reshaping the configuration at any level.

STATE CAPABILITY, LEADERSHIP, AND STRATEGY PREFERENCE

This book provides a dualist theory that stresses the importance of both political leadership and a state's capability in decision making. A strategy is composed of goals, and the approaches to achieving these goals. A state's capability determines its objective interests, namely, the goals of its strategies, while a state's leadership determines the approaches to achieving that state's interests. Therefore, foreign strategies are jointly determined by these two variables. On the one hand, the anarchical nature of the international system requires all policy makers to define their strategic interests prudently, according to their state capability; on the other hand, it gives policy makers room to develop the distinct strategic approaches through which to pursue national interests (see figure 3.1).

This section derives corollary 2, which links the anarchical nature of the international system to different strategic preferences. In fact, it makes a methodological connection between theories at the levels of the international system and of policy making, which no-

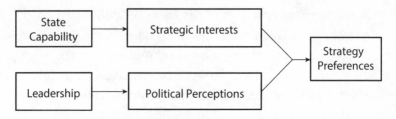

FIGURE 3.1 Joint impacts of capability and leadership on strategy preferences

tionally accounts for the presence of both capability resources and operational capacity in decision making.[10] This corollary helps to explain why states that have successfully risen usually invent new strategies rather than imitating existing strategies that have succeeded in history.

Corollary 2: In the Anarchical International System, All States Engage in Self-Help for Their Own Strategic Interests but Adopt Different Foreign Strategies to Pursue Them

Realism assumes that states can rely on no one but themselves for survival because of the absence in the anarchical international system of organizations that constitute legal military force monopolies.[11] In fact, both pursuing and protecting security interests depend on states' native capability, including adopting the appropriate foreign strategies. According to the "self-help" doctrine that reflects the anarchical character of the international system, corollary 2 can be discussed in two aspects: how different state leaderships lead to different strategies in the same international system; and how different international leaderships result in different international orders.

(1) Different Types of State Leadership Adopt Different Strategies for Pursuing Strategic Interests

State capability serves as a basis for defining states' strategic interests, as well as for limiting strategic choices. Waltz says, "The units of an anarchic system are functionally undifferentiated. The units of such an order are then distinguished primarily by their greater or lesser capabilities for performing similar tasks."[12] Because achieving different interests entails different capabilities, lesser states usually define their strategic interest at a lower level than great powers do. Accordingly, they adopt different security strategies. Take America, Japan, and the Vatican as examples: the United States protects not only its own security but also that of its allies; Japan protects no other states' security and partially entrusts its own security to the United States; and the Vatican fully entrusts its security to Italy. It is a popular phenomenon in an anarchic system for lesser states to entrust their security to a more powerful state or an alliance, because their own limited military capability cannot guarantee their survival.[13]

States' differing capabilities apart, different types of state leaderships are also instrumental in states' adoption of different strategies. In this regard, we can find also that states of similar capability adopt different security strategies. For instance, most of the lesser states, such as Japan, West Germany, India, and Egypt, made alliances with one of the two superpowers—the Soviet Union and the United States—for their security in the 1960s. Nevertheless, China was an exception under the leadership of Mao Zedong during that period, adopting the strategy of standing against both superpowers. This strategy certainly failed to protect China's security but nonetheless illustrates the fact that political leadership has an impact on strategic preferences at least equal to that of state capability. When state capability remains unchanged, political leadership becomes the determining factor.

(2) Different Types of International Leadership Advocate Different International Orders

Many realist theorists believe that rising states and dominant states invariably settle any power struggles between them through war. Shepard Clough says, "At least in all the cases which we have passed . . . cultures with inferior civilization but with growing economic power have always attacked the most civilized cultures during the latter's economic decline."[14] Gilpin says, "As its relative power increases, a rising state attempts to change the rules governing the international system, the division of the spheres of influence, and, most important of all, the international distribution of territory. In response, the dominant power counters this challenge through changes in its policies that attempt to restore equilibrium in the system. The historical record reveals that if it fails in this attempt, the disequilibrium will be resolved by war."[15] Mearsheimer argues that all great powers must employ an offensive strategy to maintain their dominant positions in the anarchical international system, saying, "Offensive realists . . . believe that status quo powers are rarely found in world politics, because the international system creates powerful incentives for states to look for opportunities to gain power at the expense of rivals, and to take advantage of those situations when the benefits outweigh the costs. A state's ultimate goal is to be the hegemon in the system."[16] Graham Allison calls the war between rising states and dominant states "Thucydides's trap."[17] These statements imply that only one strategy can be deployed to deal with the conflicts between rising states and dominant states— that of war.

Corollary 2 challenges this logic and argues that there is more than one strategy whereby a great power can obtain or maintain its dominance, just as the dominant species in an ecosystem can achieve its numerical advantage through multiple strategies, such as pure breeding speed (rats), or lower offspring mortality (hominids). It is true to say that offensive strategies have been popularly adopted by powerful states in our history, but they are not the solely viable ones. In any given era, the dominant state will encounter an international system, international norms, and military technology entirely different from those of the previous era. That state has a greater chance of improving its power through a newly invented strategy than by imitating the existing ones. For example, before World War I the European powers competed for hegemony by conquering colonies outside Europe. During World War II, Germany, Italy, and Japan did so by annexing their neighbors but suffered defeat. Different from the European powers, the United States and the Soviet Union contended for hegemony via proxy war during the Cold War. Since the second decade of the twenty-first century, history has witnessed the struggle for power between the United States and China through nonviolent strategies including trade war that are in stark contrast to those adopted by the United States and the Soviet Union.

Alliance Strategy versus the Nonalignment Principle

The nonaligned movement was founded by the leaders of five third-world countries (India, Yugoslavia, Egypt, Indonesia, and Ghana) in the 1950s. The principle of nonalignment has since evolved into a kind of strategic ideology shared by many developing countries. Since the Cold War, whether or not to make alliances has come to be regarded no longer as a strategy geared purely to security, but rather a strategic preference imbuing concerns about political morality. For instance, alliance has gradually been framed as a negative political concept in China. As a self-identified developing country, China has officially labeled alliance as denoting a Cold War mentality and persuaded its strategic partners to accept this view. Russia, for instance, agrees with China that alliance is a policy synonymous with a Cold War mentality, even though it still maintains alliances with certain former Soviet Republics.[18] The United States and Western countries, meanwhile, regard alliance as a moral strategy for protecting their collective security, based on both common strategic interests and shared democratic ideology.

Despite the fact that China, the present powerful rising state, and some developing countries disvalue the alliance strategy, the author nevertheless believes that alliance remains an effective moral strategy through which leading states may win international support and also establish their authority. Alliance is a public good based on the leading states' protection of lesser states' security. Through making an alliance, a rising state can improve its strategic credibility and international influence, so facilitating changes in the international power distribution, and thus gaining the chance to establish its leadership over the whole international system. Once consolidated, the leadership can establish new international norms that enable it to change the normative order and even the entire international system.

Certain scholars in both China and the United States argue that alliance can easily lead to war, and that the lesser ally in an alliance with a leading state could drag that state into an unnecessary military conflict. In reality, the political leadership is the determining factor of whether or not a leading power can either successfully deter potential wars by making alliances or be passively dragged into unnecessary wars. Recent critics of the alliance strategy are now frustrated by a solid study of the function of alliances in war-making policy. Michael Beckley's research on US alliance history concludes: "In sum, the empirical record shows that the risk of entanglement is real but manageable and that, for better or worse, US security policy lies firmly in the hands of US leaders and is shaped primarily by those leaders' perceptions of the nation's core interests. When the United States has overreached militarily, the main cause has not been entangling alliances but rather what Richard Betts calls 'self-entrapment'—the tendency of US leaders to define national interests expansively, to exaggerate the magnitude of foreign threats, and to underestimate the costs of military intervention."[19]

That the head of an alliance that has become involved in war is immoral or irresponsible is a misconception. Holding the opposite view in this regard, I would argue that indiscriminate refusal to use military force is a policy of national suicide, as well as an immoral principle, and antithetical to the behavior of a humane authority leadership. In the anarchical international system, small states seldom have enough military capability to protect their security and must rely on a powerful state for protection. A leading state's adoption of a policy of absolute nonuse of military force amounts to a denial of its duty to protect international order and justice. Other states consequently perceive such a leading state as one lacking both moral integrity and strategic credibility, and hence to whom lesser states cannot entrust their security, instead forcing them to rely on their own military capability. When the leading state refuses to maintain international order through military force, the whole system falls into a chaos wherein war predominates over peace in a system dominated by realpolitik norms.

INTERNATIONAL LEADERSHIP AND NORM CHANGE

IR realism assumes that human nature is selfish, and thus that states controlled by human beings must also be driven by self-interests.[20] This assumption is backed up by the theory of evolution, which holds that the force of natural selection as evident in animal behaviors is attributable to selfish survival needs, while hypotheses based on group altruism are demonstrably implausible. Beyond natural instincts, human behavior is also shaped by social norms and expectations. For example, psychologists have found that children who have been consistently exposed to adults that display violent behavior are more likely to give aggressive responses than children who are not; also that children who have been abused are more likely to be abusers themselves upon reaching adulthood than others in the same cohort.[21] These studies demonstrate the role that environment plays in shaping behavior. Based on this knowledge, I derive the third corollary as below.

Corollary 3: Pursuit of Self-Interest Is the Primary Motivation of State Actions as Well as the Selective Force behind the Creation of International Norms

There is a popular misconception that some states adopt foreign policy according to their national interests, and some do according to international norms. The truth of the matter is that every state adopts a foreign policy based on concern for its own interests as well as the constraints of international norms in any interstate system. Since both interests and norms have an impact on states' policy decisions, we will explain corollary 3 from two aspects: what impact interests and norms have respectively on policy making; and how interests drive leading powers to establish international norms.

(1) The Pursuit of Self-Interest Is the Primary Dynamic of State Actions, but It Is Also Impacted by Social Norms

It is true to say that self-interest is the primary motivation of state actions, but social perceptions and expectations are also influential

in the shaping of policies that states make. In regard to what constitutes human nature, Xunzi once clearly distinguished *xing* (性, inherited traits) from *wei* (伪, nurtured traits). He said: "As a general
rule, 'inherited traits' are given by nature, what cannot be learned,
and what requires no application to master. . . . What must be
learned before a man can do them and to what he must apply himself
before he can master them are called 'nurtured traits.' This is the
distinction between inherited traits and nurtured traits."[22] The pursuit of self-interest is an inherited trait. It generates the same influence on every decision maker because it is the natural instinct of all
human beings. Nevertheless, according to Xunzi, policy makers
have different social perceptions, or nurtured traits, owing to different upbringings, including education. These different perceptions
may lead policy makers to adopt different strategies when dealing
with similar problems.

Policy makers' social perceptions may affect the process of policy making in two ways. One is the influences they have on policy
makers' ranking of national interests, that is to say, which national
interests are given priority in a specific situation. The other is
through their impacts on policy makers' strategic preferences as
regards achieving those interests. I suggest that objective national
interests are defined by state capability, and that their existence is
not determined by people's perceptions, although policy makers'
social perceptions do indeed affect which interest they consider
most important and what strategy is most appropriate for obtaining
said interests. This characterization of national interests is what
distinguishes my view on national interests from Alexander
Wendt's. I believe that national interests are objective, while Wendt
suggests that national interest is subjectively construed by social
perceptions.[23]

(2) The State's Pursuit of Self-Interest Is Also the Force
behind the Establishment of New International Norms

Classical realism assumes that "states are rational actors characterized by a decision-making process leading to choices based on national interests."[24] According to this assumption, the pursuit of self-

interest is also the driving force behind leading states' effort to establish new international norms. Military force and international norms are the two fundamental means used in concert to maintain a sustainable international order; neither is sufficient to achieve that goal alone. For instance, the foremost priority of a dominant state's national interest is to maintain the international order it has established in favor of its own strategic interests. In order to keep that order as long as possible, the dominant state must establish a set of international norms for other countries to follow. These norms stabilize the international order and reduce its maintenance costs. Although international norms constrain the actions of the dominant state, that state will nevertheless benefit more than any other country from the order it has enforced, because these norms will provide it with strategic advantages that far outweigh any disadvantages. This is why a dominant state provides the world with public goods such as international order. When the norms generate more cost than benefit for the dominant state, however, it will revise them accordingly. For instance, after the 2008 global financial crisis, the United States proposed the Trans-Pacific Partnership (TPP) and the Transatlantic Trade and Investment Partnership (TTIP) to replace the World Trade Organization (WTO), in order to maintain its dominant position by formulating more liberal trade norms. Trump's administration also views WTO norms as unfavorable to America, but contrary to Obama's administration, with its strategic preference, Trump's administration believes that protectionist norms are favorable to American economic interests.

Rising states can be another important force behind the reform of existing international norms, which have generally been established in favor of the dominant state. When a rising state dramatically reduces its disparity in capability with the dominant state, it will seek to reform the existing international norms in the direction favorable to itself. As the reform of international norms requires the capability of providing public goods in related fields, a rising state usually advocates reform or the creation of new norms in areas where its capability is greater, or at least equal to that of the dominant state. For example, after 2010 China became the country with the world's largest foreign reserves but had difficulties finding profitable projects for investment. In order to make full use of those reserves, in 2013, China initiated the establishment of the Asian Infrastructure Investment Bank (AIIB). A main difference between AIIB and other international development banks is the absence of any political prerequisite to loans.

Strategic Credibility and International Norms

It is commonplace for IR scholars to emphasize the function of rewards and punishments in the establishment of new international norms. However, this understanding ignores the fact that, for leading states, establishing new international norms based on high strategic credibility is by far the more efficient approach. This could be more important to rising states because they have less material capability than the dominant state as regards doling out rewards or imposing punishments. When a rising state achieves higher strategic credibility than the dominant state, however, the new norms it proposes will be more attractive to lesser states than the ones the dominant state advocates. This argument does not deny the effectiveness of rewards and punishments in establishing new norms but suggests that leading by example is a more competitive mechanism for creating new norms. This mechanism rests on a leading state's pursuance of what it preaches, that is to say, setting itself as an example to other states in the same international system.[25] Through the consistency of actions and advocated codes, the leading state will improve its international strategic credibility and gain the influence it needs to reshape international norms.

In fact, the functions of strategic credibility in shaping international norms are the same for both rising states and dominant states. Specifically, retaining high strategic credibility is more important for the maintenance of an existing international order than for establishing a new one. Generally, it is possible for a dominant state to establish an international order entirely by virtue of its material capability, but it cannot continuously maintain that order through material capability alone. The durability of an international order is based on the premise that most states adhere to international norms. To what extent those states stick to the existing norms greatly depends on the dominant state's credibility as regards following the norms that it advocates. Thus, there is a positive correlation between the leading state's strategic credibility and the durability of the international order it establishes.

A recent example supporting the above argument is America's violation of the norms of strategic arms control. The Bill Clinton administration and the George W. Bush administration adopted different policies toward international arms control and nuclear proliferation. During the Cold War, the United States globally promoted the Treaty on the Limitation of Anti-ballistic Missile Systems (ABM) as the cornerstone of world peace. In the late 1990s, however, the Bill Clinton administration considered opting out of the ABM Treaty in order to deploy the National Missile Defense system. However, fearing this action might severely impair America's international strategic credit, Clinton did not authorize the Pentagon's plan.[26] Bush's administration did not place the same value as the Clinton administration on international strategic credit. George W. Bush not only denounced the ABM Treaty soon after coming to power in 2001 but also lifted the US sanctions of 1998 on India's illegal nuclear tests.[27] To make things worse, just two years later, the United States went back on its word by enacting a nuclear cooperation with India, a nonsignatory to the Nuclear Non-proliferation Treaty.[28] America's inconsistent policies toward nuclear proliferation reduced America's strategic credibility, and a weakened nonproliferation regime ensued wherein North Korea and Iran endeavored to implement their nuclear plans.

CHANGES IN INTERNATIONAL ORDER AND SYSTEMS

Changes in power distribution are often directly related to the changed international status of rising states and dominant states. During the process of change in power distribution, rising states must demand international power commensurate with their increased capability, while dominant states must protect their original power, which, owing to their declining capability, they can no longer support. Therefore, the power struggle between a rising state and the dominant state becomes inevitable and causes serious disturbances to the international order. Based on this common knowledge, we can derive the following corollary.

Corollary 4: The Zero-Sum Nature of Power Brings About a Structural Contradiction between Rising States and Dominant States, as Well as Disturbances to the Existing International Order

Power rests on the relationship between superior and inferior actors; thus one's gain in power entails another's loss. Therefore, international power competition between rising states and dominant states is a zero-sum game.[29] Based on this assumption, we can discuss corollary 4 in two aspects: how the nature of power generates a structural contradiction between rising and dominant states; and how power struggle disturbs the international order.

(1) The Structural Contradiction between the Rising State and the Dominant State Is Inevitable Because Both Pursue Domination within a Closed System

The structural contradiction between a rising state and a dominant state stems from the redistribution of power between them during changes of configuration. This contention is inevitable, because it emerges naturally, along with the process of the narrowing disparity in capability between them, as well as the transition of international leadership from a dominant state to a rising state. Under the present situation where we lack galactic travel or communications with any alien civilizations, the current international system is a closed one in which the international power sums to one; fractions of this power are then distributed among all states according to the relative capability of each. In our history, those independent international systems that lacked substantial contact with each other possess the same nature as the modern global system in terms of power distribution.

The distribution of leadership power is mainly arranged according to the international structure of the major states' capability. Consequently, rising states will attempt to seize more power, while the dominant state refuses to share its power with the rising state, even as its relative capability declines. Therefore, the nature of the structural contradiction is that of the struggle between maintaining and changing the existing structure of international power distribution. The Anglo-German naval arms race from 1898 to 1912 serves as a good case to illustrate the concept of structural contradiction.[30]

For rising states, the structural contradiction is also manifested in the rising state's dilemma wherein external pressure on it increases in tandem with their expanding influence. The rising state's dilemma somewhat resembles Newton's Third Law, which states that "for every action there is an equal and opposite reaction." Similarly, the rapid growth of a rising state will impose a strong impact on other states, mainly the dominant state, the inevitable results of which are either desperate resistance or confrontation. The growing capability of a rising state expands its interests overseas, thus leading to conflicts with others' interests. The more overseas interests a rising state acquires, the more conflicts with other states it must face, and the more these conflicts will accumulate till they reach the level of strategic confrontation or threats. A recent example of the rising state's dilemma is the emergence after the 2008 Beijing Olympic Games of comments in international public opinion on "China's Responsibility." Many countries, mainly the United States, blamed China for not undertaking international responsibility consistent with its capability.[31] This opinion intensified after 2010, when China's GDP replaced Japan's, making China the world's second-largest economy.

(2) International Order Becomes Unstable Because of Disagreement over Power Redistribution

International order is the state of affairs wherein players in a given international system settle their conflicts through nonviolent approaches according to interstate norms.[32] This means that as long as no states resort to military solutions, the general international order can be maintained. Resuming order through violent actions is also under the chaotic condition. Nevertheless, there is no military monopoly in the anarchical international system; therefore, any state that is dissatisfied with the current situation may use its military might to achieve the interests it claims. The core of international order is the structure of power distribution among states. Owing to humans being born hungry for power, neither the dominant state nor the rising state is satisfied with the existing power distribution in an international system. Although the dominant state has more power than other states, it still pursues more. For instance, upon becoming sole superpower after the collapse of the Soviet Union, the United States was in possession of more international power than any other country, but US president George H. W. Bush nevertheless called for the establishment of a new international order.[33] This is a case of the dominant state seizing more power from its rivals, rather than a rising state seizing power from the dominant state.

The international configuration constitutes the material basis for an international order. Any changes in configuration, therefore, will undermine that order. Since the dominant states enjoy more international power than rising states do, they stress the importance of maintaining the existing order, or to be more exact, the existing structure of power distribution. Meanwhile, the rising state advocates establishment of a new order, which entails a redistribution of international power according to the changed capability structure. Because the configuration is composed of both the capability structure of major states and the strategic relations between them, the leading state, which has more allies than any of its rivals, has the best chance of reshaping the international order according to its own blueprint.

It would be a misconception to assert that leading states' moral actions, including those that gain it high strategic credibility, constitute a panacea for shaping the international order. The international order is rather maintained by both the capability and moral policies of leading states. National capability is the precondition for effective moral actions. In other words, the moral actions of leading states can play a positive role in maintaining international order, largely because leading states have larger material capability than lesser states. Without superior capability, no leading state would be able to maintain international order through moral actions alone.

Types of International Leadership and System Change

Changes in international order, no matter whether the order is disturbed or resumed, do not prefigure a change of the entire international system, because the order and the system are two totally different entities. Gilpin defines an international system as "an aggregation of diverse entities united by regular interaction according to a form of control," and international order as "the governance of an international system."[34] Hedley Bull also makes a distinction between international system and order. As he defines the former, a "system of states (or international system) is formed when two or more states have sufficient contact between them, and have sufficient impact on one another's decision, to cause them to behave—at least in some measure—as parts of whole"; and the latter as "a pattern of activity that sustains the elementary or primary goals of the society of states, or international society."[35] Based on their definitions, this book defines the system as a complex whole and the order as the state of a system.

The international norm is the shared component of the international order and the international system, which could be the reason why many people confuse the two. As the shared component of these two entities, international norms perform the function of defining the normative character of a given international order or international system. For instance, based on the principles of free trade and fair trade, an international community can establish two different sets of international trade norms. The normative order of international trade will be decided according to which set of norms states follow in their trade contacts. This logic can also be applied to defining normative character changes in a given international system. Although sharing one component, the international order and system each have two components that are different from the other's, which is often ignored by IR students. The components of an

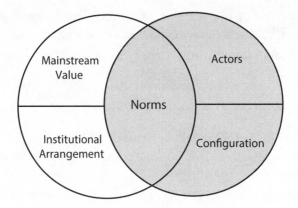

FIGURE 3.2 Components of international order and international system

international system include actors and a configuration, while those of an international order include mainstream values and institutional arrangements (see figure 3.2).

The distinction between the international system and the international order implies that any given international system could be in order or disorder. The same goes for a domestic system, which can be either at peace or in the throes of a civil war. We can illustrate the difference through the analogy of a mechanical watch and an electronic watch. Mechanical and electronic watches are two different systems, but both are in good order if they keep good time, and if they do not run correctly, then neither is in order. In our history, the international order has frequently been disturbed by wars within a given international system, and that system has proved able to survive these wars and have its order restored. For instance, the ancient Chinese tributary system and the modern sovereignty system are two different types of international systems that sometimes maintain peace and sometimes do not.

International order can be categorized into two domains—structural order and normative order. The former refers to the structure of power distribution, which is mainly represented by the arrangement of international institutions, such as the privilege of permanent membership of the UN Security Council. The latter refers to the character of norms, mainly illustrated by the principle of norms, such as nuclear nonproliferation. Evelyn Goh says, "Beyond power distribution, an order transition involves significant alterations in the common goals and values, rules of the game and social structures of international society."[36] Changes in either structural order or normative order will cause conflicts between major states, which sometimes may escalate into military clashes, that is, disorder. In general, changes in structural order will more likely lead to armed conflicts than those in normative order.

Because international order and system are different substances, they change under different conditions. When it has transitioned from the leadership of a dominant state to that of a rising state, the international order is usually undermined. Nevertheless, transformation of the international system often hinges on a change in the type of international leadership; otherwise the system may remain the same after the order has been resumed. For instance, according to the types of international leaderships defined in chapter 2, the leadership offered by European colonial powers before World War II was one of tyranny, and that by the United States and Soviet Union during the Cold War was one of hegemony. In these two periods, the two different types of leadership established different international norms. Annexation, a common norm prior to World War II, was prohibited after World War II. The United Nations adopted the charter, asserting, "All Members shall refrain in their international relations from the threat or use of force against the territorial integrity or political independence of any state, or in any other manner inconsistent with the Purposes of the United Nations."[37] Along with the changes in both international configuration and norms, therefore, after World War II the international system changed from one type to another.

Whether the success of a rising state will change the type of international system depends on the quantity of system components that change in type by virtue of the successful rising state. Since the international actors, international configuration, and international norms are the three key components of an international system, changes to any two or to all three of them will transform the system

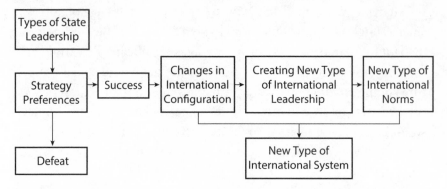

FIGURE 3.3 Types of rising states' leadership and changes in international systems

as a whole from one type to another.[38] The international configuration often changes from one shape to another as a rising state replaces the dominant state as the new international leader. Based on the new configuration shape, the international system may change if the rising state offers a new type of international leadership and establishes new norms.

Figure 3.3 illustrates the relations between the types of state leadership of rising states and possible changes in international systems. The type of state leadership determines the rising states' strategy preference, but their strategy may lead to two different results—success or defeat. If the rising states successfully change the international configuration by catching up with or even surpassing the dominant state in terms of comprehensive capability, they will have the chance to offer to international society a new type of international leadership and to shape new international norms for the sake of maintaining the new order dominated by them. As long as rising states bring about changes in both international configurations and norms, the type of international system will change accordingly.

SUMMARY

This chapter explores the logics and mechanisms of international power transition on the basis of fundamental realist assumptions. From these assumptions moral realism derives four corollaries: (1)

improvements or declines in states' leadership lead to changes in relative capability between major states and eventually in the international configuration; (2) all states engage in self-help for their own strategic interests in the anarchical international system but adopt different foreign strategies to pursue them; (3) pursuit of self-interest is the primary motivation of state actions as well as the selective force behind the creation of international norms; and (4) the zero-sum nature of power brings about a structural contradiction between a rising state and a dominant state, as well as disturbances to the existing international order.

These corollaries, moreover, are not mutually exclusive but may overlap. For example, corollary 1 argues that the difference in leadership determines the change in international configuration, while corollary 2 assumes that different leaderships have different strategic preferences, and that all states engage in self-help for strategic interests in an anarchical system. Corollary 3 assumes that pursuit of self-interests is the primary motivation of state action, arguing that leading states establish international norms to stabilize an order in favor of their own interests, while corollary 4 argues that conflicting interests between leading states destabilize international order.

Obviously, these four corollaries are abstractions of a highly complex international political reality but nevertheless theoretically connect the three levels of analysis—leadership at individual level, policy making at state level, and configuration as well as norms at the system level—by attributing changes in international configuration, norms, orders, and systems to the leadership types of rising and dominant states. We can see that the types of political leadership play a crucial role in all four corollaries. They determine the growth of state capability in corollary 1, foreign strategies for international competition in corollary 2, the types of international norms in corollary 3, and the stability and durability of international order in corollary 4.

Although the types of international leadership determine the types of international norms and the stability of international order, changes in international order do not necessarily bring about any transformation of international system, because they are different substances. The international system refers to an assemblage of components (actors, configurations, and norms) forming international society as a unitary whole, while the international order refers to the state of the international system, and whether or not actors settle disputes peacefully according to norms. Although the international norm is the shared component of these two substances, it defines only their normative trait and does not make them the same.

4

Power Redistribution and World Center

夫先王之所以王者，资邻国之举不当也。
(Ancient kings became the world leaders, which benefited from the wrong policies of their neighboring states.)

GUANZI

The previous chapter attributes international power redistribution to the different capabilities between the national leaderships of rising states and the dominant state. The bipolarization that occurred in the second decade of the twenty-first century is a case illustrating that argument. Nevertheless, the current bipolarization is coincidently accompanied by the shift of global geopolitical center. Although both cases resulted from power redistribution, they happened under different conditions. This chapter will discuss three aspects of the issue. They are the key factor driving the present bipolarization between China and the United States; the conditions that could spark a global cold war; and the conditions for forming the new global geopolitical center. The analysis of current bipolarization is guided by corollary 1: improvements or declines of state leadership lead to changes in relative capability between states and eventually in international configuration; the analysis of conditions sparking a cold war is guided by corollary 2: in the anarchical international system, all states engage in self-help for their own strategic interests, but adopt different strategies to pursue them.

LEADERSHIP AND BIPOLARIZATION

The present bipolarization of the world does not mean that China has obtained power parity with the United States, but its international status is improving toward a superpower as well as a pole in the coming bipolar configuration. Although China's current power has not yet reached the top position together with United States, it is already much larger than other major powers according to the contemporary distribution of national power. In some Europeans' eyes, "the power gap between the two leading states today, the United States and China, and the third ranking power is similar to that between the two top-ranked superpowers and the great powers in 1950."[1]

The present bipolarization is mainly attributable to the narrowed disparity in comprehensive capability between China and the United States. How rapidly the disparity in Sino-American comprehensive capability can be reduced depends on how quickly not only China's capability, but also that of the United States, grows. If America's capability were to grow as rapidly as China's, however, their disparity in capability would enlarge rather than reduce, because America's comprehensive capability is still greater than China's. Under such a scenario, bipolarization would cease, and the United States would regain the capability necessary to consolidate its unipolar leadership. If, however, China maintains a more rapid growth in capability than the United States, the state of bipolarization will continue. Whether the rate of the United States' growth in capability can equal that of China in the next decade depends on the political leaderships of the two countries. This argument is consistent with corollary 1 mentioned at the beginning of this chapter.

As Chinese political institutions have fewer constraints on national leadership than is the case in the United States, there could

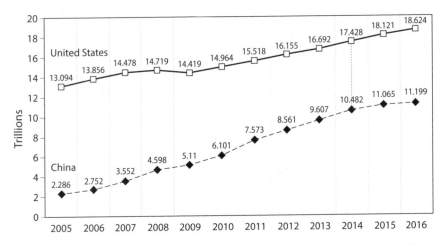

FIGURE 4.1 GDP of China and the United States 2005–16 (US$) *Source*: World Bank, https://data.worldbank.org/indicator/NY.GDP.MKTP.CD?end=2016&locations=US-CN&start=2005

be two different trends of the present bipolarization. If the Chinese government carries out more political reforms over the next decade than its American counterpart, the bipolarization will be paced up; otherwise it will stop if the Chinese government commits more strategic mistakes and retrogression than the United States. Figure 4.1 shows that China's disparity in GDP with the United States almost stopped decreasing from 2014 and started growing from 2015.

Academia holds two opposing views on whether or not the United States has relatively declined. One group argues that it is impossible for the United States to decline, even in the relative sense. There are three primary grounds for this view. The first one is historical experience. At the end of the 1960s, certain people believed that the Soviet Union would arise and overtake the United States,[2] and in the 1980s and the early 1990s, there were those who thought that Japan would arise and eclipse the United States.[3] However, history has proven wrong both prognostications of America's decline. This implies that predictions of China's rise and its overtaking of America will follow the same historical track and be proven also to be mistaken.[4] The second argument is that, as a democracy, the United States has stronger self-rectifiability than China. America's presidential election system will enable the United States to adjust its policy in a more timely way than China could, which would prevent China from catching up with and surpassing America. Robert Kagan argues that "the American system, for all its often stultifying qualities, has also shown a greater capacity to adapt and recover from difficulties than that of many other nations, including its geopolitical competitors."[5] The third one is a theoretical argument about the durability of an American-dominated unipolar world. Nuno P. Monterio says that "unipolarity is in principle durable and, indeed, more likely to last in a nuclear world like ours, in which the expected costs of great-power war are terrifically high. Durability is not guaranteed only by the high costs of war, however. On the contrary, it also depends on a second factor, namely the strategy of the unipole regarding the economic growth of major powers."[6]

The other group argues that America's relative decline is already happening, and that it is losing its world number one status in more and more domains. David Lake argues, "Over the longer term, however, it is almost certain that China will emerge as a superpower equal to the United States. With its vast population, large territory, and rapidly growing economy, China's aggregate economy will likely surpass that of the United States sometime in the second quarter of the twenty first century."[7] The argument of this group is often based on economic data such as that of the United States being unable to repay its international debts, whereas China has become America's biggest creditor. As at the end of 2012, the annual wealth produced in America could not clear the country's year-end debt, which amounted to $16.2 trillion—$1.2 trillion higher than the country's $15 trillion GDP that year.[8] In 2013, Obama explicitly stated that the United States' budget would not be balanced over the next decade.[9] After Trump took office, growing numbers of intellectuals blamed the United States' worsening financial deficit on his tax policy. Edward J. McCaffery said that "the Trump plan would be a 'massive' increase in the debt and deficit."[10] Those arguing that America is in relative decline even believe that China will use its creditor status to check US growth.

Although in agreement that America's relative decline has indeed occurred, my explanation differs from that implied by the financial analysis. America's relative decline is superficially a result of government debt policy. The fundamental reason, however, is that the United States lacks a political leadership capable of implementing political reforms at home, which primarily disenables it from averting China's narrowing of the disparity in capability between them. America's indebtedness grew steadily during the administrations of Ronald Reagan, George H. W. Bush, George W. Bush, and Barack Obama. However, different from these, Bill Clinton's administration made the distinctive achievement. His administration repaid the previous one's debts and also endowed on America's finances an accumulated surplus of more than $200 billion.[11] This feat by the Clinton administration implies that whether or not America resolves its debt problem will depend not on the market but rather on the ability of governmental leadership, and especially of political reforms. Political reforms are the key factor in the growth of both China's and America's comprehensive capability. Whichever of the two countries makes the more effective reforms than the other side will decide whether China or the United States wins the strategic competition in the coming decade. Conversely, the slower reformer or stronger contrarian will encounter relative decline.

Changes in the type of national leadership occur for various reasons, in particular that of the state's unfavorable status in an international system. The backward position of a state often encourages that state's leadership to implement reform. By contrast, the more comfortable a state is with its status, the weaker the resolve of its leadership is to reform. The problem the United States faces is one of a relative decline rather than an absolute decline. This means that America's absolute capability in relation to itself grows continuously at a pace quicker than that of most major powers, but slower than China's. The nature of relative decline is such that the US government can easily cite its improvements through historical comparisons with itself, and special comparisons with major states other than China. Comparing America's economy in 2015 with that of 2010, National Security advisor Susan Rice said, "As a nation, we are stronger than we've been in a long time. Since President Obama took office, we arrested the worst financial crisis and repaired the biggest collapse in world trade since the Great Depression."[12] Trump is different from Obama in many respects but is the same as his predecessor as regards the pride he takes in American superpower status and the achievements of his administration. After his visit to East Asian countries, he said, "Everywhere we went, our foreign hosts greeted the American delegation, myself included, with incredible warmth, hospitality, and most importantly respect. And this great respect showed very well our country is—further evidence that America's renewed confidence and standing in the world has never been stronger than it is right now."[13]

When the United States possesses so much more comprehensive capability than China does, it is difficult for any American leadership to relish reform with the same fervor as the Chinese leadership. Both are faced with resistance from interest groups that oppose reforms that go against their interests. Interest groups will make good use of both legal rights and social resources to defend their particular interests tooth and nail. A leadership capable of political reform, therefore, must have both the courage and the ability to overcome these interest groups. Such ability usually comes through political practice rather than electioneering saber rattling. Since the beginning of the twenty-first century, China has experienced three leaderships, and the US leadership has experienced four administrations. Nevertheless, the Chinese government has implemented many more reforms, including political reforms, than has the American government. Currently, the change in capability disparity between China and the United States is determined more by which of the two suffers less from political retrogression rather than which of the two implements more political and social reforms.

Although the Chinese and American leaderships play key roles in the current bipolarization, we should not forget that the leaderships of other major states also influence that process through their policies toward China and the United States. Bipolarization will gather pace if these major states take pro-China stands, but slow down if these countries stand with America. At present, several of the major powers are headed by aggressive national leaders. The list includes Vladimir V. Putin of Russia, Shinzō Abe of Japan, Narendra

Modi of India, and Recep Tayyip Erdogan of Turkey. All of them prefer confrontation to conciliation, and unexpected choices to normal policies. This type of leadership often worsens strategic relations and intensifies the strategic rivalry between major powers. Thus, it lays a suitable ground for bipolarization to pace up.

BIPOLAR CONFIGURATION NOT EQUAL TO COLD WAR

Many people worry that the strategic competition between China and the United States under the present bipolarization will bring about a world regression to the Cold War, as in the second half of the twentieth century, especially if China abandons its nonalignment principle and, like the United States, makes allies.[14] This kind of understanding confuses a bipolar configuration with a cold war. A bipolar configuration refers to two great states of similar capability with international followers, whereas a cold war refers to an ideological contest through military confrontation with proxy war strategy as the primary medium of rivalry. History shows that a bipolar configuration can exist in three different situations. They are: war, cold war, and peace.

During 431–404 BCE, Athens and Sparta were the two most powerful city-states of ancient Greece. They formed a bipolar configuration in the Mediterranean region, and the Peloponnesian War shortly followed.[15] This case illustrates a bipolar configuration in war. During 579–546 BCE, the State of Jin and the State of Chu were two hegemons in the Chinese interstate system that formed a bipolar configuration. After engaging in military confrontations, including many wars, for more than eighty years, the two giants signed a peace agreement that included the provision: "Jin shall attack any that injure Chu, and Chu shall do the same when Jin is injured."[16] This peace treaty created a superficial alliance, which, after taking on a bipolar configuration, made their relations much less violent. This case shows that a bipolar configuration can exist in a state of war as well as of peace.

Two historical events in 1988 and 1991 respectively also highlight the distinction between a bipolar configuration and a cold war. In

1988, history witnessed the first visit during the Cold War of an American president to the Soviet Union, when the two countries reached an agreement on reducing strategic nuclear arms.[17] After signing the agreement, the American president Ronald Reagan announced in Moscow that the Cold War was over, and that America would no longer regard the Soviet Union as an evil empire.[18] If we use that announcement as the criterion, therefore, the Cold War ended in 1988. However the bipolar configuration did not accordingly end but rather continued until the Soviet collapse at the end of 1991. This case also demonstrates that a cold war and a bipolar configuration are not at all the same thing, and that one does not necessarily follow on from the other.

Three necessary conditions applied to the forming of the Cold War. They included nuclear weapons to prevent strategic rivalry from escalating into direct war between the United States and the Soviet Union; ideological rivalry as the core of strategic competition; and zero economic and social contacts between the two superpowers. The absence of any one of these conditions precludes forming a cold war today. Nuclear weapons play a positive role in preventing direct war between China and the United States, just as they did between the Soviet Union and the United States. Meanwhile, the core conflict between China and the United States is not derived from ideological confrontation, and the two giants have extensive social contacts in all fields. This situation, therefore, is fundamentally different from that between the United States and the Soviet Union. The following paragraphs discuss in detail the reason why the present strategic rivalry between China and the United States is not of a cold war style.

(1) In view of their mutually profound knowledge of nuclear weapons, China and the United States will do their utmost to prevent any strategic contest between them from escalating into war. In the early period of the Cold War, many people were unaware that the function of mutual deterrence that nuclear weapons performed could save the world. In the 1960s, Thomas C. Schelling made the character distinction between nuclear and nonnuclear weapons in his study of the relationship between nuclear weapons and limited

war.[19] From then on, strategists gradually understood the function of mutual nuclear deterrence, and by the 1980s this specialized intelligence had become common knowledge. Nuclear weapons prevented global war from breaking out after World War II and also prevented any direct war between the United States and the Soviet Union. Although the United States accelerated development of antimissile systems after the collapse of the Soviet Union, such improved systems had yet to undermine the function of nuclear deterrence. The United States has an advantage over every country with regard to antimissile systems but nevertheless exercises extreme caution as regards direct military conflicts with nuclear powers. For instance, even though the United States strongly opposed Russia's annexation of Crimea, the Obama administration was nonetheless cautious about providing lethal military aid to the Ukraine government, which had been fighting against Russian military volunteers in eastern Ukraine since the middle of 2014.[20] Wary that Trump's administration may launch a preventative attack against North Korea, the US Congress is considering enacting a law that prevents Trump from ordering such a premeditated attack without the prior consent of the Congress, as required by the Constitution.[21]

Both possessing profound knowledge of nuclear deterrence strategy, neither China nor the United States considers the possibility of victory in a nuclear war, even though they keep modernizing their nuclear and conventional arsenals. They understand that the cost of nuclear war in a competition for hegemony is unaffordable. They are also unwilling to bear the costs of proxy war for strategic competition, because nuclear proliferation increases the danger of escalating proxy war to full-out war. In the next decade, Sino-American military competition will be more apparent in arms modernization than in the risk of direct war between them. The further shrinkage of their disparity in capability will also inhibit the possibility of proxy war between them, as compared to such a risk between the Soviet Union and the United States.

(2) The core confrontation between the United States and the Soviet Union was derived from ideological opposition during the Cold War, but the core competition between China and America is

geared to material interests in the twenty-first century. Ideological confrontation closely relates to the survival of a regime and leaves no room for conciliation. Therefore, it often sparks a life-or-death struggle, as when both the United States and the Soviet Union publicly defined the other side as an evil power. Strategic rivalry for material interests, including international power, can be extremely intense, but it relates to international influence or status rather than regime survival. Therefore, China and the United States were reluctant to publically define the other side as the enemy during the period through the presidencies of the second term of Clinton, George W. Bush, and Obama, preferring instead to maintain a relationship of "neither friend nor foe," or of "superficial friends."[22] Such superficial friendship provides opportunities for each side to initiate conciliation should their strategic competition escalate to potential military clashes. In December 2017, the Trump administration publicly defined China as a strategic rival to the United States, but this mainly refers to an economic competitor rather than an ideological rival.[23] Being aware that a cold war may result from states mutually defining each other as strategic rivals, the Chinese government purposely downplayed this issue. As long as China constrains itself from an ideological contest with the United States, it is still possible for the world to avoid sliding backward into a cold war.

If we compare the American-Soviet strategic contest to a boxing match, that between China and the United States could be compared to a football game. The former relies mainly on brute force, whereas the latter, although featuring physical collisions, depends less on violence as the primary competitive medium.[24] That no one can promise there will never be another cold war is certain, but no such risk will arise in the next decade. Even though it is possible that the Trump administration will launch new wars during this presidency, they will likely be waged against a much lesser state than China. It is possible also that China may become involved in military conflicts over the next decade. However, there is only a very slight risk that China and the United States will engage in a direct war.

(3) Globalization reduces the vulnerability of interdependence, thus making a new cold war unlikely. Many people agree with Ken-

neth Waltz's argument that the economic interdependence between the French and Germans could not prevent World War I, because it shows that amid the throes of strategic rivalry, great powers give little thought to the economic damage that war inflicts.[25] Therefore, they argue, post–Cold War economic globalization will not prevent war between a rising state and the hegemon.[26] These people, however, overlook the difference between globalization and bilateral interdependence, both of which generate sensitivity between two economically interdependent countries. Globalization, however, reduces the vulnerability of two interdependent economic entities, while bilateral interdependence does exactly the opposite. Robert O. Keohane says, "The vulnerability dimension of interdependence rests on the relative availability and costliness of the alternatives that various actors face."[27] Globalization generates the availability of alternative markets for economic interdependent states and reduces the cost of transferring business from one country to another. In the age of globalization, each interdependent country can find alternative markets elsewhere, and at a lower cost should any of them face economic sanctions from their original economic partners. For instance, Japanese enterprises quickly transferred their investment from China to ASEAN countries during the political confrontations between China and Japan in 2012 stemming from their disputes over the Diaoyu/Senkaku Islands. Japan's direct investment in ASEAN from January through June 2013 underwent a sharp 88.7 percent increase to 998.6 billion yen, while its FDI to China fell 18 percent from a year earlier to 470.1 billion yen.[28]

After the collapse of the Soviet Union, democratization and marketization created the global market. Democratization of East European countries led to the dissolution of the Council of Mutual Economic Assistance and transformed Eastern and Western markets into a single global one. Marketization opened up the closed markets of many developing countries. Apart from a few exceptions like North Korea and Cuba, most countries open their domestic markets to foreign capital and products. Foreign trade and overseas investment have become two main means for China and the United States to access foreign markets and natural resources, both of which are far more effective than war as regards wealth accumulation.

(4) In addition to globalization, computer technology is also a helpful factor for preventing a new cold war in the twenty-first century. Owing to the rapid development of computer science, technology is the most important medium for accumulating national wealth and reduces the importance of natural resources in economic development. Therefore, China and the United States do not need to wage war to compete over natural resources. Personal computers became popular in the 1980s, and the Internet became a daily-use instrument in the 1990s. Computer technology and the Internet accelerate human inventions and productivity to such an extent that human productivity has surpassed its consuming capability. China and the United States are the countries that have the most advanced capability as regards technological inventions and are able to invent new products for trade sufficient for all the natural resources they need. Hence neither needs to control geographic areas of natural resources with military force. In the twenty-first century, the biggest problem humankind faces is no longer that productivity cannot meet consumption demands, but rather that humanity lacks the capability to consume all the goods it produces. This problem is known as "global overcapacity."

As regards obtaining natural resources, war becomes a less efficient strategy than foreign investment. China possesses the world's largest foreign reserves, and the US dollar is the most widely held currency in the Allocated Reserves. This means that both China and the United States possess strong monetary means to obtain natural resources globally. In addition, rapid technological development is continuously replacing natural resources with newly invented materials and energy. This means that China's and the United States' economic growth will depend less on overseas natural resources and more on their respective technological inventions. For instance, improved shale gas technology has dramatically reduced American oil imports.[29] In the future, therefore, China and the United States will compete for technological superiority and the consumer market, rather than for natural resources. Technology superiority rests on

advanced university education at home rather than military competition abroad, which also helps to distinguish the US-China strategic
rivalry from the Cold War between the United States and the Soviet
Union.

CONDITIONS FOR FORMING A WORLD CENTER

With the establishment of the BRICS summit and the G20 summit,
and especially since China became the world's second-largest economy in 2010, discussions about the shift of the global geopolitical
center have gained pace. The current bipolarization makes this geopolitical issue a more worldwide matter. However, ideas as to exactly where the geopolitical center will shift vary considerably. One
Argentine scholar, for example, holds that it is shifting from the
West to the East and from the North to the South,[30] while certain
Chinese scholars believe that the center of the global economy is
moving toward Asia.[31] In 2010, in response to a Mexican reporter's
question about this theory, Chinese foreign minister Yang Jiechi
said, "There is indeed a kind of thinking which considers the world's
center of power to be shifting to the East from the West, but I don't
agree with this opinion."[32] These differing notions as to the direction
of the shift of the international geopolitical center are largely attributable to the absence of any distinction between power redistribution and configuration change, as well as of objective criteria for
judging the international geopolitical center.

Criteria for Defining the Global Geopolitical Center

Halford John Mackinder, a British geopolitical strategist, argued,
according to his World War I experience: "Who rules Eastern Europe commands the Heartland; who rules the Heartland commands the World-Island; who rules the World-Island controls the
world."[33] Although his argument is very popular among IR scholars, many historical events do not support his view. During World
War II, Nazi Germany dominated Eastern Europe, but after losing
the war the country was ultimately divided into the two entities of

East Germany and West Germany. During the Cold War, the Soviet Union took control of Eastern Europe, which instead of becoming strong enough to rule the entire world later collapsed into fifteen countries. Eastern Europe was thus assimilated via the European Union (EU), where, again, it did not make the EU more powerful but rather undermined integration among its members. [34] The 2016 trend of EU disintegration implies the process of a shifting of the global geopolitical center away from Europe. After the Cold War, the United States became the most militarily influential power in Eastern Europe by virtue of its eastern expansion of NATO. This, however, was not the reason why the United States became the sole global superpower; it was rather the collapse of the Soviet Union that resulted in a US-dominated unipolar world. If the Soviet Union had not fallen, the bipolar configuration would have continued. In addition, American military domination of Eastern Europe did not lead to its command over the continent as a whole even after the collapse of the Soviet Union, and especially after Putin came to power.

A world center is determined not by its natural geographical position, but by the capability of the countries that reside there. Specifically, there are two necessary conditions for an area to become the international geopolitical center. First, it must contain the world's most influential states; that is to say, one or more leading states in possession of material force, especially military force, and political capability of a level that exceeds the reach of secondary states. Material capability enables those leading states to lead the world, and political capability makes them models for lesser states to follow. Second, an international geopolitical center should be a hotbed of intensive international rivalry between contending powerful states. History shows that the strategic rivalry between leading states is manifested in two situations: one wherein the focus is on dominating the geopolitical center in which they reside; the other wherein power rivalry expands from the geopolitical center to peripheral areas. Absent the rivalry for ruling the locale of leading states, that area cannot become the international geopolitical center. Therefore, the first situation reflects the fundamental condition whereby an area becomes the geopolitical center, while the second is an extension of the first.

In the 150 years leading up to the end of World War II, Europe was generally acknowledged as the geopolitical center of the world. During this period, European powers competed for overseas colonies as well as for domination of Europe. Europe was hence both the stomping ground for global competitors and the arena wherein those great powers competed for its domination. Britain, France, and Russia, among other countries, for instance, competed for control over the Balkan Peninsula, a strategic rivalry that led to the Crimean War. Hitler's aggressive expansion within Europe also caused wars there. Africa, meanwhile, was a colonial continent over whose command European powers constantly vied. The absence of global influential states on that continent, however, precluded its becoming the global geopolitical center. Europe's global supremacy having been undermined by two world wars, it was indeed the rise of the Soviet Union that salvaged and reinstated its status as the central area of international politics.[35]

During the Cold War, the United States and the Soviet Union were the world's most powerful states, and also the major strategic rivals in the global system. As the location of the Soviet Union, one of the two "poles," Europe was also a focus of fierce strategic competition between these two superpowers. Europe was thus able to retain its status as the central area of international politics throughout the Cold War. In 1946, Winston Churchill, the then British prime minister, said in his famous speech in Fulton: "From Stettin in the Baltic to Trieste in the Adriatic, an iron curtain has descended across the Continent."[36] It is precisely because the core strategic rivalry between the two superpowers happened to be in Europe that this "iron curtain" descended across this continent rather than any other region. With the exception of the United States and Canada, all members of NATO and of the Warsaw Pact Organization resided in Europe. This phenomenon implies Europe, on the one hand, as the geological location of global competitors, but on the other, as the core area of the strategic rivalry between the United States and the Soviet Union.

The above analysis of the two necessary conditions for being an international geopolitical center can also be applied to the judgment of a geopolitical center in ancient independent interstate systems. Notwithstanding various differences otherwise, both modern global systems and ancient interstate systems are anarchical in nature; thus their geopolitical centers are determined by the location of the most powerful states, which doubles as the core area of strategic rivalry between those states.

Bipolarization and the Shift of the Global Geopolitical Center

The United States is the only country to have remained the most powerful global competitor in both the Cold War bipolar configuration and the unipolar configuration of the post–Cold War period, but Europe was regarded as the international geopolitical center throughout both epochs. Therefore, there is a misconception at large that the geopolitical center will remain in Europe for however long the United States maintains its status as the strongest superpower, no matter whether the global configuration is bipolar or unipolar. However, the current bipolarization between China and the United States refutes that view.

The United States can be identified as both a Pacific country and an Atlantic country, but its geographic location is unchanged. Since the end of World War II, the United States has remained the world's most powerful state and seems likely to continue as top superpower for the next decade. As the United States remains a superpower in an unchanged geographic location, therefore, it can hardly be the force behind the current shift of the international geopolitical center. Methodologically, it should not be regarded as a major variable in an analysis of the direction in which the center is shifting. After controlling America as a constant, we should compare the changes in capability gap between European powers and East Asia states, which is the key variable determining the shift of the international geopolitical center in the coming decade.

Although European states and America both experienced relative declines in capability after the financial crisis of 2008, each has had different impacts on the shift of the geopolitical center. Within the next decade, the relative decline of the United States will not alter its world superpower status, and as a global competitor the United States will undoubtedly still be a major strategic player in East Asia. However, the relative decline in European states has diminished their global influence to a level lower than some East Asian countries. Lord Green, the chairman of Asia House, says, "Europe has retreated from being the self-defined center of the world to what it had been before the 15th century—a corner of the Eurasian land mass."[37] The combined GDP of China and Japan, respectively the world's second- and third-largest economies, plus ASEAN, Korea, Taiwan, and Hong Kong, is larger than the GDP of the EU and Russia combined. The military expenditures of European states and East Asian countries and regions reflect the same situation. In 2016, twenty-eight members of the EU reported €199 billion (approximately $238.8 billion) of government expenditure on defense;[38] meanwhile China's budgeted expenditure on defense was $146 billion,[39] and that of Japan and South Korea were $44 billion[40] and $36 billion[41] respectively.

In addition, perhaps the most important factor that could make Europe lose its status as global geopolitical center is that no European state, including Germany and Russia, has sufficient capability to be a global competitor, and therefore none of the European countries possesses the potential to become a superpower. China, meanwhile, is rising as a new superpower in East Asia, and becoming a global strategic competitor. All in all, therefore, the current shift of the geopolitical center is being driven by the conversion of disparity in national capability between major European states and China.

The rapid growth of the national capability of China as an up-and-coming superpower not only brings about a power redistribution that changes the international configuration from unipolar to bipolar but also drives the shift of the global geopolitical center from Europe toward East Asia. In the 1980s, the promisingly rapid economic growth of Japan and the "four Asian tigers," South Korea, Taiwan, Hong Kong, and Singapore, failed to make East Asia the global geopolitical center. Apart from the existence of the Soviet Union as a superpower, the other main factor in this nonfulfillment is that of Japan's lacking the potential to become a superpower after World War II owing to its being an economic power and not a country of comprehensive capability. In striking contrast to Japan's rise in the 1980s, which was based purely on economic growth, China's rise has been built on the construction of its comprehensive capability since the 1999 US bombing of the Chinese embassy in Belgrade. China's rise reduces not only its economic gap with the United States, but also notable disparity in the domains of politics, military, and culture. As a result, China has become the United States' chief rival for global leadership in the twenty-first century, and it was listed as the first strategic threat to American interests by Trump's administration.[42] No European state, including Russia, qualifies as a global competitor of the United States. Therefore, America's biggest strategic competitor is now in East Asia rather than Europe.

China's rise provides East Asia with a superpower wielding world-class influence and also makes the region a core area of strategic competition between superpowers. As previously mentioned, the second necessary condition for a region to become the global geopolitical center is that whereby global powers jostle for supremacy over it. In 2010, the Obama administration adopted the "pivot to Asia" strategy, later renamed the "rebalance to the Asia-Pacific" strategy. This strategy of America's implies that East Asia is fast becoming the focal point of strategic rivalry between global powers.[43] In view of America's weakened relative capability, the narrowing geographical range of its global strategy toward the new center is to be expected. The United States may then deal with the present challenge of the real rising power in East Asia. The purpose of America's pivot-to-Asia strategy is thus to maintain its influence and predominance in the new geopolitical center of world power. The US troop withdrawals from the Middle East, and an expanded US military presence in East Asia, moreover, clearly confirm that East Asia is becoming the new center of world power. Faced with the reality that China is an emerging superpower, the United States is fearful of losing its domination over East Asia. In recent years, American strategists have repeatedly claimed to be an East Asian country in private conversations with Chinese counterparts, and consequently that America cannot tolerate being squeezed out of East Asia. Even though Trump's administration determines American strategic interest from an economic perspective, it could hardly define any other region as of greater importance to the United States in this era than East Asia. Although the Trump administration coined the term "Indio-Pacific" for the sake of differing from Obama's administration, Northeast Asia and Southeast Asia are discussed before any other region in the section entitled "The Strategy in a Regional Context" in the *National Security Strategy* of 2017.[44]

While China's rise leads to the emergence of a new superpower with global influence in East Asia and endows larger economic and military capability on East Asia than Europe, the United States joins China in increasing their disparity in capability with other major powers, such as Japan, Germany, Russia, the UK, France, and India, in the coming decade. This bipolarization has inevitably caused intense rivalry between China and the United States in East Asia.[45] The power redistribution caused by China's rise is thus accompanied by the change of configuration from unipolar to bipolar, and the shift of the global geopolitical center from Europe to East Asia. In the history of East Asia, the strategic competition between the central dynasty and a major power in this region, such as the Han Dynasty–Hun, Song Dynasty–Jin, and Ming Dynasty–Manchu rivalries, provides good examples of the linkage between intensive rivalry and power transition between leading states.[46]

Evolving Fields of Strategic Competition

Historically, a shift of the world center was generally accomplished through warfare, so military supremacy was always intensely pursued in order to enhance strategic competitiveness.[47] The strategic competition between the Soviet Union and the United States during the Cold War also supports the general knowledge of the strategy popularly at play in hegemonic rivalry. Nevertheless, this knowledge must confront the challenge of the rising strategy that China has adopted in the twenty-first century, whereby it prioritizes economic development over military might. The country's rising strategy, however, is predictable rather than unreasonable, according to corollary 2, as mentioned at the beginning of this chapter. China's strategic preference does not reflect the uniqueness of Chinese leadership in history but is rather geared to the different historical era it now faces. In an age where nuclear weapons inhibit direct war between major powers, technological innovations constitute the main wealth-generating resources. In addition, globalization brings easy access to foreign markets and natural resources; thus it is reasonable for China to adopt a historically untried strategy for its rise in the twenty-first century. China's economic-oriented strategic preference has effectively induced Sino-American strategic rivalry in an economic rather than military context, although it does not rule out the possibility of military conflicts, including proxy war, between them in the future.

Strategic competition for global domination consists of both economic and military rivalry. Although China is now the world largest trader in goods, and has the most foreign exchange reserves, it falls far behind the United States in military capability. China's annual military expenditure is less than one-third that of the United States, whose military budget for the fiscal year 2018 is nearly $700 billion.[48] China's real military prowess also has yet to catch up with Russia's, owing to its lack of modern war combat experience. In other words, mathematical military capability, or that measured according to the monetary value of military assets, does not necessarily equal physically measured military might, or that measured according to real offensive and defensive capabilities. Because the economic disparity between China and the United States is relatively small and the military gap remains wide, economic competition between these two countries will be far more intense than any militaristic vying between them.

A global geopolitical center also entails a region that is a hotbed of global powers wielding world-class ideological impacts. During the Cold War, both the Marxist-Leninist communism of the Soviet Union and the capitalism practiced by the United States were global ideologies. The resultant ideological confrontation had a strong impact not only on their foreign policies but also on those of other countries. After the Cold War, the liberal vision shared by the United States and European states became the sole dominant global ideology, to the extent of being regarded as the soft power of Western countries.[49] Since 2016, however, the dominance of liberalism as a global ideology has been challenged by anti-establishmentarianism in the United States and populism in Europe. The diminished influence of liberalism implies that Europe is losing its status also as an ideological world center.

Although China's ideological influence in the world is less significant than America's, it is nevertheless becoming increasingly persuasive. Martin Jacques argues in *When China Rules the World* that Chinese values "will remain pervasive and, with China's growing influence, acquire a global significance."[50] Foreign strategists and policy analysts usually refer only to the ideas of deceased Chinese thinkers and strategists like Laozi, Confucius, Zeng Guofan, Liang Qichao, Mao Zedong, and Deng Xiaoping. Nowadays, however, foreign strategists, policy analysts, and academics are paying attention to the strategic thinking of living Chinese. In 2008, Mark Leonard, a British policy analyst, published *What Does China Think?*, the first book by a foreign strategist on China's modern strategic thinking in the twenty-first century.[51] In 2010, Chung-in Moon, a South Korean strategist, published a book on the same theme under the title *Grand Strategies of China's Rise: In-Depth Dialogue with Leading Chinese Intellectuals*.[52] That the ideas of those living in a rising state are being studied by international strategists and policy analysts signifies that the rising power is also gaining ideological influence in the world sphere. In any event, the future of a rising power depends, to a much larger extent, on the ideas of living people than on those of the long gone.

SUMMARY

China-US bipolarization is the result of the shrinking disparity in comprehensive capabilities between China and the United States, but the fundamental reason for it is the differing levels of efficiency of the Chinese and American leaderships. After Clinton's administration, the United States witnessed three leaderships, none of which carried out political reforms as efficient as the Chinese government did. Inefficient leadership has mainly disenabled the United States from preventing China's reduction of the disparity in capability between them. As aggressive leadership prevails in most major states, bipolarization will likely gather pace over the next decade.

It is quite possible that a bipolar world will be formally established in the next few years, but the strategic competition between China and the United States will be in a different style from that between America and the Soviet Union in the Cold War. The US-China strategic competition and the US-Soviet strategic rivalry are the same in nature, but different in form and content. In accordance with the reduced disparity in capability between China and the United States, these two countries will be involved in all-around rivalry, but there is little danger of their falling into a direct war, mainly owing to the nuclear weapons they both possess. There is also a slight possibility that the world may witness a new cold war, because of the combined roles of globalization, improved computer technology, and less possible ideological confrontation between China and the United States.

A type change in international configuration is caused by power redistribution among leading states but does not necessarily result in a shift of the global geopolitical center. There are two necessary conditions for forming the global geopolitical center. First, the region must be an area where at least one leading strategic competitor is located. Second, the region must be crucial, to the extent that domination of it is a precondition for gaining leadership of the world. It is the latter that drives rival leading states to compete over control of that region. Today, the power redistribution caused by

China's rise and America's relative decline are changing the post–Cold War configuration from unipolar to bipolar. Coincidently, this bipolarization is concurrent with Europe's decline. The engine driving the present shift of the global geopolitical center, therefore, is the combination of China's rise and Europe's decline, rather than America's relative decline.

5

Leadership and International Norms

其身正, 不令而行; 其身不正, 虽令不行。
(Righteous leaders are followed; corrupt leaders are resisted.)
CONFUCIUS

As changes in international norms result from state interactions, students of IR have a misled tendency to ignore the fact that leading states play a far more dominant role than lesser states in the shaping of new international norms. That international norms change according to leading states' conduct of foreign affairs in an international system is the theme of this chapter. The analysis of this argument is guided by corollary 3: pursuit of self-interest is the primary motivation of state actions as well as the selective force behind the evolution of international norms. That is to say, the desire of leading states to set up or maintain an international order that favors their domination is the engine that drives them to promote new international norms. As different types of international leadership have different strategic preferences, interactions between leading states and other states can either promote international cooperation or intensify international conflicts. Since leading states' conduct of their foreign policy is crucial to shaping new norms, therefore, it is necessary to study exactly how they establish new norms in the anarchical international system.

EARLY STUDIES OF LEADERSHIP AND NORM CHANGE

Early studies of the role of leadership in international politics were mainly carried out by theorists of decision making. Behaviorist scholars of the 1960s studied foreign policy making from the perspective of political leaders' personal characteristics, educational background, religious beliefs, political experience, and professional knowledge. Some of their conclusions about types of leaders are helpful in addressing this topic. Richard C. Snyder and his colleagues, for instance, distinguished two types of leaders: one identifiable through in-order-to motives, and the other through because-of motives.[1] Based on these two types of leaders, James E. Dougherty and Robert L. Pfaltzgraff argue that the former consciously creates or reforms norms, while the latter does so unconsciously.[2] I agree with them insofar as types of leadership constitute a determining factor in reforming international norms, but I would not use their typology to categorize international leadership, because it cannot explain antithetical actions by the same type of leaders when practicing the same international norms. Take for example US presidents Lyndon B. Johnson and George W. Bush, both of whom are leaders typified by in-order-to motives. Johnson advocated the Treaty on the Non-proliferation of Nuclear Weapons (NPT) and restricted cooperation with illegitimate nuclear powers, yet George W. Bush violated the NPT by engaging in nuclear cooperation with India, which is not a party to the treaty.[3] The category of international leadership in chapter 2 will be used for analysis in this chapter.

Theorists focused on international norms widely agree with Martha Finnemore and Kathryn Sikkink that changes in leading states are prerequisite to changes in the character of international norms. They hold that the formulation of new international norms usually goes through three phases: (1) leading states propose new norms; (2) the majority of states follow the proposal; and (3) the norms are internalized or socialized as universal principles guiding international behavior.[4] Although this analytical model is useful, its dialectic methodology fails to make the distinction between independent and dependent variables. On the one hand, it argues that changes in people's perceptions change international norms, but on the other suggests that international norms construct people's perception of national interests.[5] To avoid the pitfall whereby perception becomes both an independent and a dependent variable in theory building, I will explore the relationship between the changes in leading states' actions and changes in international norms. That is to say, the type of international leadership is the independent variable, and the type of international norms is dependent on the leadership type. Leading states selectively promote the norms in favor of their interests rather than being persuaded into accepting all good norms including those unfavorable to their interests. Therefore, different types of leading states advocate different norms. To avoid arbitrary judgment, in this book, a leading state's actions are used as the criterion through which to define its type of leadership, and its impact on international norms is judged according to chronological sequence. In other words, the leading state's actions should take place before any changes in international norms.

Finding that the new norms promoted by leading states sometimes succeed but can also fail, G. John Ikenberry and Charles A. Kupchan studied the processes and conditions through which leading states had successfully advanced new international norms. They identified three mechanisms whereby dominant states socialize other states into new international norms. They are normative persuasion, external inducement, and internal reconstruction.[6] Normative persuasion initially entails the elites of other states' internalization of the new norms advocated by a dominant state and their subsequent adoption of new policies. External inducement and internal reconstruction involve first changing the policies of lesser states and then effecting changes through these states' acceptance of the new norms.[7] In this model, the three mechanisms overlap with each other, and internal reconstruction is especially questionable.

The first problem is that normative persuasion has some overlap with external inducement. Diplomatic persuasion includes informing the lesser states of the potential benefits of behaving according to a given conduct principle and harms of not doing so. This kind of persuasion is similar to external inducement. The second problem is that external inducement is often incorporated into the efforts of internal reconstruction to change the national leadership of a lesser state. For instance, America forced the Japanese government to accept new norms after World War II by changing Japan's constitution and government, such that the Japanese government accepted the international norm of migrant labor under America's pressure.[8] The third problem is that internal reconstruction confuses the process and outcome of socialization. Ikenberry and Kupchan argue that normative persuasion consists in a lesser state first internalizing new norms and subsequently changing its policies.[9] But in fact, this mechanism does not include any process of a country's internalization but directly assumes such an outcome. In reality, however, the internalization of a norm consists in its process of socialization among the people of a country, rather than just a few of its policy makers. The acceptance of the dominant state's persuasion by a lesser state's policy makers does not equate to that country's internalization of the new norm. Although inducement and internal reconstruction can make the leaders of a secondary state accept the dominant state's norms and reflect them in its policies, this does not signify that state's socialization of the norm. Policy makers' acceptance of a new norm, regardless of whether they are persuaded, coerced, or reconstructed into doing so, represents only the beginning of the socialization process rather than its outcome.

TYPES OF LEADERSHIP AND TYPES OF NORMS

Based on the assumption that the two core functions of leadership are to provide direction and exercise influence, this section will analyze the impact that international leadership imposes on the change in type of international norms, and through what approaches international leadership exercises its influence on other states. To understand the relationships between international leadership and international norms, it is necessary also to discuss the accordant categories of relations between leaderships and norms, as well as the mechanisms for shaping new norms through interactions between leading states and other countries.

Categorization of International Norms

To understand the impact that different international leaderships have on changes in international norms, we must examine the different conducts of the four types of leadership: humane authority, hegemony, anemocracy, and tyranny. Since types of international leadership refer to the principles that guide the decision making of leading states, the type of a given international leadership can be determined by leading states' foreign policy, just as spitting, or not, in a public place signifies an individual's level of concern about public health issues. A leading state may provide different types of international leadership at different times, and for various reasons. Therefore, we need to characterize the international leadership of a leading state according to its main conduct over a given period.

When analyzing the accordance between leadership types and norm types, a clear definition of an international norm is as important as defining international leadership. Stephen D. Krasner says, "Norms are principles of behavior defined in terms of rights and obligations."[10] Based on this definition, I would define international norms as behavioral principles in regard to the rights and obligations accepted by the majority of states in an independent international system. This definition includes the norms of both violent and nonviolent conduct.[11] It also serves as a reminder that a dominant state's foreign policy principles should not be regarded as international norms until they have been accepted by the majority of international members, because it is only then that they will be popular and influential enough to influence the actions of the majority of states.

International society is composed of both natural and social characters, which means that international norms relate to either one of the two. This reality calls for distinctions between types of interna-

TABLE 5.1: TYPES OF INTERNATIONAL NORMS

| System Characters | Conduct | |
	Consistent	Inconsistent
Social	Moral norms	Double-standard norms
Natural	Realpolitik norms	Coward-bully norms

tional norms according to the essential conduct of foreign affairs when rooted in the natural or the social characters. Xunzi said, "Sage kings try to win men; hegemons to acquire allies: tyrants to conquer others' land."[12] Borrowing from Xunzi's categorization of leading states' foreign policy principles, we can modify it into four types of international norms—realpolitik, coward-bully, double standard, and morality—shaped respectively by tyrannical, anemocratic, hegemonic, and humane authority leaderships. The realpolitik and coward-bully norms are rooted in the innate character of international society, while the double-standard and morality norms are rooted in the nurtured character of human society. Both the morality and realpolitik norms result from the consistent behavior of leading states, while double-standard and coward-bully norms result from the inconsistent actions of leading states (see table 5.1).

Driven by their innately human character, tyrannical states will follow the realpolitik principle, also known as the survival of the fittest/social Darwinism. Guided by this principle, a tyrannical leadership's actions will be reflected in its ensuing norms. Realpolitik norms refer to the principle of achieving national interests through coercive measures, mainly military force. This phenomenon is illustrated by European states' practice of the principle of the right of conquest and occupation when competing for colonies from the sixteenth to the nineteenth centuries.[13] Realpolitik norms are based on the inborn nature of human beings and serve as a popular principle of state conduct in the absence of the constraints of more progressive social norms. This is similar to the second law of thermodynamics that says, "The entropy of an isolated system never decreases." Without the external intervention of human self-actualization, the natural state of any social interaction tends toward chaos. Confucius believed that it is natural for states to strengthen their security through military might. He said: "The origins of wounding lie far back. It was born along with mankind. . . . Wasps and scorpions are born with a sting. When they see danger they make use of it so as to protect their bodies. Human beings are born with joy and anger; hence, troops arise, and they came into being at the same time human beings did."[14] In other words, humans instinctively use violence as a means of self-protection and for the sake of interests.

Coward-bully norms often result from the actions of anemocratic leadership. Also driven by innate human nature but without political principles, anemocracies follow the coward-bully principle, which refers to browbeating the weak but fearing the strong. This type of leading state usually bullies lesser states when in possession of a larger material capability than its rivals and ignores its own strategic credibility in an international system. However, when faced with tough states, no matter whether they are big or small, anemocratic states will avoid conflict owing to a timid mentality. For instance, the Trump administration launched a direct military assault in April 2017 against the Assad regime in Syria in response to the threat that the Syrian government appeared to constitute to its own people by virtue of its use of chemical weapons, yet it dared not make any military response to North Korea's nuclear tests in August of the same year.[15]

Moral norms refer to the principles that guide states toward achieving their interests through the legal means applicable to a specific historical period. For example, by 1997, 165 states had signed the Convention on the Prohibition of the Development, Production, Stockpiling and Use of Chemical Weapons and on Their Destruction (CWC).[16] This convention prohibits states from using chemical weapons in warfare. The moral principles guiding foreign policy are based on cultural education and become the norm when the majority of member states agree on them for the sake of peaceful settlement of conflicts. When moral norms are weakened, realpolitik principles automatically resume power as the norms dominating states' behavior. Different from the tyrannical and anemocratic leaderships, leading states that display humane authority observe moral principles that are known, based on the social character of international society, as progressive courtesy.

Double-standard norms are much more popular than the other three types of norms in the history of interstate relations. As international society consists in both natural and social characters, realpolitik principles and moral principles often simultaneously direct states' actions. In most cases, hegemonic states apply realpolitik principles when dealing with enemies, and moral principles with friends or allies. Since this kind of practice became popular in the international system, we have defined such a scenario as a double-standard norm. For instance, the United States has scarcely criticized its ally Saudi Arabia for its poor human rights record, yet it imposed sanctions on its enemy Cuba for such transgressions during the Cold War.

Mechanisms Shaping International Norms

The actions of leading states decide the type of their leadership, and the actions of these states encourage other states to follow the principles of conduct that they adopt. When the majority of states adopt that principle it becomes socialized into an international norm, as shown in figure 5.1.

When analyzing the relationship between types of international leadership and international norms, the former is an independent variable, and the latter is the dependent variable. Changes in the type of international leadership bring about changes in international norms through leading states' interaction with other states. As such, the intervening variable, that is to say, the interaction between leading states and other states, is the medium through which

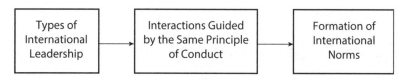

FIGURE 5.1 Types of international leadership and formation of international norms

the leadership type alters international norms. The intervening variable can take on the values of conventional interaction, which strengthens existing norms, or unconventional interaction, which leads to the emergence of new norms.

Leading states cannot impact international norms other than through their interactions with the member states of a given international system. It is widely agreed that the existence of several independent international systems prior to the fifteenth century was attributable to the absence of interaction between states on different continents.[17] The interstate norms of those contemporary systems, therefore, were different. Interaction is a mechanism through which to establish international norms, but it does not guarantee that all member states in a given system (whether a regional or a global one) will respond to other states' actions under the same principle of conduct.

To understand the different effects of interactions between leading states and other states, therefore, it is necessary to clarify the distinction between conventional and unconventional interactions. An action that accords with existing norms comes under the category of conventional interaction, while one that violates those norms is referred to as an unconventional interaction. Conventional interactions strengthen existing international norms, while unconventional interactions change them. Changes in the types of international norms, therefore, stem from unconventional interactions between states.

Understanding how the interactions between leading states and other states influence existing norms entails differentiating between the mechanisms of international norm changes and their outcomes. Wendt suggests that there are three pathways to internalizing international norms: force, price, and legitimacy.[18] This categorization, however, obfuscates the mechanisms and outcomes of internalization of international norms. Internalization refers to the process whereby a conscious behavior becomes a subconscious one. As such, actions consistent with norms born of reward seeking or punishment avoidance constitute conscious rather than subconscious behavior. Thus, they are not the outcome of internalization but

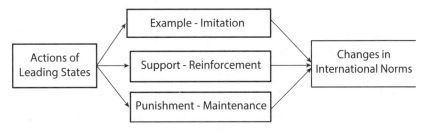

FIGURE 5.2 Mechanisms through which states change international norms

rather illustrate the mechanisms of punishment and reward used in internalization. By contrast, behaviors based on legitimacy are sub-conscious actions and are the outcomes rather than the mechanisms of internalization.

Based on the above distinctions, we suggest that consent rather than coercion is the most efficient way for leading states to wield influence when shaping new international norms. Consent is greatly facilitated by a leading state setting itself up as an example to convince others of the benefits of following its principle of conduct. Robert Gilpin says that "the 'governance' of the international system is in part maintained by the prestige and moral leadership of the hegemonic power."[19] Here, I would replace Wendt's pathways with three mechanisms through which all types of leading states change international norms. They are: (1) example-imitation: setting up an example for other states to emulate; (2) support-reinforcement: rewarding states that enact a similar principle of conduct; and (3) punishment-maintenance: penalizing those that violate that principle. When the majority of states convert their principle of conduct to one that is in compliance with that of leading states, it can be said that such a principle has evolved into an international norm (see figure 5.2).

The example-imitation mechanism takes effect by convincing lesser states to imitate the behavioral principles of leading states. A leading state enjoys more international power than other states, and this fact persuades other states that its behavioral principles constitute important reasons for its success; hence, they will imitate the leading state's behavior principles. The leading state's example, moreover, has influence on both the targets and the observers of its actions. During the Spring and Autumn period, Zheng Zijia, a minister of the Zheng State, wrote in a letter to Zhao Xuanzi, the executor of the Jin State: "Small states follow the great states in a human way when large states have virtue; small states will behave like deer and risk danger in desperation when great states have no virtue."[20] Generally speaking, when addressing conflicts with other states, a leading state's adoption of negotiations as a means of resolution is likely to encourage other states to follow moral principles, while its decision to use force to settle the conflict is likely to make other states resort to realpolitik principles. The former promotes the internalization of moral principles into norms and the latter that of realpolitik principles into norms. Whether or not the example-imitation mechanism consolidates the existing norms or shapes new norms depends on whether or not the leading powers' behavioral principles are consistent with existing norms.

Example-imitation differs from normative persuasion as proposed by Ikenberry and Kupchan. Normative persuasion appeals to the instinctive psychological behaviors of reward motivation and punishment avoidance, while leading by example allows lesser states to choose whether or not they wish to emulate such behavior. In other words, when a leading state leads by example, it respects other states' free will and allows international society at large to judge whether or not it wishes to follow the line of the leading state without the threat of using coercion. The other difference between leading by example and normative persuasion is that the former requires a leading state to practice what it preaches, while the latter precludes a leading state from practicing the norm that it tries to persuade other states to follow. For example, the United States violated the NPT treaty by engaging in nuclear cooperation with India, yet it successfully persuaded other states to follow the NPT and impose sanctions on North Korea's nuclear tests.[21]

The support-reinforcement mechanism is one whereby a leading state's support of other states' actions that are consistent with a principle it advocates reinforces other states' belief in that particular principle. For example, after World War II, the United States consistently supported Israel's military attacks on its neighbors, a policy that reinforced Israel's belief in realpolitik principles. Another example is the United States' adoption of a double-standard principle after the Cold War through its support for separatist movements in other countries, that is to say, supporting separatist movements in non-Western states but not in Western states. This policy encouraged other Western states to practice the same principle on this issue. An existing international norm is reinforced when a leading state supports the actions of other states that are consistent with that norm. The support-reinforcement mechanism, however, also makes it possible for an existing norm to be replaced by a new one if the leading state supports other states' violation of that norm.

The punishment-maintenance mechanism refers to a leading state's adoption of punitive policies toward states that violate the type of behavior principles that it advocates. When a leading state imposes punishment on a state for violating existing norms, its punitive policy helps to maintain those norms by increasing the costs of such violations and encouraging other states to adapt their behavior in ways that conform to those norms. For instance, Iraq's annexation of Kuwait in 1990 violated the UN Charter, which prohibit the use of force to violate the territorial integrity or political independence of a sovereign state.[22] In response to these violations, the United States punished Iraq through the Persian Gulf War in January 1991.[23] This punitive action made Iraq and other states understand that they must abide by relevant UN conventions. Such punishment helps to maintain existing norms in the two respects whereby it inhibits states' belief in principles that oppose existing norms, and increases their consciousness of existing norms. However, if the punishment targets the action of a state that does act in accord with existing norms, then the punitive policy of leading states can by the same token reduce other states' consciousness of existing norms and deepen their belief in antithetical principles. For instance, the United States imposed a half-century trade embargo on Cuba for having a political system different than America's. This policy resulted in Latin American states' mistrust of nonintervention norms based on the UN Charter, and their adoption of the principle of military intervention into any South American state in which a coup has occurred.

Each of the above three mechanisms could operate through either conventional or unconventional interactions between leading states, and between leading and lesser states. In most cases, when the behavioral principle of leading states is consistent with existing norms, it will lead to conventional interactions, but otherwise to unconventional interactions. Therefore, the former strengthens existing norms, and the latter helps to shape new norms.

CHANGE IN THE TYPE OF INTERNATIONAL NORMS

The previous two sections respectively raised four types of international norms and proposed three mechanisms through which to establish new international norms. This section will apply these categories to a discussion on the accord between leadership types and type changes as reflected in international norms. Based on case histories, this section will also discuss the direction of the evolution of international norms.

Norm Types Shaped by International Leaderships

(1) When the international leadership is a tyrannical one, its actions tend to erode moral norms and drive other states to follow realpolitik principles. Tyrannical leading states often support or encourage their allies' adoption of aggressive stances toward enemies, which objectively fosters their belief in realpolitik principles. Motivated by its own interests, a tyrannical leadership may even adopt realpolitik actions in response to the moral actions of others when a realpolitik policy promises to generate greater profit. Such actions effectively punish those adhering to moral principles, so objectively weakening other states' belief in moral norms and pushing them toward adoption of realpolitik principles.

During the latter half of the Warring States period, the State of Qin established a typical tyrannical interstate leadership. The state's adoption of a brutal policy in accordance with realpolitik principles caused other states to perceive the Qin as a predator state[24] that violated interstate agreements and annexed the territory of states that did adhere to interstate treaties. The Qin's savage actions caused other states to adopt a realpolitik policy toward it. For example, in peace negotiations with the State of Zhao, Qin proposed that Zhao could end the war by ceding to it six of its cities. Yu Qing, a minister of the Zhao state, advised King Huiwen of Zhao: "Qin is a state of beasts and has no respect for the rites. Qin's demands are endless while our lands are limited. Zhao will vanish if we try to meet Qin's endless demands with our limited lands."[25] The King of Zhao accepted this advice in the belief that continuing the war against Qin was more conducive to survival than signing a peace treaty with Qin. He consequently formed an alliance with the State of Qi to carry on the war of resistance against Qin.[26]

(2) The coward-bully actions of an anemocratic international leadership cause conspiracy and deception to prevail as normal behavior. Under the guidance of the coward-bully principle, the inconsistent actions of anemocracies stem from their irresponsible interstate leadership. This is in sharp contrast to the double-standard principle of hegemonic states. Unlike hegemonic states, which value the strategic confidence of their allies, anemocracies take little account of strategic relations with their allies. Owing to this lack of strategic credit, therefore, no other country trusts one that is an anemocracy, including its so-called allies. *Zuo Zhuan* (The Chronicle of Zuo) notes, "Without true credibility, even exchanging royal members as hostages cannot help to make alliance reliable."[27] When anemocratic leaderships have no strategic credit, the behavior of lesser states will be even worse in regard to keeping promises, because their strategic interests are even fewer and their capabilities weaker than those of the leading state. Maintaining strategic credibility is thus impossible, and strategic conspiracy and deception become the prevailing international norms.

During the transition period (476–406 BCE) from the Spring and Autumn period to the Warring States, no truly hegemonic states undertook interstate leadership, and most major states were anemocracies. Thus, the coward-bully principle became the norm that the majority of states in the Chinese interstate system followed. The coward-bully norm also often prevails in countries embroiled in civil war, such as the warlord period during the first two decades of the Republic of China (1911–28), and the situation in Libya, Syria, and Yemen since 2011. This is because a country in the midst of a civil war constitutes an anarchical system, which is the same as an international system. Leading actors in such a purely anarchical social system are mainly driven by innate human nature.

(3) When the international leadership is a humane authority, its actions are consistent with moral principles that help to shape moral norms at the expense of realpolitik norms. Leading states' moral actions strengthen other states' belief that following moral principles is beneficial to increasing their capability and prosperity. Xunzi said: "He who establishes morality becomes a sage king."[28] This statement indicates that the promotion of moral norms is a necessary, albeit not sufficient, requisite for a humane world leadership. A state of humane authority is based on possessing material capability much greater than that of other states, and a foreign policy that is guided by moral principles. Thus, the state has to possess the capacity both to reward the states that adhere to moral principles and to punish violations, for the sake of establishing or maintaining moral norms. The observance of moral principles by leading states governed by human authority thus legitimizes their use of force to shape or keep moral norms.

In chapter 1, morality is defined at the governmental level. It is, therefore, just that an international leadership that is a humane authority establishes or maintains international moral norms through military approaches. Chinese ancient thinkers who defined morality as just goals rather than nonviolent strategies regarded the purpose of promoting moral norms as legitimizing the military actions taken by a humane authority leadership. The *Lüshi Chunqiu* (Springs and Autumns of Master Lü), an encyclopedia written in the late Spring and Autumn period, observes, "The ancient sage kings used military force for justice and never abandoned troops."[29] An ancient legendary case illustrating this view is that of the war that King Yu, the first King of the Xia Dynasty, waged against three minority tribes in the early twenty-first century BCE.[30] Even Mozi, an ancient Chinese pacifist philosopher who opposed all wars, believed that this was a just war.[31]

(4) Hegemonic leadership adopts foreign policy according to double-standard principles, whereby other states also treat allies according to moral principles and deal with enemies according to realpolitik principles. The actions of hegemonic leadership promote the double-standard principle in the formation of international norms, while the moral actions of such leadership help to promote the moral principles that guide their interactions with allies. In order to maintain hegemony, therefore, a hegemonic leadership needs to establish strategic credibility among its allies through adoption of a moral policy. As Zhifu Huibo, an assistant minister of the State of Lu in 529 BCE, said, "Trust is of supreme importance to alliance."[32] In order to consolidate and expand its alliances, a hegemon must provide its allies with security protection according to moral principles, and the mechanism through which it promotes such moral principles is the same as that of humane authority leadership, namely, the carrot and the stick.

Hegemons' actions guided by realpolitik principles compel their enemies to respond in like manner, thus promoting the realpolitik principle as the norm between them and their enemies. For instance, after the collapse of the Soviet Union, the then Russian president Boris Yeltsin had a strong desire to join the Western camp and to act according to the international norms observed among Western countries. The American-led NATO, however, took advantage of Yeltsin's practice of Western norms to expand eastward and compress Russia's strategic space. NATO's aggressive response to Russia's respect for Western norms diminished Russia's confidence in them. When Vladimir Putin came to power, therefore, Russia resumed its foreign policy based on realpolitik principles.[33] In 2008, as members of NATO turned a blind eye to Georgia's use of military means to resolve the South Ossetia issue, Russia not only sent troops into Georgia but also backed the self-proclaimed republics of Southern Ossetia and Abkhazia's call for independence from Georgia.[34]

The double-standard principle followed by hegemonic leader-ships is determined by their relations with allies and enemies and causes no conflicts in the direction of norm changes. Through the three mechanisms of example-imitation, support-reinforcement, and punishment-maintenance, these double-standard actions drive other states to follow the double-standard principle in decision mak-ing by applying moral principles toward allies and realpolitik prin-ciples toward enemies. For instance, Western countries tolerate Israel's possession of nuclear weapons but cannot tolerate Iran's nuclear programs. Double-standard behavior is a universal phenom-enon consistent with the natural and social characters of the inter-national system. In fact, double-standard principles are applied not only to the different relationships the hegemonic leadership has with its allies and enemies, but also to those it has with states of both similar and different status. A typical case is the NPT, initiated by the then two superpowers the United States and the Soviet Union, based on the principle of distinguishing between nuclear and non-nuclear states. This treaty has been widely accepted and became a global norm in the field of nuclear arms control.[35]

Direction of the Evolution of International Norms

The theoretical question about the direction of the evolution of in-ternational norms has arisen in regard to whether changes in the types of international norms are on a one-way track or a two-way path. Wendt categorizes international norms into three types: the Hobbesian, Lockean, and Kantian cultures.[36] Hobbesian culture re-fers to confrontational norms between enemies; Lockean culture refers to rival norms between competitors; and Kantian culture refers to norms of cooperation between friends.[37] Wendt believes in the one-way evolution of international norms, arguing, "In conclusion, I address the question of progress over time, suggesting that although there is no guarantee that international time will move forward to-ward a Kantian culture, at least it is unlikely to move backward."[38]

His linear view of history lacks historical evidence and defies theoretical logic. If we were to limit our observations of European history to the period since the end of World War II, the direction of changes in international norms might support Wendt's view. But from a longer and broader historical perspective, we find that international norms are not evolving toward a progressive ultimate end. An ancient example is that of the changes in interstate norms of the pre-Qin Chinese interstate system. The dominant norm during the Spring-Autumn period (770–476 BCE) was hegemonic rivalry, when the annexation of other states was prohibited. This was replaced during the period of the Warring States (475–221 BCE) with the annexation norm. A modern case is that of the norm change from "Lockean culture," established by the League of Nations after World War I, to "Hobbesian culture," which endured through to the end of World War II.

The direction of changes in the type of international norms is uncertain, because there is no guarantee that a new international leadership is any more moral or benevolent than its predecessor. We cannot rule out the possibility that the new dominant state will advocate principles of conduct that are less moral than those supported by previous leading states in certain historical periods. History has witnessed random changes in the types of international leadership between humane authority, hegemony, anemocracy, and tyranny. For instance, the interstate leadership in the ancient Chinese system changed from humane authority to tyranny when King Jie succeeded to the throne as the last ruler of the Xia Dynasty in the middle of the seventeenth century BCE, and a similar change occurred in the interstate leadership of the Shang Dynasty during the reign of King Zhou during 1075–1046 BCE.[39] These two historical changes in interstate leadership are tied to the changes in the interstate norms of that Chinese system from moral principles to realpolitik principles.

Since the end of the Cold War, the international leadership of the United States has also experienced random type changes according to modern standards. The foreign policies of Bill Clinton, George W. Bush, Barack Obama, and Donald Trump all displayed different principles of conduct. The principle of multilateralism, adopted by Clinton and Obama, follows the double-standard principle. Bush's unilateralism is a kind of realpolitik principle. And Trump's America-first policy is in line with the economic coward-bully principle. Obama's foreign policy principles represent a progressive return to those of the Clinton administration. The principles of Bush and Trump, meanwhile, constitute historical retrogression.

Changes in international norms can be divided into the two categories of degree changes and type changes. Degree changes in international norms often take a long time to effect type changes when there is no change in the type of international leadership. This is why one type of norm may maintain predominance for a hundred years or more. It would be wrong, however, to say that all changes in the type of international norms are the result of degree changes. When reviewing the history of international relations we can also observe rapid changes in the type of international norms in the wake of a sudden change in the type of international leadership. Therefore, we need to make observations covering a long period of world history before judging the role that leadership types play in the degree or type changes in international norms.

It is possible for international norms to undergo a type change when rising states take over leadership from previously dominant states, because the new leading states may provide a type of international leadership different than the previous one. It is true to say that most international leadership transitions do not change the leadership type, because the rising power and the old dominant state are of the same type. However, the chance of a sudden change in the type of international norms arises when the type of the new leading state differs from that of the previous one. In 1945, after the end of World War II, for example, the United States and the Soviet Union replaced the European powers as the global leading states. Different from those European tyrannical states during World War I and World War II, both of the two hegemonic states adopted double-standard principles in their foreign policy making. The United States established NATO in 1949, and the USSR established the Warsaw Treaty Organization of Friendship, Cooperation, and Mutual Assistance (Warsaw Pact) in 1955, thus splitting the world into Western and Eastern camps.[40] In attempts to gain the upper hand, both the United States and the Soviet Union adopted the strategy of supporting their own allies and opposing each other's. Their foreign policy rapidly raised double-standard principles to the level of a predominant international norm.

The durability of a type of international leadership promotes the socialization and internalization of the international norm it espouses. A type of international leadership that endures for a long period signifies that leading states have continuously interacted with other states according to a given type of principles of conduct. These interactions enable that type of principle to be socialized internationally and internalized in many countries. Thus, that type of principle becomes, or is maintained, as the dominant international norm. For example, American culture has an inherent belief in democracy.[41] After the Cold War, the United States became the sole superpower, and it increased its efforts to promote democracy and oppose autocratic regimes throughout the world. Consequently, by the beginning of the twenty-first century the majority of nations in the world, at least verbally, claimed to be democratic entities, regardless of their actual political institutions. Meanwhile, humanitarian intervention, a term coined in the early 1990s, became a dominating international norm in the post–Cold War period, when the majority of states supported democratic movements and opposed autocratic regimes in other states. Both the collapse of Eastern European socialist regimes in the late 1980s and the color revolutions of Arab countries in the 2010s illustrate the internalization and socialization of liberalist norms advocated by American leadership since the end of World War II.

SUMMARY

The four types of international leadership—humane authority, hegemony, anemocracy, and tyranny—may create four corresponding types of international norms: moral, double standard, coward-bully, and realpolitik. The formation process of a new type of international norm is often a combination of internalization and socialization through interactions between new leading states and other states.

The formation of a new type of international norm occurs through unconventional interactions, whereby the interactions between the new leadership and other states accord with a principle that differs from the existing norms. Conventional interactions consolidate existing norms rather than effect changes to international norms. Unconventional interactions are not necessarily wars, and a peaceful transition of international leadership could be followed by peaceful changes in the type of international norms. However, wars are inclined to change the type of international norms far more quickly than peaceful transitions. In any event, the leadership type differences between rising states and the previous dominant states account for the changes in the type of international norms.

In regard to the formation of a new type of international norm, there are three mechanisms: example-imitation, support-reinforcement, and punishment-maintenance. Among the three mechanisms, example-imitation plays the fundamental role in shaping international norms, because no dominant state can establish new international norms that it does not practice itself. The support-reinforcement and punishment-maintenance mechanisms induce or force other states to behave according to the norms advocated by the dominant states but play secondary roles in the socialization and internalization of new norms. The example-imitation mechanism, on the other hand, can convince other states to follow the leading states' behavioral principle according to their own free will. The internalization of a new behavioral principle is the precondition for its socialization into the widely accepted norms guiding the majority of members of an international society. Thus, leading by example is a more effective approach for dominant states to shape international norms than the other two mechanisms.

Changes in the type of international leaderships between different types of leading states occur less often than transfers of leadership among the same types of leading states, and there is also uncertainty as to the change of direction toward a better or worse leadership. Therefore, the direction of international norm evolution is nonlinear, and each change in the type of international norms depends on whether or not there is a type difference between the rising state and the previous dominant state. History has witnessed random changes in international leadership types as well as in international norm types. The present norms guided by American liberalist values have maintained unchanged for two decades or more but face the possibility of being replaced by new norms, either progressive or retrogressive, in the future. Whether or not the liberalist norms will change in the foreseeable future, it is certain that no international norms can remain forever, and the direction of norm evolution is uncertain.

6

International Mainstream Values

得道者多助, 失道者寡助。
(He who is just shall be assisted, he who is not shall lose assistance.)

MENCIUS

When distinguishing the international order from the international system in chapter 3, we noted that both international mainstream values and international norms are components of international order. As international norms are formed under the guidance of international mainstream values, the character of the former will change along with changes in the latter. Thus, the normative character of the international order changes in accordance with changes in mainstream values and norms. When rising states espouse values different than those of the previous dominant states, value conflicts become part of the strategic competition between rising states and dominant states. This chapter will analyze value competitions under the guidance of corollary 4: the zero-sum nature of power brings about a structural contradiction between rising states and dominant states, as well as disturbances in an existing international order. The following discussion on value competitions will focus on the current challenges to liberalist values, the coming ideological competitions for regional domination, and the possible modernization of humane authority values.

VALUE CHALLENGE AND COMPETITION

A look at the history of the twentieth century shows that no modern ideology has been able to maintain itself as an international mainstream value for more than three decades. Rather, several modern ideologies have become elevated to such a status, including nationalism in the 1910s, fascism in the 1930s, communism in the 1950s, nationalism again in the 1960s, and liberalism in the 1990s. However, none of these modern ideologies wielded dominant influence over the modern international system for as long as Confucianism did over the ancient Chinese interstate system. During the Cold War, communism, represented by the Soviet Union, and capitalism, represented by the United States, were the two contending global ideologies, and the competition between them shaped the normative character of that era's international order. Liberalism rose to preeminence after the collapse of the Soviet Union and subsequently influenced the international value system to the extent that the post–Cold War era is known as the liberal order. However, as we near the end of the second decade of the twenty-first century, liberalism has begun to falter because of the growing challenges of other ideologies that threaten to undermine its dominance.

Decline of Liberalism

Liberals espouse a wide array of views depending on their understanding of the intended purpose of liberal principles. For this reason, the meaning of "liberalism" diverges in different parts of the world. In the United States, liberalism is associated with the welfare-state policies of the New Deal programs initiated by President Franklin D. Roosevelt,[1] while the ideas of laissez-faire economics exist simultaneously within current American conservatism.[2] In Europe, liberalism is most commonly associated with a commitment to government responsibility and social welfare, whereas in Latin America and many postcommunist countries it often relates to socialism and is hence generally referred to as social liberalism.[3] In China, liberalism refers politically to Western democracy and economically to a market economy.

Despite the above differences, liberalism in any country generally affirms the principles of equality, freedom, democracy, civil rights, secular government, international cooperation, and the resultant programs in support thereof. Liberalism first became a distinct political movement after achieving a degree of popularity among Western philosophers and economists during the Age of Enlightenment. In the first half of the twentieth century, Western liberalism spread from European democracies to other parts of the world, mainly owing to the dominance afforded by their victories in both world wars. In the aftermath of World War II, the United States became the de facto leading exponent of liberalism, and its hegemonic power signified that international norms were influenced by the American liberalist values of equality and freedom. This is exemplified in chapter I, article 1, clause 2, of the UN Charter reflecting the UN directive: "To develop friendly relations among nations based on respect for the principle of equal rights and self-determination of peoples, and to take other appropriate measures to strengthen universal peace."[4]

Liberal democratic governments achieved great social progress across Western Europe during the Cold War, a development that would reinforce their values in almost all fields as liberalism came to be viewed as a Western ideology in direct opposition to the oppression of the communist East. With the subsequent success of the US-directed Western camp in its strategic competition with the Soviet-directed Eastern camp, liberalism became the dominant international ideology in the post–Cold War period. The triumph of the Western world led many to believe in the preeminence of liberal values. Francis Fukuyama went as far as to say, "What we may be witnessing is not just the end of the Cold War, or the passing of a particular period of post-war history, but the end of history as such: that is, the end point of mankind's ideological evolution and the universalization of Western liberal democracy as the final form of human government."[5]

The history of liberalism has been permeated with competition from other ideologies—conservatism, secularism, constitutionalism, nationalism, socialism, fascism, communism, Islamic fundamentalism, and more. Despite the aforementioned predictions to the contrary, however, today it faces challenges once more. In 2016, anti-establishmentarianism gained momentum; in the United States it took the form of Trumpism, while in Europe and other democratic countries it became known as populism.[6] Although liberal parties in many countries continue to wield power and influence both domestically and abroad, Brexit and Trump's victory in the presidential campaign of 2016 dealt a serious blow to the global standing of liberalism. People in the UK and the United States are now ideologically divided, and liberalism is far less dominant than in the past.

However, the root causes of the decline of liberalism in Western countries differ from those in non-Western countries. In the West, this trend has been mainly the by-product of the inadequate response of democratic governments, in the wake of the financial crisis of 2008, to the need to resume their domestic economies. Faced with the inefficiencies of democratic governance, many liberalists, including former UK prime minister Tony Blair and political theorist Fukuyama, have made critical comments on this very issue.[7] Yoni Appelbaum, a senior editor for politics at the *Atlantic*, warns that "with democracy in retreat abroad, its contradictions and shortcomings exposed at home, and its appeal declining with each successive generation, . . . the greatest danger facing American democracy is complacence. The democratic experiment is fragile, and its continued survival improbable."[8]

Younger Americans, for instance, have lost faith in the ability of American democracy to deliver on its promises.[9] Among people born before World War II, more than 70 percent highly value living in a democracy, while for those born after 1980 the number shrinks to less than a third.[10] The situation in the United States is not unique; there is a similar decline of liberalism across most democracies. In

Australia and New Zealand, for example, the generation gap with regard to democratic values is comparable with that in the United States.[11] Results of a survey of European millennials show that only 32 percent selected democracy as one of their top five most important social values.[12] Increasingly, liberalists in the West seek to reform liberalism, to the extent that some now refer to their political ideals as liberal progressivism, while others style themselves as progressive liberals.[13]

Meanwhile, the argument for liberalism in non-Western countries has been undermined by both the slowing economic growth of Western countries in comparison to rising states, and the foreign policy double standards that the former have demonstrated. When it comes to economics, global millennials are much more likely than older generations to express positive opinions about the Chinese communist government and its ability to rapidly improve living standards when compared to Western governments. People in developing countries admire China's policy of setting clear national priorities that invest greatly in the future and as a consequence are increasingly open to nondemocratic forms of government. In 2011, almost half of global millennials were agreed that the idea of a strong leader was preferable to a democratic parliament and elections.[14]

In addition, the perception that Western countries maintain foreign policy double standards further undermines the popularity of liberalism. For example, the policies of Western governments toward Arab states have been inconsistent with the professed goal of promoting liberal values in the region. Saudi Arabia, despite the overtly undemocratic nature of its government by virtue of being a totalitarian absolute monarchy, has received unwavering support from America because of its status as an important strategic ally, yet the United States has opposed the secular regime of Syria since the so-called Syrian uprising of 2011. Assistance from the United States to Saudi Arabia has moreover extended to its military intervention into other Arab states, as demonstrated by the provision of military aid to antigovernment forces in Syria and the use of military assets to suppress antigovernment forces in Yemen and Bahrain. Furthermore, the Arab Spring movement that pledged to rid the Arab world of dictators has resulted in new dictatorships rather than liberal governments.[15] In fact, quantitative research shows that both military and economic forms of American intervention are more likely to hinder rather than to promote human rights abroad,[16] suggesting the likelihood of a decline, rather than an increase, of liberalism in the Middle East.

Competing Ideologies in China

The decline of liberalism as a mainstream global political value creates an opportunity for other ideologies to compete for influence. Its successor is likely to originate in a country that achieves greater political and economic success than the United States. Looking ahead over the next decade, China appears to be the only country with the potential to narrow the disparity in comprehensive capability with the United States to a degree sufficient to become a new superpower. Today, people in democratic countries regard China the same way as Europeans once did the United States—as an uncouth land of opportunity and rising economic might.[17] Consequently, people in many countries fear that the current liberalist order may be replaced by a new order shaped by Chinese values.[18] Christian Reus-Smit has indeed noted "a fear that as power shifts to the East, [the] non-Western great powers will seek to reshape international order according to their own values and practices."[19] Former Australian prime minister Kevin Rudd recently remarked, "Very soon we will find ourselves at a point in history when, for the first time since George III, a non-Western, non-democratic state will be the largest economy in the world. If this is the case, how will China exercise its power in the future international order? Will it accept the culture, norms and structure of the post-war order? Or will China seek to change it? I believe this is the single core question for the first half of the twenty-first century, not just for Asia, but for the world."[20]

In 2017, the Chinese government announced its plan to significantly increase soft power before 2035, publicly stating that China's modernization "offers a new option for other countries and nations who want to speed up their development while preserving their independence; and it offers Chinese wisdom and a Chinese approach to solving the problems facing mankind."[21] This statement implies a desire on the part of the Chinese government to advance its official ideology and exert global influence. In fact, after the Nineteenth Party Congress held in October 2017, the Chinese Communist Party sent thirty international propaganda delegations abroad to introduce its programs and opinions in almost eighty countries and regions.[22] However, the ideological situation in China is complicated. For one thing, the official ideology advocated by the Chinese government is inconsistent with the popular traditional values espoused by ordinary people. In addition, even Marxism, the official ideology that ostensibly guides domestic political life, differs from the exceptional Chinese traditional culture applicable to foreign policy. In general, there are four ideologies competing for influence on China's foreign policy making:

(1) Marxism, the official ideology of the Chinese Communist Party, but which has limited influence on actual foreign policy. The Chinese government has stated that Marxism should guide all areas of its work, such that "in developing this culture, we must follow the guidance of Marxism, base our efforts on Chinese culture. . . . We must continue to adapt Marxism to China's conditions, keep it up-to-date, and enhance its popular appeal."[23] Nevertheless, the Chinese government seems unable to mention Marxism when explaining its foreign policy. In fact, the government has not claimed to use Marxism as a guiding principle in its foreign policy since the adoption of the opening-up and reform policy in 1978, clearly because of the contradiction between the core idea in Marxism of class struggle and the emphasis on international cooperation imbued in the opening-up principle. The later adoption of peaceful development as a fundamental principle made guiding foreign policy through Marxism impossible. Implemented in 2004 with Hu Jintao as party secretary, the principle of peaceful development has since become the orthodoxy guiding China's foreign policy, to the extent of being immutable.[24] Since class struggle is the core of Marxism, it cannot possibly harmonize with peaceful development. A return to class

struggle in foreign policy making would, on the contrary, endow on China a much more aggressive international image.

(2) Economic pragmatism, the ideology most popularly accepted by both the government and the ordinary people of China in the wake of Deng Xiaoping's political reforms of 1978. As the potential for another world war substantially decreased, economic prosperity became the reference point for judging the appropriateness of an ideology in China. The country's economic achievements over the last four decades have laid a strong social base for the values of economic pragmatism. Although the Chinese government has not specified economic growth as its primary priority since 2013, most Chinese people still regard the economy as the basis of national comprehensive capability and therefore support the elevation of economic interest to the level of a main policy objective. Economic pragmatism has largely established its legitimacy in China through the Marxist argument whereby the economy is the basis of the political superstructure. This is a perspective that shares certain similarities with American economic nationalism as represented by Steve Bannon,[25] whereby, with regard to foreign policy making, both define strategic interest from an economic perspective and stress the importance of foreign trade. At the same time, neither relishes international responsibility, rather sharing the common desire to shake off the burden of maintaining world order. It was with this intent that Deng Xiaoping adopted the principle of *tao guang yang hui* (韬光养晦, keeping a low profile), while Trump advocates that of "America first."[26]

(3) Liberalism, the most popular ideology among Chinese intellectuals. During the early 1980s, when Hu Yaobang served as the party secretary general, liberalism guided reforms in all fields, which mainly involved imitating the American model. Nowadays, it is popular only among intellectuals. Although the influence of liberalism on China's political reform stopped short after the Tiananmen incident in 1989, it still had considerable impact on the making of economic and foreign policies. We can observe the sustained influence of liberalism after the Cold War, when China's foreign policies were guided by the principle of keeping a low profile, which mainly

reflected liberalist values. However, its impact on economic reform weakened after the global finical crisis of 2008 and became irrelevant to the making of foreign policies after the Eighteenth Party Congress in 2012. When the principle of keeping a low profile was replaced by *fen fa you wei* (奋发有为, striving for achievement) in 2013, liberalism ceased altogether to influence China's foreign policy.[27] Today, China supports the principle of free trade for practical reasons, having become the world's largest trader, and not because of any liberalist influence on policies. As long as China continues to narrow the gap in capability with the United States, liberalism will never regain the same degree of influence in China that it had in the 1980s.

(4) Traditionalism, which, even though it is not the official ideology, is today gaining momentum among everyday Chinese people as well as intellectuals and politicians. Traditionalism does not exclusively refer to Confucianism, but rather to a combination of all schools of ancient Chinese thought. Despite their differences, each of these schools emphasizes the significance of political leadership, as well as the role of strategic credibility, in constituting a base for the solidarity and durability of that leadership. In this regard, they argue that a superpower's foreign policies should prioritize its strategic reputation. To this end, the ancient idea of *wang* (王, humane authority) promotes the values of *ren* (仁, benevolence) and *yi* (义, righteousness) in guiding decision making.[28] Traditionalism also advocates the strategy of leading by example, thereby emphasizing the importance of a leadership that produces demonstrable achievements. This school of ideology encourages China to improve its international strategic reputation by shouldering more international security responsibility, especially that of providing neighbors with security protection.

Although traditionalism is not the Chinese government's official ideology, scholars of both traditionalism and the Chinese government agreed that foreign policy should be guided by Chinese traditional political wisdom rather than any ideology rooted in Western culture, including Marxism. For instance, in 2011 the government issued the white paper *China's Peaceful Development*, which stated unequivocally, "Taking the path of peaceful development is a strategic choice made by the Chinese government and people, in keeping with the fine tradition of Chinese culture, the development trend of the times, and the fundamental interests of China."[29] In this statement the phrases "development trend of the times" and "fundamental interests of China" reflect the objective factors, and "fine tradition of Chinese culture" the subjective factor. This official document reflects the Chinese government's intent to take traditional political values into account when formulating its foreign policy. Although the Chinese government adjusted its foreign policy guidelines from "keeping a low profile" to "striving for achievements" in 2013, it has nonetheless maintained Chinese traditional values as a source of guidance for its decision making. For instance, at the conference on the diplomatic work toward surrounding countries, new foreign policies were explained in light of Chinese traditional values such as *qin* (亲, closeness), *cheng* (诚, credibility), *hui* (惠, beneficence), and *rong* (容, inclusiveness).[30] These four Chinese characters also appeared in the foreign policy section of the Nineteenth Party Congress report.[31]

Along with the earlier mentioned change in foreign policy guidelines, China has also adjusted its diplomatic posture from that of an ordinary power to that of a major power, indicating a shift in the government's perception of its current capabilities. At the World Peace Forum in 2013, Chinese foreign minister Wang Yi explained this change through the lens of ancient Chinese philosophy: "The unique features of China's diplomacy originate in the rich and profound Chinese civilization. Throughout its five-thousand-year history, the Chinese nation has developed the humanistic-oriented concept of loving all creatures as if they were of your species and all people as if they were your brothers, the political philosophy of valuing virtue and balance; the peaceful approach of love, non-aggression and good-neighborliness, the idea of peace as of paramount importance and harmony without uniformity, as well as the personal conduct of treating others in a way that you would like to be treated, and helping others succeed in the same spirit as you would want to succeed yourself. These traditional values with a unique oriental touch provide an endless source of invaluable cultural assets for China's diplomacy."[32]

Regardless of whether or not these benevolent Chinese traditional thoughts have seen application in real policies, the Chinese government has claimed, at least rhetorically, to be guided by them when formulating foreign policy. In fact, citations of ancient Chinese sayings are now a prerequisite for Chinese leaders' policy speeches. However, the possibility that such Chinese traditional values embrace those of economic pragmatism and generate a hybrid that guides China's foreign policies cannot be ruled out, since economic pragmatism is still very popular among both everyday people and bureaucrats.

DEVALUATION OF STRATEGIC CREDIBILITY

The current global decline of liberalism, in conjunction with the ideological competitions within China, could lead to a world without mainstream values. There is little hope for liberalism to survive the current challenges from nonliberalist ideologies and resume its dominance as a global influence as long as Trump's administration continues undermining the United States' international reputation and American leadership, and fails to grow the United States' capability faster than China's. It is also less possible for China to provide a nonliberalist ideology for the world unless it adopts the principle of humane authority. At the present time, the most possible scenario is that no ideology dominates at the global scale while major ideologies, including liberalism, compete for regional domination or influence on countries of a given type. These states could be categorized by proximity of geographical location, by similarity of political system/culture, or by size of economy.

An Era without a Dominant Ideology

Chapter 4 analyzes the trend of bipolarization headed by China and the United States, whereby the two giants will continuously enlarge their capability disparity with other major states. This trend means that unless the United State or China can replace liberalism with a new ideology as the mainstream value, no other country will have the capability to do so. With regard to collective capability, unless the United States and China provide a joint leadership for the world, such as the "G-2" or "Chimerica" coined respectively by C. Fred Bergsten and Niall Ferguson,[33] there is no group with the potential to advance a new ideology to replace liberalism's global influence. According to corollary 4, the structural contradiction between China and the United States is a zero-sum game; thus, that they would make joint efforts to establish a new global ideology is unimaginable.

Despite the Trump administration's pursuit of anti-establishmentarianism, it has little chance of becoming a dominant ideology in the West, let alone globally. The rise of anti-establishmentarianism has dramatically undermined the domination of liberalism in the United States, but it has not yet become popular enough to overwhelm liberalism. Although most Americans still identify themselves as either Democrats or Republicans, nowadays they are also more likely to identify themselves as liberals or nonliberals. This phenomenon implies that liberalism is still the strongest competitor of anti-establishmentarianism, neither of which can achieve absolute dominance in the United States, let alone abroad. Appelbaum says, "America no longer serves as a model for the world as it once did; its influence is receding. At home, critics on the left reject the notion that the US has a special role to play; on the right, nationalists push to define American identity around culture, not principles."[34]

Anti-establishmentarianism not only splits Americans at home but also undermines the political solidarity of the West. In Western countries, liberals believe that international treaties and agreements are necessary for peace and security. After the Cold War, the United States established its world leadership based on multilateral liberal regimes that depended heavily on Western countries' support. Nevertheless, the Trump administration, guided by the mentality of anti-establishmentarianism, is walking away from many of these regimes, one after the other, as it did from the Paris Climate

Agreement, the TPP, UNESCO, NAFTA, and more recently by scrapping the nuclear deal with Iran.[35] These policies distanced the United States from its traditional allies, making it impossible for the United States to establish a set of new global values with collective support from Western countries.

The ideological competition within China enacts a similar role as it does in the United States, in that it disenables China from proposing a global dominant ideology over the next decade, even if China becomes the world's largest economy. There are two necessary conditions for a great state to establish a global influential ideology. The first is the existence of a popular ideology pursued by both the government and its people at home. The existence of four competing ideologies in China precludes any one from gaining a dominant influence; this is also the reason behind the Nineteenth Party Congress's advocation of "cultivation and practice of socialist core values."[36] The Chinese government is cognizant that it needs first to establish a popular ideology at home before it can effectively promote such an ideology globally. Therefore, it is trying to establish a universal ideology that combines Chinese traditional values with Marxism. The Nineteenth Party Congress report states, "To develop socialist culture with Chinese characteristics is to follow the guidance of Marxism, base our efforts on Chinese culture, and take into account the realities of contemporary China and the conditions of the present era."[37] During a panel discussion at the Nineteenth Party Congress, Wang Qishan, a Politburo Standing Committee member, summarized this idea as "the embrace of the fundamental tenets of Marxism into the Chinese traditional cultural essence."[38] However, this is no easy task, because of the opposing creeds of Chinese traditional values and Marxism, whereby the former advocates harmony and the latter struggle.

The second necessary condition is the existence of political cultures in certain countries that make them amenable to accepting the ideology advanced by a great power. Although imitating China's economic policy is entirely feasible to other countries, owing to its economic achievements, following the example of China's official ideology or political system is less so. According to China's amended constitution of 2018, "Chinese Communist leadership is the most fundamental character of socialism with Chinese characteristics."[39] This judgment means that communist rule is the precondition for the achievements of China's economic model, and that it would be impossible for noncommunist countries to attain the same success simply by copying such a model. At present, there are few communist countries, including China's neighbors, and also few states in which the opposition party is a communist organization that could potentially gain national power.

Besides their impotence with regard to establishing a global influential ideology, the current Chinese and American governments hesitate to become embroiled in any ideological rivalry. Cognizant that ideological rivalry was the core cause of the Cold War, both have so far purposely constrained their competition from spilling over into the ideological domain—the precise opposite of what the United States and the Soviets did during the Cold War. The *National Defense Strategy* issued by Trump's administration states, "We will not seek to impose our way of life by force."[40] When the international media interpreted the Nineteenth CCP Congress report as a press release on China's plans to advance its model to the rest of the world, the Chinese government quickly declared that it "has no intention to ask other countries to copy the Chinese model."[41]

Since neither the United States nor China is able to offer a global dominant ideology in the coming decade, the coming bipolar world is likely to be different from that during the Cold War. Instead of a competition between two global influential ideologies, there could be kaleidoscopic competition between various ideologies for regional domination or influence in certain types of states. For instance, Shias and Sunnis will compete for domination of Muslim countries, mainly in the Middle East; liberalism and populism will contend for votes in Western countries, mainly European states; socialism and capitalism will continue their rivalry in Latin American countries; statism and civicism will vie for people's support in developing countries; communism and economic pragmatism will contend in communist countries; and religions and secularism will struggle for power in theocratic states.

One-Man Decision Making without Strategic Credibility

Since the United States and China could either independently or jointly establish a dominant global ideology in the coming decade, the international normative order will possibly be shaped mainly by the common trait of foreign decision making in major states. The present decline of liberalism is accompanied not only by challenging ideologies but also by the one-man decision making now prevalent in major states. Kishore Mahbubani, a Singapore senior diplomat, has observed that "a wave of strongmen rulers has been elected, many of whom have clearly non-Western identities. This list includes Shinzo Abe of Japan, Recep Tayyip Erdoğan of Turkey, Narendra Modi of India and, looking back further, Vladimir V. Putin of Russia."[42] President Trump is not on the list, but he actually qualifies to head it. Although more research is needed on the correlation between the wave of strongmen rulers and the decline of liberalism, it is obvious that those leaders prefer one-man decision making to collective decision making.

Because the phenomenon of one-man decision-making mechanisms has prevailed in both democratic and nondemocratic countries, we should analyze its traits from the leadership level rather than the state or system level. In the one-man decision-making mechanism, foreign policy is also decided by a leading group instead of one person. The core difference between collective decision making and one-man decision making is apparent in the sequence of institutional feasibility studies and decisions. The former carries out feasibility studies before making decisions; the latter does the opposite. One-man decision making is often carried out through personal consultations between the supreme leader and a few of his personal confidants, after which the related institutions are tasked with finding the best way to implement the decision. This type of decision making undermines a state's strategic credibility and increases mutual suspicions between states in several ways.

(1) Inconsistent policies reduce other states' confidence in one's policy and commitments. The one-man decision making mechanism inevitably entails more policy changes than does that of collective decision making, owing to the absence of predecision feasibility studies. Wrong decisions lead to poor results; therefore they are followed by policy adjustments. But adjustments made through the same mechanism are highly likely to result once more in the wrong policy. This type of decision making, therefore, exacerbates the inconsistency of a country's foreign policy. Keren Yarhi-Milo, a faculty of Princeton University, noted that Trump "has flip-flopped on policy positions, publicly undermined the efforts of members of his own administration, and backpedaled on diplomatic agreements, including the Paris climate accord and the Iran nuclear deal. . . . As the president undermines the nation's credibility at home and abroad, allies will hesitate to trust American promises, and US threats will lose some of their force."[43] In fact, Trump's type of leadership is no exception in this era, but rather representative of many major states. For instance, on March 6, 2017, China said it would fight the United States, "at any cost" after Trump threatened $100 billion in new tariffs on Chinese goods, but four days later, on March 10, China promised to open its market further, and to lower import tariffs on products, including cars.[44] When most major states' foreign policies so frequently swing in opposite directions, mutual distrust and suspicions will prevail among states.

(2) States that issue radical policies are constantly on the alert for those proposing more rational policies and are reluctant to cooperate. Because collective decision making allows governmental institutions to present their different opinions, the final decision is often a balanced combination of different policy suggestions. By contrast, one-man decision making leaves no room for that, because the supreme leader is disdainful of the different ideas raised by technocrats. Absent professional involvement in decision making, it is highly possible to make radical decisions, including adjustments to correct previous radical policy. For instance, although Indian prime minister Modi paid a state visit to China in May 2015 and signed

twenty-four agreements,[45] in June 2017, he abruptly sent troops across the border between China and Bhutan to stop China's road construction in the Doklam area.[46] This radical decision brought about a military confrontation between China and India that lasted more than two months. Since then, China's policy toward India has been less cooperative. Most major states that adopt radical foreign policies are constantly on guard against cooperative initiatives by any other, opting instead for a bullying strategy. A typical case in point is the mutual threat of trade retaliation between China and the United States in the spring of 2018.[47]

(3) Unpredictable policies of major states increase mutual suspicion and distrust between states. One-man decision making is rooted in supreme leaders' personal power overwhelming national interests. When protecting national interests undermines the supreme leader's power, he will protect his personal power at the cost of national interests. For instance, in 2016 Turkish president Erdogan suddenly improved relations with Russia after an attempted coup, convinced that the coup had been planned by the CIA.[48] A country's national interests constitute a more substantive basis for other countries to judge them than does a leader's preoccupation with personal power, thus foreign policies driven by the supreme leaders' personal interests are less predictable than those by national interests. When one-man decision making prevails in most major states, unpredictable foreign policies will catch states off guard and inevitably result in mutual suspicion and distrust.

The Common Practice of Conspiracy and Secret Diplomacy

Chapter 5 illustrates the argument that international norms may retrogress in the realpolitik direction by giving examples of historical cases in some periods. The world seems likely to prove this once more in the coming decade, in light of an emerging conspiracy mentality, reflected in the defying of international norms, violating of agreements, and breaking of promises between states amid the present bipolarization. Since 2017, the issue of North Korea's nuclear weapons has repeatedly illustrated the conspiracy mentality of all related players in this issue.

Trump's policy toward North Korea's nuclear weapons has swung constantly between military solutions and diplomatic negotiations. For instance, his administration announced that Vice President Mike Pence would reject any interaction with the North Korean delegation during his attendance of the 2018 Winter Olympic Games in Pyeongchang, South Korea. Pence ignored Kim Jong Un's sister, Kim Yo Jong, who was sitting in the box next to him during the opening ceremony, and later said, "I didn't believe it was proper for the United States of America to give any countenance or attention in that forum to someone who's not merely the sister of the dictator, but is the leader of the propaganda effort."[49] In fact, Pence had arranged a secret meeting with the head of the North Korean delegation at Pyeongchang, which the DPRK scrapped, earning him a stern rebuke from the State Department soon after he returned home.[50]

China's policy toward North Korea's nuclear weapons is also somewhat inscrutable. After the US-China summit at Mar-a-Lago in early April 2017, China supported America's suggested sanctions on North Korea. This policy further deteriorated the already uncomfortable relations between China and North Korea. In January 2018, one of China's official newspapers, *Global Times*, publicly criticized Kim Jong Un's threats to destroy the United States with nuclear weapons.[51] But two months later, in March, China, without preamble, suddenly invited Kim Jong Un to visit Beijing, and *Global Times* made a 180-degree about-turn by advocating the inheritance of the China-DPRK traditional friendship.[52] After the summit, China's media quoted Kim as saying: "The issue of denuclearization of the Korean Peninsula can be resolved, if South Korea and the United States respond to our efforts with goodwill, create an atmosphere of peace and stability while taking progressive and synchronous measures for the realization of peace."[53] Meanwhile, North Korea's media aired a forty-minute documentary on the event, in English, that mentioned nothing about denuclearization.[54] As neither side released any substantive comment on the summit, the media buzzed with conjecture.

Russia has also adopted an inconsistent policy on the issue of North Korea's nuclear weapons. For instance, Russia voted for the UN's sanction on the DPRK on December 22, 2017, but a few days later, Russian tankers were caught smuggling oil to North Korea.[55]

According to the example-imitation mechanism discussed in the previous chapter, leading states' conduct on the issue of North Korean nuclear weapons will act as examples that influence lesser states' foreign affairs behavior. Chinese ancients noted the prevalent phenomenon whereby the weak imitate the bad behavior of the strong, a point they drove home with a story, known as *dong shi xiao pin* (东施效颦, an ugly girl imitates a beauty's frown). Today, the irregular policies of leading states will also play a role in shaping the mentality of advocating conspiracy among states. When leading states' foreign conduct is irresponsible and untrustworthy, the common practice will prevail in the international community of preferring secret diplomacy to open diplomacy, conspiracy to dialogue, sanctions to negotiations, protectionism to free transactions, political chicanery to strategic credibility, military bullyragging to strategic deterrence, and bilateralism to multilateralism.

The untrustworthiness of leading states' policies will diminish lesser states' willingness to participate in global governance and regionalization. The essence of global governance is the distribution of responsibility for the handling of common problems or threats to most states. Leading states' display of lax responsibility for global governance renders them untrustworthy, giving lesser states no reason to believe that they can benefit from participation in global governance, because no multilateral cooperation can achieve its goals without a strong international leadership. Meanwhile, lesser states will value their sovereignty more than ever when handling regional and global problems, something that is highly likely in light of the current prevalence of decentralization within international organizations, including the EU.

BEYOND LIBERALISM

The previous section analyzed the retrogressive trend of international values apparent in the decline of liberalism and prevalence of one-man decision making in major states. However, the impermanence of international leadership types gives rise to the chance in future of a progressive international leadership. The current China-US bipolarization implies two things, namely, that China will further reduce the disparity in capability with the United States; and that an ideology more advanced than liberalism can be established by combining the fine traditions of the two countries' political thoughts. Reus-Smit proposes that the relevant principles through which to establish international norms are not necessarily homogenous, but may be combinations of different types.[56] Since American liberalism still has global influence, and China officially claims to guide its foreign policy according to Chinese traditional fine values, it is possible for either a Chinese or American leadership of the millennial generation to pursue an advanced ideology by learning from the other. Therefore, this section will discuss the possible combination of the three values of liberalism—equality, democracy, and freedom, with the three Chinese traditional values of benevolence, righteousness, and *li* (礼, rites).

Before discussing how to combine these values, we must first define the concepts of "fairness" and "justice" as they relate to international politics, and so avoid any possible misunderstandings stemming from their everyday use. American philosopher John Rawls defines "justice as fairness,"[57] a definition that considers the principle of justice as a closed system discrete from other societies rather than as one participant in relations between states. However, an international system comprises different domestic societies wherein justice and fairness mainly apply to judgments of institutions, and rarely of individuals. Thus, in such a setting justice and fairness refer to different matters. For instance, we distinguish a just from an unjust war, but never a fair from an unfair war, in the same way that we distinguish fair from unfair trade, but never just from unjust trade.

Therefore, I define justice as being in accordance with righteousness of result, and fairness as being in accordance with a morality favorable to the disadvantaged.

Benevolence's Embrace of Equality

The Christian tradition values the concept of equality as one enjoined by the natural law of life.[58] Nevertheless, owing to inherent genetic differences and divergent social environments, disparities between human beings are natural phenomena, apparent in variances in intelligence, strength, height, weight, and athleticism, as well as in social differences rooted in family background, education, peers, and so on. Focusing on equality without taking these differences into consideration is equivalent to advocating the law of the jungle—that of unquestioned equal rights and zero distinctions between the advantaged and the disadvantaged. The individualist value of liberalism thus often leads to conflict rather than cooperation among human beings. Even when defined in terms of competitive opportunity,[59] under circumstances where violent means are the best option for winning competitions, absolute equality can still result in life-and-death rivalry. The war between different religious groups in Libya since 2011 is a case in point.[60]

Benevolence is the core idea and social norm of Confucianism, one whose essence as a governing principle calls on state leaders to empathize with and care for their peoples. Thus, it can find application in the management of relations between the strong and the weak, the rich and the poor, and those occupying high and low ranks at work, so helping to reduce social conflicts emanating from disparities between the powerful and the disadvantaged. As the members of an international system are divided into different classes according to their capability, the principle of equality without benevolence places the lesser states in an unfavorable position. They will consequently fight ceaselessly to attain equal power.

By embracing the merging of equality with benevolence, we can popularize the value of fairness on a global level. For instance, "first come, first served" is a principle of absolute equality. It gives those first in line the opportunity, for example, to take a seat on a bus, but it is not fair to the aged or infirm. A norm of fairness dispels this conflict by requiring that the able-bodied, whether or not among the first in line, yield their seats to those in greater need of one. Another popular example is that of the Olympic Games boxing rules. To ensure equality, the established rule is that the loser is the fighter who fails after a knockdown to get up before the referee has counted to ten. However, to ensure fairness, boxers are divided into classes according to weight, so giving boxers in an ascending scale of weight an equal chance to win championships. In this case, the classification of boxers constitutes the prerequisite for referees to make a fair judgment based on the skill that the contestants display in a match.

This same principle of differentiated treatment is equally applicable in international politics. For instance, the concept of "common but differentiated responsibilities," which arose at the Stockholm Conference in 1972, and was accepted by the United Nations Framework Convention on Climate Change in 1992 and the Kyoto Protocol in 1997, reflects this ideal.[61] On the issue of reducing CO^2 emissions, the international community has embraced the principle whereby the developed and developing countries take common but differentiated responsibilities.[62] The Lomé Convention signed in February 1975 between nine members of the European Community (EC) and forty-six developing countries in Africa, the Caribbean, and the Pacific (ACP), also embodied this equitable principle. Through this convention, the EC countries offered preferential economic treatment to members of the ACP group.[63] These treaties suggest the possibility of a greater emphasis on fairness over equality in future international principles.

Righteousness's Embrace of Democracy

Democracy is one of liberalism's major contributions to human political life, and the legalization of governmental actions through popular support is at its core.[64] In a modern civil society, every citizen judicially and equitably claims ownership of national sovereignty and state power. However, owing to the logistical issues generated by large populations, it is impossible for all citizens to participate directly in the decision making on state affairs. Therefore, the representative system is the obvious choice for the execution of state power through democratic procedures.[65] The active principle in the democratic procedure is that of majority consent through secret ballot. However, while the democratic process of decision making legitimizes governmental decisions, it cannot guarantee that those decisions are just. For instance, in 2003 the US Congress authorized the White House's decision to attack Iraq based on alleged evidence that Iraq possessed weapons of mass destruction. Although this authorization legitimized American military action against Iraq, the war was eventually proven to be unjust after revelations that invalidated the alleged evidence.[66]

In fact, not even international legitimacy automatically ensures that a state's actions are just. As international society is an anarchical system, the power distribution among members of international institutions is mainly arranged according to their varying levels of capability. Therefore, a just outcome achieved solely through international institutions' procedures is rare. As regards the issue of pure procedural justice, as held by liberalists, Rawls says, "Even though the law is carefully followed, and the proceedings fairly and properly conducted, it may reach the wrong outcome. . . . The injustice springs from no human fault but from a fortuitous combination of circumstances which defeats the purpose of the legal rules."[67] He adds, "Pretty clearly, perfect procedural justice is rare, if not impossible, in cases of much practical interest."[68] For instance, members of the Arab League made the decision to expel the Syrian government led by Bashar al-Assad from its ranks and offer military assistance to antigovernment forces in Syria, all through a democratic process. This democratic decision internationally legitimized the subsequent support provided to rebel militants in Syria but thus escalated a war that resulted in tens of thousands of civilian deaths and over a million refugees.[69] In humanitarianism terms, therefore, the Arab League's decision was unjust.

Righteousness is an ancient Chinese moral code shared among a number of philosophical schools, including Confucianism, Daoism, and Moism. Although righteousness has broad connotations, at its core is upright, reasonable, and proper behavior. Mencius said: "Benevolence is man's mind and righteousness is man's path."[70] In other words, only by choosing the just way can one implement benevolence. The difference between righteousness and democracy is that the former stresses the results of a policy while the latter emphasizes its legitimacy. Allison says, "For Americans, democracy is the only just form of government: the authorities derive their legitimacy from the consent of the governed. That is not the prevailing view in China, where it is common to believe that the government earns or loses political legitimacy based on its performance."[71] In reality, there are many unjust results stemming from legitimized policies. For instance, the UN is designed to maintain world peace, but it is also dominated by the leading powers—the five permanent members of the Security Council. It is common practice among the leading powers to undermine the UN's democratic regulations by using veto power to achieve their particular unjust purposes.

The value of righteousness can help constrain the unjust legitimacy of leading states' conduct through requiring justice in both form and result. By fusing democracy with righteousness, we can popularize the value of justice and help to ensure that the resolutions of international organizations are legitimate in form and just in result. When the two are unified, justice is upheld. For instance, most countries exercised sanctions against the apartheid regime in South Africa during the Cold War. Not only did such actions carry legitimacy in the form of a UN resolution adopted by a majority of UN members, but, more importantly, the anti-apartheid policies were just in nature and in accordance with the principle of righteousness. The combination of the two explains why this particular use of sanctions was not regarded as an intervention into domestic affairs.[72]

When comparing justice and democracy, the former proves to be a more useful value in promoting social fairness. At the same time, justice does not repel but rather draws support from democracy. In fact, justice can utilize democracy as a means of achieving greater social fairness while preventing unjust results. Rawls set forth two principles of justice: principle 1 is freedom and equality; principle 2 is a combination of equal opportunities and differentiated treatment. Principle 2 aims to achieve justice based on the value of fairness, which cannot be achieved by democracy alone.[73] In addition to ensuring the legitimacy of the actions of leading states through democratic procedures, therefore, it is necessary also to ensure that the results of their actions are just by assessing decisions according to the principle of righteousness. For instance, as the polarization between the rich and poor intensifies owing to globalization, priority needs to be given to the principle of justice over that of democracy in order to promote common development in our age. The principle of democracy alone ensures only that every country, regardless of its wealth, has the equal right to decide its own development agenda. By contrast, the principle of justice calls on developed countries to provide economic aid to developing states amounting to 0.7 percent of their GDP in efforts to eliminate or mitigate polarization.[74]

Rites' Embrace of Freedom

Freedom is also a core value of liberalism. Rooted in man's inherent attributes, the desire for freedom is an instinct common to all animals. This primal need provides legitimate justification for freedom in human society, as man's desire for longevity does for the right to live. But human beings are a social species for whom the community is a precondition for survival.[75] Building a social order, however, requires sacrificing some degree of freedom to the norms that regulate an individual's behavior.[76] The tension between individual freedom and the greater social order exists in both domestic and international systems. Although social norms can be implemented within a domestic system through the monopolization of force, violence and chaos will inevitably prevail when actors utilize such ability to protect their interests in an international system. Hence, the balance between the freedom of individual states and the international order becomes a crucial political issue.

Rites constitute a Chinese traditional value applicable not only to political affairs, but also to the affairs of ordinary people in their daily lives. Rites refer to social norms or customs formed according to given ethics. Although a formality, a rite plays a more extensive role than law in maintaining social order. Confucius says, "If you do not learn rites, your character cannot be established."[77] Laws deter illegal actions by punishing law-breaking behavior after the fact, while rites preemptively restrain people's uncivilized behavior through moral formats. Rites are a more extensive restraining force than laws, because they function in areas unrelated to the law. Laws protect freedom of speech but are unable to curb the hurling of abuse, while rites can restrain people from uttering obscenities. Freedom without the constraint of rites can easily give rise to violent conflicts. For instance, the 2012 American movie *Innocence of Muslims* is legally consistent with the principle of freedom of speech but nonetheless caused widespread protests in many Muslim countries that resulted in numerous deaths and injuries.[78] In 2015, two brothers later identified as terrorists attacked the Paris office of the French satirical weekly magazine *Charlie Hebdo* in response to its publication of satirical cartoons and nude caricatures of Muhammad. The attack killed twelve people and injured eleven.[79]

Rites are the foundation of civility and advance the social significance of human life beyond the principle of freedom. Because man values the meaning of life, the major difference between humans and animals is not discernible exclusively in the degree to which they pursue freedom, but rather in the former's pursuit of freedom with a meaningful purpose. Rites help to guide humans toward civilized behavior, thus enriching the meaning of life. Freedom without civility may lead to a regression of human society to one more akin to that of animals and beasts. Xunzi said: "Birds and beasts have parents but no parental affection; they distinguish between male and female but do not make the distinction between man and woman."[80] In Chinese culture, extremely uncivilized behavior, such as incest or maltreatment of the aged, is regarded as inhuman or bestial. Human civility, therefore, lies in the ability to distinguish between social goods and ills. For example, all animals have the freedom to excrete, but civility prohibits humans from excreting indiscriminately, as an animal might. It is through civility that humanity constantly advances while other animals remain forever in an uncivilized state. The conventions and formalities of the Oriental and Western etiquettes may differ, but the observation of such proprieties is a shared social norm.

The embrace of freedom alongside the social recognition of rites will improve human civility, thus reducing the danger of violent conflicts among human beings. Allison has expressed concern regarding the potential for a civilizational clash between China and the United States due to "the profound differences between American and Chinese conceptions of the state, economics, the role of individuals, relations among nations and the nature of time."[81] He notes, "Chinese culture does not celebrate American-style individualism, which measures society by how well it protects the rights and fosters the freedom of individuals."[82] However, what he does not realize is that Chinese culture advocates the recognition of rites for the sake of preventing the social violence to which individual freedom gives rise. Should both rising and dominant states guide their competition for international power in accordance with the principle of civility, such competition will be peaceful and may possibly be healthy as well. With the Trump administration's characterization of China as the United States' major rival, as noted in its *National Security Strategy*,[83] it has become increasingly necessary for these two giants to consider ways of regulating their competition in a civilized manner.

In the twenty-first century, innovation has become a primary method of wealth accumulation. It reduces dramatically the need to control natural resources as part of the power competition between rising and dominant states. Thus, it is possible for China and the United States to establish norms of civility that regulate their competition for global domination in a peaceful manner. The shift of world power throughout history has often been accompanied by wars between rising states and dominant states that are classic manifestations of the incivility of international society. Establishing international norms in accordance with the value of civility will help to reduce the risk of war between all states, including rising and dominant powers. Crystallization of the value of civility amid the establishment of new international norms not only transcends liberalism but also advances human civilization.

SUMMARY

International mainstream values play a guiding role in establishing international norms. In keeping with this maxim, the decline of liberalism will inevitably generate challenges to the liberalist international order and the current norms established under the guidance of the United States. After enjoying a dominant status for three decades, the values of liberalism are now being challenged by the rise of competing ideologies—anti-establishmentarianism in the United States, populism in Europe, traditional values in China, Islamic fundamentalism in the Middle East, and economic nationalism in both developed and developing countries.

During the present bipolarization, neither the United States nor China is able to replace liberalism with a set of new values as a dominant global ideology. The coming decade may witness a bipolar world with many different ideological competitions for regional domination or influence on certain types of states. The current prevalence of one-man decision making in major states is bringing about a historical retrogressive trend. Decision makers in many states will prefer secret diplomacy to open diplomacy, conspiracy to dialogue, sanctions to negotiations, protectionism to free transactions, political chicanery to strategic credibility, military bullyragging to strategic deterrence, and bilateralism to multilateralism. States will value sovereignty and privilege more than before and become less open to global governance and regionalization.

Although the coming decade may witness a bipolar world with a retrogressive normative order, millennials in China and the United States may provide an advanced leadership when they come to national power. American liberalism still wields greater influence than any other ideology at this time, and China's rise will expand the international influence of Chinese traditional values. These two factors offer the chance to combine the Chinese traditional values of benevolence, righteousness, and rites with the liberalist values of equality, democracy, and freedom, thus modernizing them in the forms of fairness, justice, and civility. Ultimately, it is the merging of these values that should prove universally acceptable to people of different countries.

7

Transformation of the International System

故可以有夺人国，不可以有夺人天下。
(You can seize a state, but you cannot seize all under heaven.)
XUNZI

Although the expression "transformation of the international system" often appears in IR writings, definitions of it do not. In fact, this phrase is used randomly to refer to changes in international orders, or configurations, or norms, or actors, rather than to the system as a whole. Such indiscriminate usage academically confuses a system change with changes in a system's components and also obscures the causes of system change. History shows that the success of rising states often leads to changes in the international order, or configurations, or norms, but that it only occasionally results in a system change and even rarely in a type change of international actors. Thus, this chapter will first distinguish between system changes and component changes, and then analyze the influence of international leadership on the transformation of international systems. Since system transformation relates to changes in international actors, norms, configurations, orders, and leadership types, the analysis of system transformation will be based on the four corollaries as discussed in chapter 3.

COMPONENT CHANGE VERSUS SYSTEM CHANGE

As there is no common criterion for judging system transformation, IR scholars hold opposing views on the international change after the Cold War. Some label the change as "an international system transformation," while others refer to it as "a change in international configuration." In 2006, Yang Chengxu, a senior policy researcher and diplomat, strongly argued that the post–Cold War period brought about a change in power configuration rather than a system change.[1] In fact, configuration was the only difference in the international system during and after the Cold War. After the change in configuration from bipolar to unipolar, international actors and norms remained the same as in the Cold War. This kind of misunderstanding occurred again when some people misjudged the current bipolarization as an international system transformation. Bipolarization of the international configuration, apparent in the narrowing disparity in capability between China and the United States, occurred in tandem with the global financial crisis of 2008. Some people perceive this change in configuration as an international system change and have indeed even labeled it "the third great system transformation of the last 500 years."[2] It would be impossible, however, to make any sound judgments on whether or not a change has occurred in the current international system as whole, or in just of one of its components.

Component Change Not Equal to System Transformation

Literature on international relations encompasses writings on a wide range of interstate systems, including the five service system in pre-Qin China, the tributary system in pre-seventeenth-century East Asia, the Westphalia system in post-1648 Europe, the Vienna system in nineteenth-century Europe, the Versailles-Washington system after World War I, and the Yalta system after World War II. These interstate systems, however, are not defined or categorized according to a common criterion, but rather to historical events, mainly power transitions, between major states. A review of IR scholars' different academic interpretations of international systems, including those of David Singer, Kenneth Waltz, Alexander Wendt, and Barry Buzan and Richard Little, reveals divergences and contending opinions on the concept of "international system."[3]

Waltz defines a system as "a set of interacting units. At one level, a system consists of a structure, and the structure is the systems-level component that makes it possible to think of the units as forming a set as distinct from a mere collection. At another level, the system consists of interacting units."[4] Besides the units and structure that Waltz suggests as components of a system, norms are also a constituent part, because units must interact according to a set of norms in a given system. Robert A. Mundell and Alexander Swoboda say, "A system is an aggregation of diverse entities united by regular interaction according to a form of control."[5] The diverse entities of an international system consist of international actors, mainly states, and the form of control may range from informal international rules to formal international laws. Stanley Hoffmann regards a set of rights and rules as an international system component that influences interaction among states.[6] David Kang defines the Chinese tributary system as "a set of institutional structures that provided an overarching framework for organizing external relations among political actors in early modern East Asia."[7] Based on the elements mentioned in the above definitions, this book regards international actors, configuration, and norms as the three key components of an international system (see back to figure 3.2). Although there is wide agreement on the components of an international system, there is no common academic criterion as to which of these three components should be used to categorize the traits of a given international system. Consequently, nor is there a common criterion through which to judge whether or not the transformation of a given international system has occurred.

Many scholars take changes in international configuration—mainly in capability structure of major powers—as transformation of international systems.[8] Some researchers, for instance, claimed that the change from the Cold War era to the post–Cold War era constituted a transformation of international systems.[9] Nevertheless, nation-states were the main international actors during these two historical epochs, and international norms were the sovereignty norms based on the Charter of the United Nations. Among the three key components of the international system, therefore, it was only the international configuration that changed—from bipolar to unipolar. Equating a change in the international configuration to a transformation of the international system as a whole thus renders meaningless the distinction between the configuration and the system. Semantic considerations apart, the primary reason why international configuration and system cannot be treated as the same thing is that equating a component change to a system change would make it impossible for researchers to distinguish between the parts and the whole.

Aware that a component change does not equate to a change of the whole system, Gilpin distinguishes three types of change in an international system according to its component changes. "Systems change" refers to a change in the nature of the actors in a system; "systemic change" to a change in the form of control of a system; and "interaction change" to a change in interactions among actors in a system.[10] In his book, Gilpin's "systems change," "systemic change," and "interaction change" equate respectively to actor change, configuration change, and norm change.[11] He defines both systemic change and interaction change as changes within a system, but systems change, that is, change of actor, as change in the character of an international system.[12] He says, "The character of the international system is identified by the most prominent entities: empires, nation-states, or multinational corporations."[13] His approach of defining actor change as change in the character of a system, however, confuses component change with system change, in the same way as that which regards configuration change as system change.

TABLE 7.1: THE COMPONENTS OF INTERSTATE SYSTEMS ACADEMICALLY DEFINED

Interstate Systems	Actors	Configurations	Norms
HUAXIA REGION			
Western Zhou Dynasty (1046–771 BCE)	Royal state and vassals	Unipolar	Enfeoffment
Spring and Autumn period (770–476 BCE)	Royal state and vassals	Bipolar, multi-polar	Hegemonic rivalry, annexation prohibited
Warring States era (475–221 BCE)	Monarchies	Multipolar	Annexation
Qin Dynasty (221–206 BCE)	Empire	Unipolar	Annexation
EUROPE			
Roman era (27 BCE–395 CE)	Empire	Multipolar, bi-polar	Annexation
Middle Ages (ca. 476–1453)	The pope and kingdoms	Multipolar	Magisterium
Westphalia system (1648–1791)	Empires and nation states	Multipolar	Sovereignty
Anti-France coalitions (1792–1814)	Empires and nation-states	Multipolar or bipolar?	Interference in internal affairs
Vienna system (1814–1913)	Empires and nation-states	Multipolar	Interference in internal affairs
MUSLIM REGION			
Post-Caliphate times (8th–14th centuries)	City-states	Multipolar	Annexation
Ottoman period (14th–16th centuries)	Empire	Unipolar	Annexation
GLOBAL			
Versailles-Washington system (1919–39)	Nation-states	Multipolar	Occupation and annexation
Yalta system (1945–)	Nation-states	Bipolar	Noninterference and nonannexation

Comparing the components of interstate systems as academically defined throughout history would help us to understand the relationship between component changes and system transformation, that is, a change of the whole system. Table 7.1 demonstrates the differences between certain academically termed interstate systems as apparent in their actors, configurations, and norms. In this table, actors refer to the major states rather than all states in a given interstate system, because only major states have the capability to influence the character of an interstate system.[14]

In table 7.1, the components of some sequential interstate systems, namely, the Anti-France Coalitions system and the Vienna system, are of one type. One or two of the components of other sequential interstate systems, namely, the Versailles-Washington system and the Yalta system, meanwhile, differ. This phenomenon raises the question of whether or not some of these academically termed international systems lack independence, for they might be continuums of the system immediately preceding them. An examination of the relationship between changes in the type of the three components and the system transformations in table 7.1 will help us to find an objective criterion for judging system transformations. Scrutiny of this table enables us to make three observations:

First, changes in the type of actors do not necessarily correlate with system transformations. The Treaty of Westphalia, signed in 1648, could be regarded as the starting point of nation-states, but this change remained confined to Europe for a century. After signing the treaty, European interstate actors experienced the evolutionary process of city-states; kingdoms; monarchies; empires; nation-states. Nevertheless, the IR community has rarely characterized European interstate systems prior to the Westphalia Treaty according to actor changes in that region. In fact, the treaty indicated the transformation of the European system not just through the appearance of nation-states, but also by virtue of sovereignty becoming the dominant interstate norm in Europe, that is, nation-states possessed independent sovereignties.[15] We can also find in this table counterevidence of character changes in an international system when no change in the type of actors has occurred. For instance, the Chinese Qing Dynasty ended in 1911, and the Persian Empire in 1908, before World War I wiped out the centuries-old Hapsburg, Hohenzollern, Romanoff, and Ottoman dynasties in Europe.[16] Since the end of World War I, nation-states have remained the most important international actors. Nevertheless, IR academia regards the Versailles-Washington system and the Yalta system as two entities of different characters before and after World War II, which implies that a transformation of the two systems took place. If we accept the judgment that these two systems are different in character, then we have to agree that international system transformations do not necessarily relate to changes in the type of actors.

Second, changes in configuration types are not necessarily indicative of system transformation. There are three basic types of international configurations: unipolar, bipolar, and multipolar. For instance, in the thirteenth century, when the interstate configuration changed from bipolar between the Southern Song Dynasty and the Jurchen Empire to unipolar under the grand unification of the Yuan Dynasty, the ancient Chinese interstate system remained an empire system. The main reason why many IR students take power redistribution as system transformation is because they have overlooked historical system transformations that did not entail configuration change. In table 7.1 we can find several cases, such as in ancient Chinese history, where the configurations of both the Spring-Autumn period and the Warring States period were multipolar, as were the European interstate configurations before and after the Westphalia Treaty. However, interstate systems transferred in these two cases, which disproved the idea that a change in the type of power configuration will lead to the transformation of international systems.

Third, changes in the type of international norms are also not necessarily indicative of system transformation. The relationship between norm changes and system transformations is a topic for further study. Many international system transformations are indeed accompanied by norm changes, as illustrated by several cases in table 7.1, and Chinese historians as well as IR scholars have categorized ancient Chinese interstate systems according to norm changes. For instance, they agree that the major indicator of system transformation from the Spring and Autumn period to the Warring States period is that of the legality of annexing other states, which had been illegal during the former period but was sanctioned in the latter.[17] Nevertheless, table 7.1 also includes certain system transformations that were unaccompanied by norm changes, namely, the annexation norms of both the Warring States period and the Qin Dynasty, of both the post-Caliphate times and the Ottoman period, and of both the Vienna system and the Versailles-Washington system. These cases illustrate that system transformations do not necessarily correlate with changes in the type of interstate norms, or at least that norm changes alone cannot construct sufficient conditions for a system transformation.

CONDITIONS FOR SYSTEM TRANSFORMATION

Table 7.1 suggests that there is no strict correspondence between changes in one component of a system and system transformations. Therefore, it would be logical to ascertain whether or not simultaneous changes in two components correlate with system transformations. As it turns out, using the criterion of simultaneous changes in any two components of international systems as the definition of system transformation facilitates a much more uniform explanation of the system transformations listed in table 7.1. Thus, we can argue that system transformation must be related to simultaneous changes in the type of at least two components.

System Transformation with Two Component Changes

The following system transformations in table 7.1 correspond to simultaneous changes in both norms and actors. During the system transformation from the Spring and Autumn to the Warring States the major actors changed from vassals authorized by the Son of Heaven to independent monarchies. The interstate norm, meanwhile, changed from prohibiting to sanctioning annexation. In Europe, the system transformation from the Roman Empire to the Middle Ages experienced an actor change from empire to kingdoms, and a norm change from annexation to magisterium, or feudalism. The system transformation resulting from the Thirty Years' War (1618–48) witnessed the change in actors from kingdoms to nation-states, and in norms from magisterium to sovereignty.[18] In these three cases, actors and norms changed in type, but configuration remained the same.

The following system transformations listed in table 7.1 correspond to simultaneous changes in configuration and norms. The system transformation from the Western Zhou Dynasty to the Spring and Autumn witnessed the change in power configuration from unipolar to multipolar, and the change in norms from enfeoffment to hegemonic rivalry, which prohibited annexation. The typical modern case is the system transformation after World War II, when the international system changed from the Versailles-Washington system to the Yalta system. This entailed the power redistribution from multipolar to bipolar, and the norm change from the principle of preoccupation and annexation to that of noninterference and nonannexation. These two cases show that system transformation may happen when actors remain the same. In the first case, the royal state and vassals remained the main actors, while in the second case nation-states were maintained as main international actors.

Finally, simultaneous changes in the type of both actors and configurations can be found in the following system transformations shown in table 7.1. In 221 BCE, the State of Qin annexed the other six monarchies, and the ruler of Qin changed his title from "monarch" to "emperor," and established the first empire in Chinese history. Combined with the change of actor from monarchies to an empire, the configurations also changed from multipolar to unipolar. Hence, the ancient Chinese interstate system transformed from a monarchical system to an imperial system. Such a system transformation also occurred in Muslim history. The Caliphate Empire in Arabia had been in decline since the middle of the eighth century and fragmented into many city-states, simultaneously changing the configuration from a unipolar to a multipolar one. The system transformation occurred along with these component changes. In the late fourteenth century, with the rise of the Ottoman Empire, Muslim states changed from city-states into an empire, and later two other empires—the Safavid Empire of Persia and the Mughal Empire of India—emerged in the Muslim world. At the same time, the configurations changed from multipolar to unipolar.[19] The above system transformations happened without any change in norms, and the annexation principle prevailed in all these interstate systems.

Disputable Cases and Judging Principles

In table 7.1, we can find that some system categories, namely, the Westphalia system, the Anti-France coalitions war system, and the Vienna system, are disputable. The three systems feature different international norms but are the same as regards types of actors and configurations. They would hence not qualify as three international systems of different characters according to the criterion whereby system transformation requires changes in the type of two components. However, some scholars argue that the international configuration during a series of seven wars waged by various military alliances between great European powers against Revolutionary France is a bipolar structure different from the multipolar one of the Vienna system, and that meanwhile the international norm had changed from the principle of secret diplomacies in the Westphalia system to that of universal peace and justice in the Anti-France coalitions system.[20] If this judgment reflects the historical reality, therefore, the two transformations between the three systems meet the required standard of two component changes; otherwise they do not.

There could, however, be an alternative definition of the European international system during 1648–1913. In general, compared to the time taken for changes in power configuration or norm types, international systems take much longer to transform from one type to another. Since the Anti-France coalitions period lasted only twenty-five years, it can be classified as a period of disturbance sandwiched between the Westphalia system and the Vienna system, rather than as an independent international system. It thus follows that the three sustained international systems throughout the whole period may be regarded as one. In fact, an independent international system lasting for two hundred to three hundred years was popular in the premodern world of empires and dynastic kingdoms. Categorizing these three continued periods as one system also meets the criterion of two component changes in order for a system transformation to take place.

Admittedly, the "two component change" hypothesis has yet to be tested thoroughly. It is difficult to construct a rigorous argument about the relationship between component changes and system transformations without having undertaken a thorough investigation of all the historical cases of interstate system transformations. Therefore, we cannot yet conclusively argue that an international system will undergo a transformation as long as changes occur in the type of any two of its three components. The above analysis provides a logical framework for deducing three principles through which to judge whether or not transformations of international systems occurred. First, an international system transformation will inevitably take place when all three components undergo type changes. Second, it is highly possible that the character of an international system will transform when two of its three components change in type. This proposition can be supported by the examples mentioned above but still requires further testing. Third, changes in one of the three components are unlikely to be indicative of any system transformation. As we can see, there are many cases of false categorizations of international systems based on the capability of one component change, especially that of configuration. This is a classic logical fallacy of equating a subset of the system with the whole.

POLITICAL LEADERSHIP AND SYSTEM TRANSFORMATION

History demonstrates that the type of international configurations changes faster than that of norms, and the type of international norms faster than that of actors. For instance, the international configuration experienced changes from multipolar to bipolar to unipolar during the twentieth century, while international norms changed just once—from realpolitik to double standard—and international actors remained the same as nation-states during the same period. The differential frequencies of change in actors, norms, and configurations explain why system transformations are more often accompanied by simultaneous changes in the type of international configurations and norms than by changes of international actors and one of the other two components. Since it usually takes centuries for international actors to change in type, this section will analyze the mechanism of system transformations that are caused by changes in the type of power configuration and norms.

In chapter 3, we analyzed the relationship between changes in power configuration and types of state leadership, and in chapter 5, we discussed the relationship between norm changes and types of international leadership. According to previous analysis, we can see that political leadership is a critical factor in bringing about changes in configurations and norms. Even though it is not yet clear whether political leadership has any direct influence on changes in the type of international actors, we can still argue that political leadership plays a crucial role in international system transformations for two reasons. First, system transformations require changes in at least two of the three components, one of which must be either configuration or norms. Second, history shows that system transformation occurs much faster than changes in the type of international actors. This means that changes in norms and configuration are more likely to bring about system transformations than changes in actor. Changes in both configuration and norms, meanwhile, are caused by changes in political leadership of leading states.

At the state level, the national leadership types of rising states and dominant states play a joint role in changing international configurations. An international configuration will change when the leadership of a rising state is able, through continued reform, to improve its national capability faster than the dominant state is, and when the leadership of the dominant state fails to prevent any rising state from reducing the disparity in capability between them. At the international level, the change in international configuration renders the rising state the new dominant state, one that may provide the world with a new international leadership quite different from that of previous dominant states. The new leadership resulting from the change in the type of international leaderships, moreover, is much more likely to establish international norms correspondingly different in type from the previous ones. When both the in-

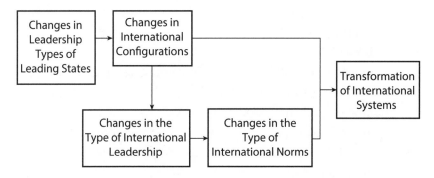

FIGURE 7.1 New types of international leadership and transformations of international systems

ternational configuration and norms experience typological change, the original international system will be transformed into a new type. Figure 7.1 illustrates the four steps from changes in the type of leading states' leadership to the transformation of international systems.

(1) The first step is the change in leadership of leading states, either rising states or dominant states, which may lead to a change in international configuration. Realistically, the states existing in an independent international system during a given historical period might range between a few and many. Changes in state leadership, therefore, can frequently happen. Nevertheless, only a few of these leadership changes lead to substantial increases or declines in their national capability, as the numerical probability is that of no substantial change. Assuming perfectly random conditions, leadership changes in a state could have one of three different impacts on that state's capability—those of rapid growth, stagnation, or decline. The international configuration will experience a type change only when the leadership change of the dominant state results in a dramatic decline of that state's capability, and when that of a rising state leads to rapid growth of its capability. This particular combination accounts for just one out of nine of the possible outcomes, and only then when assuming perfectly random situations. Historically, leadership that results in rapid growth of rising states or dramatic declines of dominant states is usually less than chance. Thus, in practice, this serendipitous synchronicity is even lower than the

theoretical one in nine. This is why rising states rarely overtake successfully the dominant states' position, such that these events happen only every half century or longer.

Many people attribute changes in power configuration to the successful achievements of rising states, but in reality the decline of dominant states is equally if not more likely to bring about changes in power configuration. Guanzi said, "When your own state is well governed but the sovereigns of neighboring states are unworthy, it will be a great advantage for establishment of a great power."[21] Guanzi thus regards the poor leadership of other states as equally important in the rivalry for interstate domination as the good leadership of one's own country. I would argue that leadership changes in dominant states are more likely than those in rising states to change the international configuration, because it is much easier for a leadership to undermine its own national capability than to improve it. That is why it takes a rising state longer to establish itself as a superpower than it does for a status superpower to ruin itself. For instance, Huhai, the second emperor of the Qin Dynasty, totally ruined the first Chinese Empire within three years of his rule (210–207 BCE). In 1985, the Soviet Union experienced a leadership change that resulted in the collapse of the Soviet Union by the end of 1991, and also in a change in the international configuration from bipolar to unipolar, despite no substantial improvement of American absolute capability during these six years. In regard to the American decline in the twenty-first century, Lebow says, "modern realist categories of analysis blind their adherents to the reasons why American influence could undergo a precipitous decline in the decades ahead. This will be because the United States proves itself to be its own worst enemy."[22]

(2) The second step is that whereby changes in power configuration produce a new international leadership, which could be of a type different from the previous one. Changes in the type of international leadership happen less often than those in state leadership, which explains why international norms change less frequently than configurations. Although changes in power configuration do not necessarily correspond to changes in the type of international lead-

ership, they do in some cases. For instance, the international configuration changed from a multipolar one before World War II to a bipolar one thereafter. It was by virtue of this change in configuration that the Soviet Union and the United States displaced the Western European powers and Japan as the leading states. Based on interaction between the United States and the Soviet Union, the two superpowers offered a hegemonic leadership that differed from the imperialist leadership of European states prior to World War II.

When the leaderships of rising states and dominant states are of the same type, the new international leadership resulting from changes in power configuration will also remain the same type. For instance, the members of leading states after World War I differed from those before the war. France, Britain, Italy, and Japan remained leading states, while Germany, Austro-Hungary, and the Ottoman Empire lost their leading positions.[23] Nevertheless, the leaderships of both the old and the new leading states are imperialist. Thus, the international leadership remained the same type after the war. Another case is the change of power configuration from bipolar to unipolar after the Cold War. This change rendered the United States the sole global leader, but the international leadership it offered remained the same type as that of its joint leadership with the Soviet Union during the Cold War.

(3) The third step is that whereby the new international leadership reforms international norms according to the new values that it advocates and practices. In order to maintain their newly achieved leading positions for as long as possible, new states constituting the international leadership will prefer to establish new international norms through which to consolidate a world order and ensure their durable domination of it. The new norms will serve as both the basis of their leading positions and the instrument for legitimizing their foreign policies. For instance, America's refusal to be a part of the League of Nations after World War I kept it outside of the world leading body, so disenabling it from establishing international norms of a new type. The United States initiated the United Nations after World War II and joined the leading body, the UN Security Council, thus changing the type of international norm from a colonial one to

a hegemonic one. This step constitutes one of the two required components for the transformation of international systems.

The norms established by a new international leadership can be divided into two categories: those differing in character, and those differing only in content from the previous ones. For instance, the norms established by the UN after World War II belong to the first category, because they stress the principle of respecting states' territorial sovereignty and prohibit annexation, and are hence contrary to the preemption doctrine. In contrast, the norms adopted by the League of Nations after World War I belong to the second category, because they are the same as those of the nineteenth century in terms of character. The arms control agreement with respect to naval capability among the United States, the UK, France, Italy, and Japan is arranged according to the principle of power redistribution and is consequently no different typologically from previous arms control norms.[24]

(4) The fourth step is that whereby the combination of changes in power configuration and establishment of new norms leads to system transformations. This final step signifies this book's unique understanding of international system transformations as distinct from other theories, namely, that system transformations happen only under the condition of changes in the type of at least two components of a given system, whereas changes in one component cannot result in system transformation. According to this standard, the Yalta system established after World War II has survived for more than seven decades. It thus not only has survived the Cold War but also has the chance of continuing for at least one more decade. This is because China, currently the most powerful rising state, does not yet possess the capability to establish new types of norms in the coming decade, even though China's rise will shape a new bipolar configuration.

This capability apart, the Chinese government has no intention of changing the Yalta system. For instance, after Japan nationalized the Diaoyu/Senkaku Islands in 2012, the Chinese government confronted the Japanese government by repeatedly stressing the importance of protecting the post–World War II system. China's *Report on the Work of the Government* in 2014 stated: "We will safeguard the victory of World War II and the postwar international order, and will not allow anyone to reverse the course of history."[25] Officially, the Chinese government regards international order and international system as the same thing, which implies that the Chinese government deems the Yalta system not yet to have ended, and that it has no intention of changing it.

The Trump administration may speed up the current change in power configuration from unipolar to bipolar, but changing the current international norms into a new type preferred by it without China's cooperation is beyond its capability. China and the United States each may have the capability to weaken the efficiency of sovereignty norms based on the UN Charter, but neither of them is strong enough to demolish them. Therefore, as long as nation-states remain as major international actors, it is highly possible for China's rise and America's decline to jointly reshape a new international order in the next decade, but the Yalta system will likely survive and not transform into a new type.

SUMMARY

International actors, configurations, and norms are the three key components of international system. Owing to the common confusion whereby a part change is perceived as a change of the whole, many people misjudge a component change in a given international system as a system transformation. As an international system comprises the three above components, transformation of it requires changes in the type of at least two of them. Changes in the type of one component alone may lead to system disorder or better order, but it cannot bring about any typological system transformation.

It takes much longer for international actors than for international configurations and norms to change typologically. Therefore, history has witnessed more changes in the type of configurations and norms than in actors. This also explains why most system transformations have been caused by combined changes in the type of configurations and norms, rather than by actor changes accompanied by a type change in one of the other two components. Owing to the fact that change in configuration happens more frequently than that in norms, system transformations often start from changes in configuration.

Changes in the type of both international configuration and norms are closely related to changes respectively in the type of domestic and international leaderships of leading states. Therefore, the transformation of international system must be influenced by changes in the type of political leadership. As it is much easier for a domestic leadership to ruin its national capability than to improve it, the decline of dominant states often plays a more important role in change of power configuration than does the rise of a new leading power. China's rise and America's decline are likely to speed up the present bipolarization and shape a new international order, but the Yalta system may survive those changes without transformation into a new type.

8

Historical Cases of System Transformation

以史为镜, 可以知兴替。
(Taking history as a mirror, one can
know the rise and fall of a state.)

EMPEROR TAIZONG

An international system transformation is a comprehensive and complex change that encompasses changes in the type of actors, configurations, norms, orders, and leaderships. Based on the analyses in earlier chapters of the relationship between leadership and changes in configuration, norms, political values, and systems, this chapter will illustrate through historical cases how types of leadership influence international system transformations. This chapter selects both ancient Chinese and modern global cases to illustrate the theoretical arguments made in this book. These cases vary across their geographical locations and sizes, their historical and cultural backgrounds, and their political systems. This huge diversity is helpful for illustrating the application scope of the theoretical arguments raised in previous chapters. Based on acknowledgment of the vast differences between ancient Chinese and modern global histories, if we can pinpoint political similarities between the system trans-formations that occurred during the two histories we might surmise that they entailed certain social laws. These similarities constitute the foundations of the theory established in this book.

ANCIENT CHINESE CASES

This section will utilize three pre-Qin periods of Chinese history to illustrate the critical role of leading states in shaping the configura-tions, norms, and character of interstate systems: the transition from the Western Zhou Dynasty to the Spring and Autumn period, the subsequent advent of the Warring States period, and the later rise of the Qin Dynasty. A noteworthy variable in this endeavor is the political leadership of leading states, which, despite undergoing many changes during each of these three timeframes, contributed to transformations in interstate norms and configurations but not the character of the system as a whole.

No System Transformation during the Western Zhou Dynasty

The interstate leadership type of the Western Zhou Dynasty (1066–770 BCE) changed from humane authority to hegemony to tyranny. Accordingly, the norms guiding interactions among states in the ancient Chinese interstate system changed from moral to double standard to realpolitik and eventually to coward-bully conventions. During this period, the types of major states stayed the same—a royal state and many feudal vassals—and the unipolar configuration stayed in place until the end of this period.

King Wu of Zhou established the Zhou Dynasty around 1066 BCE, after the collapse of the Shang Dynasty. This marked the be-ginning of the Western Zhou–dominated interstate system,[1] wherein the so-called five service norms were the conventional principles guiding interactions among feudal vassals. These interstate norms originated in the reign of King Tang of the Shang Dynasty, who, at the Jinghao Conference in the seventeenth century BCE, constructed the *Hou, Dian, Nan, Cai*, and *Wei* norms, which all feudal vassals observed.[2] King Wu of Zhou revised and renamed these norms the *Dian, Hou, Bin, Yao*, and *Huang* and strictly enacted them, as did the succeeding Zhou rulers King Cheng and King Kang.[3] When feudal vassals failed to observe the five service norms, each of the three kings of Zhou firstly inspected his own behavior according to the norms and revised the shortcomings, and then he issued warnings to those vassals that violated the norms. The rulers exerted punitive measures only against the vassals that continued to flout these norms despite receiving warnings.[4] In this way, Zhou took the lead in practicing and maintaining the five service norms. Under the leaderships of King Wu, King Cheng, and King Kang, most vassals in that system observed the five service norms; there were thus fewer instances of war than the period after the ascendance of King Zhao, the fourth king of the Zhou Dynasty.[5] In other words, there was relatively peaceful order of the interstate system under the first three kings' leadership in Zhou Dynasty.

King Zhao of the Zhou Dynasty ascended the throne in 1001 BCE.[6] Thereafter, the rulers of Zhou ceased their strict observation of the five service norms and persistently initiated wars against tribes in the peripheral areas of the Chinese interstate system.[7] A typical case is the war King Mu of Zhou waged during 965–964 BCE against the Quanrong tribes that dwelt in the Northwest periphery. According to the five service norms, those tribes were expected to pay respects only occasionally to the King of Zhou, and not required to offer quarterly tributes. Jigong Moufu, a minister, tried to dissuade King Mu from declaring war on the Quanrong on the excuse of their failure to pay quarterly tributes, which, according to the five service norms, were not expected of them. Jigong Moufu warned King Mu of the serious repercussions that would follow the war. Rejecting Jigong Moufu's advice, King Mu fought and, owing to Zhou's superior military might, won that war. The victory, however, severely undermined the norms guiding relations between the Zhou Dynasty and the tribes in the Northwest periphery (*Huang* ordinance), and the Quanrong tribes stopped paying respects to Zhou.[8]

Having violated, under the leadership of King Mu, norms guiding relations with tribes in the Huang ordinance, Zhou nevertheless continued to abide by the conventions applicable to the vassal states of the Hou and Bin ordinances, whose civilizations were similar to that of Zhou, and against whom King Mu accordingly did not wage war. Hostilities against the Quanrong tribes nevertheless transformed the dominant norms in the Chinese interstate system from the moral type to the double-standard type. This change was the result of hegemony replacing the interstate leadership of humane authority.

After King Li of the Zhou Dynasty came to the throne in the year 858 BCE, Zhou violated the norms guiding relations with both feudal vassals of similar civilizations and tribes of different ones in the peripheral areas. According to the interstate norms of that time, areas of marshland were shared by Zhou and the feudal vassals. King Li, however, allowed his royal family members to violate this norm by monopolizing those areas. This breach provoked military rebellions by several vassals in defense of their marshlands.[9] By the time King Xuan of Zhou took the throne in 827 BCE, the Zhou interstate leadership had evolved into a tyranny, whereby Zhou no longer observed norms relating to the feudal vassals, notably the State of Lu, with which it shared common ancestry. King Xuan went so far as to violate the primogenitary norm by requiring the State of Lu to name Xi, the younger son of the ruler of Lu, as crown prince. Outraged, the people of the State of Lu murdered Xi and proclaimed Boyu, the eldest son, as their ruler. King Xuan's response was to declare war on the State of Lu in 795 BCE (the thirty-second year of his reign). Although Zhou was the victor, this war undermined relations with the feudal vassals, and military conflicts became commonplace throughout the Chinese interstate system.[10] The type of predominant norms guiding interstate relations thus evolved from double standard to realpolitik.

When King You succeeded to the Zhou Dynasty throne in 781 BCE, the type of interstate leadership transformed from tyranny to anemocracy. King You violated the primogenitary norm and also deposed the crown prince, supplanting him with a bastard child. He furthermore openly violated interstate norms between allies. In 779 BCE, the third year of his reign, and for no reason other than to amuse his favorite concubine, King You lit the war beacons, ostensibly signifying an attack from marauding nomads, and the allied feudal states accordingly sent in troops to save him.[11] In the aftermath of these events, interstate norms transformed from realpolitik to coward-bully. Feudal vassals no longer followed alliance norms, and fraud and deception became the popular strategies of both Zhou and the feudal vassals. When the Quanrong tribes invaded central China in 770 BCE, most of the Zhou allies refused to respond to King You's call for help, and the Quanrong army eventually slew King You at Mount Li.[12] After these events, Zhou lost its domination, and the interstate configuration changed from unipolar to multipolar. The history of the Western Zhou system thus underwent the change from order to chaos.

System Transformation to the Spring and Autumn Period

It was the combined changes in interstate configuration from unipolar to multipolar and in interstate norms from coward-bully to double standard that induced the system transformation from that of the Western Zhou to the Spring and Autumn period. Chinese historians agree that there was no hegemonic rivalry during the Western Zhou period, but that it became the main feature of interstate relations in the Spring and Autumn period (770–476 BCE).[13] Some Western scholars also analyze differences between the Western Zhou and the Spring and Autumn periods from the power structure perspective. They suggest that the decline in the Zhou Dynasty's capability is a major factor of hegemonic rivalry in the Spring and Autumn period. Kalevi Holsti argues, "In the latter period of the Chou [Zhou] dynasty, there was considerable discrepancy between the official rules, traditions, and myths that were supposed to govern relations between political units and the actual behavior of independent states. . . . But the practice during the Spring and Autumn and

Warring States periods did not accord with the myths and customs appropriate to the feudal order. In a system of many powerful, ambitious and independent states, such rules were anachronisms. Instead, the main units developed rules or customs that reflected the major political and military characteristics of the system."[14]

The decline of Zhou's capability brought about not only a new power structure but also a new type of interstate leadership. This change is hence the driving force behind the norm alterations from the Western Zhou to the Spring and Autumn period. The interstate leadership of hegemonic states in the Spring and Autumn period differed from that of the humane authority under the first three kings of the Western Zhou and of the anemocracy under its last king, King You. When Zhou lost dominance of the system, all feudal vassals became equal, and larger vassals pursued hegemonic positions rather than maintain the system's order. That no states undertook responsibility for system order signified the cessation of humane authority interstate leadership as seen during the early Western Zhou period. As the larger vassals were hegemonic in type, they inevitably followed double-standard principles in their foreign policy making. Typically, norms guiding the resolution of conflicts within alliances differed from those applicable to non-allied states. In setting out to impress on allies the hegemon's credibility, such hegemonic double-standard principles differed also from the coward-bully norms prevalent in the late period of Western Zhou.

The State of Qi and the State of Chu were two hegemons in the early Spring and Autumn period that respectively established their own alliance. This became an important factor in promoting double-standard principles as interstate norms. Having replaced the unipolar configuration of the Western Zhou system, Qi and Chu shaped a bipolar configuration by establishing alliances aimed at hegemonic rivalry. In efforts to win the hegemonic competition amid their rise, the two hegemons expanded their military cooperation with other lesser states and transformed temporary cooperation into durable alliances. This strategy accordingly reinforced the stability of the other side's alliances.

In the year 651 BCE (the ninth year of the reign of Duke Xi of Qi), the State of Qi established the Kuiqiu Alliance with the States of Song, Lu, Wei, Xu, Cao, and Zheng, all of which reached a covenant that included principles relating to domestic affairs, diplomacy, ideology, and certain other fields. The covenant, for example, stipulated, "Upon entering the alliance, all allies will forget past grudges,"[15] a provision that restricted members of the alliance from annexing other members' territory. The alliance laid emphasis on the importance of respecting the king of the Zhou Dynasty, even though he was no more than a political figurehead of interstate authority. For the sake of interstate legitimacy, the alliance reinstated laws issued by the king of the Zhou Dynasty. For instance, it forbade obstructing rivers or springs, storing excessive grains, deposing the crown prince, marrying concubines, and women's participation in political affairs.[16] These stipulations improved political confidence among allies and reduced wars between members of the same alliance. It thus made the interstate system far more stable than it had been under coward-bully norms. Of course, the Kuiqiu Alliance norms did not apply to relationships between members of this alliance and nonmember states. The main reason why the Kuiqiu Alliance double-standard norms lasted so long was that the State of Qi, as its leader, consistently observed the alliance covenant. Compared with the major part of the Western Zhou period, however, interstate relations in the Spring and Autumn period were violent and chaotic.

System Transformation to the Warring States period

The Spring and Autumn period was followed by the Warring States period (475–221 BCE), an interstate system quite different from its predecessor. The configuration in both of these interstate systems was multipolar, but the actors transformed from vassals to monarchies, and interstate norms changed from double standard to realpolitik. Accordingly, compared to the Spring and Autumn period, interstate relations in the Warring States period were violent, and the order of its system was chaotic, mainly because there was neither a single-state interstate leadership nor a collective interstate leadership in that system.

Yang Kuan says, "Wars primarily aimed at hegemonic rivalry during the Spring and Autumn period, but at annexation during the Warring States period."[17] His opinion is widely shared by Chinese historians. In fact, the main difference between the Spring and Autumn period and the Warring States period was not that the former did not carry out annexation, but rather that annexation was regarded as a violation of interstate norms in the former but became both prevalent and legitimate in the latter.

Owing to the popularity of annexation as an interstate norm, the number of states dramatically reduced during the Warring States period. At its onset there had been at least twenty-six states in the interstate system,[18] but by the middle of the period annexation wars had eradicated most of these, leaving the Wei, Zhao, Han, Qi, Qin, Chu, and Yan as the seven remaining most powerful states.[19] Based on their dramatically enlarged territory, population, and military capability, these states declared their rulers *wang* (王, king) and transformed from vassals to monarchies. In 256 BCE, the State of Qin annexed Zhou, and King Nan of the Zhou Dynasty was demoted from Son of Heaven to duke of West Zhou.[20] This meant that all actors became independent states, and that royal states no longer existed. The annexation wars continued for a century or more, ending with the victory of the State of Qin, which annexed the six other states within the Chinese interstate system and established the first East Asian empire in 221 BCE.[21] Ying Zheng, the king of Qin, crowned himself emperor and became known as *Qin Shihuang* (秦始皇, the first emperor of the Qin Dynasty).

The founding of the Qin Dynasty transformed the Chinese interstate system from absolute anarchy to relative hierarchy, wherein actors transmuted from monarchies to a single empire along with non-Chinese kingdoms and tribes, and the configuration changed from multipolar to unipolar. Thereafter, the type of Chinese interstate system became known as the empire-centered tributary system. When the tributary system is consolidated, interstate relations are in order; otherwise, they are chaotic.

CASES IN MODERN HISTORY

No events in modern history have larger legacies in shaping international politics than World War I and World War II. Although equal in importance, their respective influence nonetheless differed in result. Notably, while World War I altered the landscape of leading states, it did not change the types of international norms and configurations. In contrast, World War II transformed the whole international system, including norms and configurations, primarily as a result of a new type of international leadership provided by the Roosevelt administration.

No System Transformation throughout World War I

Transformations of international system are often implemented through wars, but wars do not necessarily change international systems. Although World War I had a dramatic impact on international relations in the early twentieth century, it failed to bring about a transformation of the international system, because there were no changes in the type of either configurations or norms. The international configuration was multipolar before and after the war, and the type of international norms remained realpolitik. Global leading states had ceased to be empires before World War I broke out. The Chinese and Persian Empires had disappeared, and the four European empires—the Hapsburg, Hohenzollern, Romanoff, and Ottoman Empires—were considerably weakened.[22] All the new leading European powers were imperialist nation-states and remained so after the war.

In the late nineteenth century and the first decade of the twentieth century, the UK was the world's dominant power and offered a tyrannical international leadership. The country's consistent adoption of realpolitik principles while carrying out global colonial expansion enabled the universal spread of realpolitik norms.[23] The UK's realpolitik principles are illustrated by the lack of credibility of its foreign policy, and its violation of international treaties. In 1896, the UK publicly acknowledged its "glorious isolation" policy, signifying that its foreign policy would never be bound by international treaties under any circumstances.[24] This policy constituted Britain's diplomatic custom of not being bound by any treaties. In 1898, the UK and Germany signed an agreement on dividing Portugal's colonies between them. One year later, the UK signed an agreement with Portugal stating that it would not invade any Portuguese colonies, thus violating its commitments to Germany.[25] In 1904, the UK made military commitments to France, and in 1907 similar commitments to Russia, both targeted at Germany. Just two years later, in 1909, however, Britain engaged in negotiations with Germany over a naval agreement. The behavior of the UK with regard to violations of international agreements, therefore, is similar to that of King Xuan of the Zhou Dynasty, and his violation of the five service norms.

The UK's policy of keeping none of its promises encouraged other states also to ignore international treaties. In the first two decades of the twentieth century, therefore, violations of international treaties were a prevailing phenomenon. International treaties were used as an excuse, rather than as a basis, for a particular policy, and diplomatic fraud and betrayal were rife. For example, Italy was a core member of the alliance that included Italy, Germany, and Austria-Hungary. However, soon after World War I broke out on July 28, 1914, Italy backed out of the alliance and on August 3 announced its neutrality.[26] On July 9, the UK notified the German ambassador to Britain that it was an ally neither of France nor of Russia, and that it was not bound by any commitments to these two countries. Moreover, two days before World War I, the UK stated that it would remain neutral and not participate in any war. As the betrayal of alliances was a widely accepted international norm at that time, Germany believed that the UK had reneged on its commitments to France and Russia. When the UK announced on July 29 that it would join the war, therefore, German emperor Wilhelm II cursed the UK for its trickery.[27]

Major states imitated the UK's realpolitik principles with regard to expanding colonies. Annexation of other states' territory or colonies became the international norm during that period, comparable to the norm of annexation in the Chinese interstate system during the Warring States period. There were many colonial wars and much territorial expansion and invasion of others' territorial sovereignty under the UK-dominated system, such as the Spanish-American War (1898), the Boer War (1899–1902), the eight-power Allied forces' invasion of China (1900), the Russo-Japanese War (1904–5), the second Moroccan crisis (1907), the Italo-Turkish War (1911–12), the Agadir crisis (1911), the Russian invasion of Mongolia (1911), the First Balkan War (1912–13), the Second Balkan War (1913), and World War I (1914–18).[28]

After World War I, the United States soon replaced the UK as the world's most powerful state. Although the United States had begun its transition from a tyrant state to a hegemonic state, the country's political value was not yet available to provide international leadership any different from that of the UK.[29] This is illustrated by an ironic historical event. American president Woodrow Wilson initiated the Fourteen-Point Plan for a collective security system, later known as the Charter of the League of Nations. Its articles included preserving the territorial integrity, political independence, and national self-determination of member states.[30]The US Congress, however, ultimately opted to veto the Treaty of Versailles, so rejecting the idea of joining the League of Nations as proposed by President Wilson. America's own decision thus deprived its leadership of the chance to establish new international norms. Instead, tyrant states like the UK, Japan, France, and Italy retained the leading role in shaping international norms after World War I.[31] In other words, tyrant leadership continued after World War I, and realpolitik norms maintained their predominant role in international politics.

Violations of international treaties continued to be the prevailing international norm after World War I, and the use of war as a means of territorial expansion also remained prevalent. This was an era of global warring states. None of the major powers observed international treaties, despite signing a number of treaties limiting states' use of force, including the Covenant of the League of Nations in 1919, the Convention of Washington Naval Arms Limitation in 1922, the Treaty for the Renunciation of War in 1928, and the Moscow Protocol in 1929. Moreover, later on, fifteen members of the League of Nations, including Germany, Japan, and Italy, withdrew from this international organization.[32] These events demonstrate the popularity and legitimacy during that period of ignoring international treaties. After the Great Depression began in 1929, major powers dramatically increased military expansion in order to expand their territories. Japan invaded northeast China in 1931; Italy invaded Abyssinia (Ethiopia) in 1935; Japan launched a full-scale invasion of China in 1937; Germany invaded Czechoslovakia the same year, and its invasion of Poland in 1939 marked the start of World War II.[33]

From the late nineteenth century to the end of World War II, the order of the international system experienced two relatively peaceful periods that preceded the two global wars. Meanwhile, the actors and norms in this system remained the same type. The configuration was multipolar before and after World War I, and it was bipolar during the war. Nevertheless, the changes in power configuration could not lead to system transformation during this period. The IR history of this period illustrates the difference between international order and international system, as well as the difference between configuration change and system transformation.

The Sole System Transformation after World War II

Different from World War I, World War II brought about a transformation of the international system. Although it did not change the type of international actors, the war did change the international configuration from multipolar to bipolar type, and international norms from the realpolitik to double-standard type. The changes in the type of these components triggered the transformation from the Versailles-Washington system to the Yalta system, the latter of which survived the Cold War and has maintained its character to the present day.

The history of international relations since the end of World War II is academically divided into the Cold War and the post–Cold War eras, the international configurations of which differ in being respectively bipolar and unipolar. Nevertheless, the international system has remained unchanged since 1945, because the types of actors and norms in these two eras are the same. During the Cold War, all major powers were nation-states, and among them were the two superpowers the United States and the Soviet Union. As the two superpowers were hegemons, both offered the hegemonic type of leadership, and the international norms they established were correspondingly double standard. After the Cold War, all major powers remained as nation-states, and the United States became the sole superpower. Although the United States garnered the most international power, its political character remained unchanged. The type of international leadership thus remained the same, and international norms continued to be guided by the double-standard principle.

The double-standard norm during the Cold War was similar to that amid the hegemonic competition between the States of Jin and Chu during the Spring and Autumn period, which, in common with the United States and the Soviet Union, were hegemonic rather than tyrant states. Jin and Chu organized their own alliances, supported their wartime allies, and sabotaged the regimes of enemy states. The United States and the Soviet Union established multilateral as well as bilateral alliances and provided security and economic aid to allies but meanwhile engaged in proxy wars and initiated coups in enemy states. The behavior of the United States and the Soviet Union, however, was better by far than that of Jin and Chu as regards observing the principle of nonannexation.

As to maintaining peaceful relations with allies, the United States might be compared with Jin and the Soviet with Chu. The similarity between the United States and Jin lies in the greater credibility of their policies toward allies as compared with that between the Soviet Union and their allies and Chu and theirs. The State of Chu initiated more military interventions against allies than Jin. The United States initiated the Marshall Plan in 1948 to help its European allies and also established NATO in 1949 to protect its allies' security. It has not since launched any military interventions against its allies. As a result, the Western camp maintained relative solidarity throughout the Cold War.[34] As to strategic credibility toward allies, the Soviet Union fell far short of the United States. In 1948, it broke the alliance with Yugoslavia and withdrew its forces from that country. In 1958, it unilaterally suspended aid treaties with China. And in 1956 and 1968, it militarily intervened respectively in Hungary and Czechoslovakia, both members of the Warsaw Pact.[35] Those actions fail to meet Xunzi's criterion for a qualified hegemon, whereby "once making an agreement with others, regardless of gains and losses, it shall not cheat partners."[36] The Soviet Union's failure to keep promises made to its allies is also an important reason for the collapse of the Warsaw Pact in 1991.[37] As leader of the socialist camp, the Soviet Union committed violations of agreements with allies that not only weakened solidarity in the socialist camp, but also set an example for other socialist countries to imitate, namely, to settle disputes through war, such as the wars in the 1970s between China and Vietnam, as well as between Vietnam and Cambodia.

During the Cold War, both the United States and the Soviet Union adopted realpolitik norms in their dealings with nonallies. To enlarge their spheres of political influence, they not only supported proxy wars militarily in Asia, Africa, and Latin America but also sometimes participated in wars, such as the Korean War (1950–53), the Bay of Pigs (1959), the Vietnam War (1961–73), the Afghanistan War (1979–88), and the Persian Gulf War (1990–91). The United States' and the Soviet Union's policies toward nonallies strengthened the realpolitik norms between enemy states. The practice of realpolitik norms between enemies is also illustrated in wars between regional powers, such as the three wars between India and Pakistan (1948, 1965, 1971), the five wars in the Middle East between Israel and its Arab neighbors (1948, 1956, 1967, 1973, 1982), the Sino-Indian War (1962), the Vietnam-Cambodia War (1978–79), the China-Vietnam War (1979), the two wars between Iran and Iraq (1980–88), and the several military invasions South Africa mounted on its neighbors.

Its status of sole superpower gave the United States more power to strengthen the double-standard norm after the Cold War. For example, on the issue of separatism, the United States and Western states have reached a tacit understanding to support separatist movements only in non-Western states. This situation has remained unchanged through to the present day. The latest example in this regard is that of the leaders of the United States, EU, and many Western countries' rejection of Catalonia's announcement of its independence from Spain based on the results of a referendum and the votes of Catalan MPs in the 135-seat regional government.[38] Meanwhile, scarcely any leaders of Western countries publicly oppose independent movements in non-Western countries, and secessionist movements in Hong Kong and Taiwan can evoke at least political sympathy, and even support, from the UK Parliament and US Congress. Moreover, on the issue of missile nonproliferation and missile technology control, the United States and Western states have prevented proliferation among non-Western states, but not among Western states themselves. Despite the fact that Saudi Arabia and Myanmar have equally poor human rights records, Western states imposed sanctions on Myanmar in this respect but not on Saudi Arabia, an American ally.

After the Cold War, certain IR scholars developed the theory of "Democratic Peace" to explain why Western states go to war with non-Western states but not among themselves. No matter whether this theoretical argument is solid or not, it is a phenomenon manifesting the double-standard norm in the post–Cold War era. Between 1990 and 2002, fifty-eight major armed conflicts occurred in forty-six different places around the world—none of them between Western states.[39] Since 1990, there have been eleven major international wars: the Persian Gulf War (1991), the Somalia War (1992), the Eritrea-Ethiopian War (1998), the war in Kosovo (1999), the war in Afghanistan (2001), the war in Iraq (2003), the Israeli invasion of Lebanon (2006), the war in Georgia (2008), the war in Libya (2011), the war in Syria (2011), and the Saudi Arabia–Yemen War (2015). Most of these wars entailed attacks by Western states on non-Western states. Among the eleven wars, only three were between non-Western states; the remaining eight were all involved with Western states, seven of which included NATO members.

SUMMARY

In comparing the transformations of the ancient Chinese system and those of the modern global system discussed in this chapter, we can pinpoint certain similarities. For instance, both the ancient Chinese cases and modern cases show that the international order is not necessarily consistent with the type of international system. Any given international system could experience times of peace and times of war. This fact makes plain that international order and international system are two different entities. Double-standard norms were favored by the interstate leaderships of both the Chinese tributary system and the American-dominated modern global system. This is similar to what Yuen Foong Khong discovered in his research on American leadership during the post–Cold War era. He says that "the United States as the hub or epicenter of the tributary system [is] analogous to that of China's during the Ming and Qing Dynasties."[40]

History shows that the directions of international system transformations are determined by the type of international leadership. As international leadership changes in random directions rather than along a progressive route, changes in system characteristics in a historical process as long as a millennium are also uncertain. From the Western Zhou period to the Warring States period, the Chinese interstate system transformed from a relatively moral one to a realpolitik one, while during the period from the late nineteenth century to the present day, the global international system transformed from a realpolitik one to a hegemonic one. These system transformations in opposite directions demonstrate that international systems do not evolve in just one way or in any predetermined direction.

It is the type of international leadership, rather than international configuration, that decides the international order. Since the end of World War II, the world order has swung between more and fewer military confrontations, while the characteristics of the Yalta system have remained unchanged. This system is characterized by double-standard norms rather than by a bipolar or unipolar configuration. The present bipolarization headed by China and the United States may result in a new international leadership that will lead to a different order from that of the post-Cold War. Whether or not the new leadership will maintain the double-standard norms or shape a set of new type norms, however, is less certain. We cannot rule out the possibility that the international system will remain the same although it has a different order from that following the Cold War.

9

Conclusion

周虽旧邦，其命维新。
(Although Zhou was an ancient dynasty, its fate
rested on reforms.)
THE BOOK OF SONGS

Through reading pre-Qin philosophical writings, I realize not only
that political leadership plays a greater role in international politics
than any other factors but also that national leadership of great powers, as an independent variable, can string together the three levels
of analysis, namely the analytical levels of decision makers, states,
and international systems. This chapter will first summarize the
theory developed in this book and then apply it to a prediction of
the joint influence of China's rise and America's relative decline in
international politics in the coming decade.

THEORY SUMMARIZATION

As noted at the outset, the purpose of this book is to establish a new
theory that explains why few rising states have been able to replace
the dominant state. The theory can indeed also be applied to ex-

plaining the decline of the dominant power as well as to the failure of most rising states. This book's theoretical explanations about power redistribution are related to the mechanisms of change in international configurations, norms, orders, and systems. Political leadership serves as the core independent variable in the theory, and its values consist in different types of leadership at either the domestic or international level. Leadership types play a key role in changing international configurations, norms, orders, and systems.

Leadership and Differential Growth

Based on the realist assumption that the pursuit of national interest constitutes the primary motivation for state actions, I argue that a state's objective strategic interests are defined by its comprehensive capability. As the capability of each state is different, its strategic interests may be discretely defined, such that maintaining world domination is the main strategic interest of dominant states; attaining world domination is the main strategic interest of rising states; gaining regional domination is the main strategic interest of regional powers; and protecting survival is the main strategic interest of weak states.

A state's capability consists of four elements, namely, its politics, military, economy, and culture. Political capability is the operational element, and the other three (military, economy, and culture) are resource elements. In other words, political capability applies a multiplicative effect on the other three elements. Should political capability decrease to zero, then the effect of the other three is reduced to nil. Thus, the improvement or decline of a state's capability is determined by the political capability of that country. A state's national strategic interests are hence redefined according to any improvement or decline in its national comprehensive capability. Any concrete interest of each sector or issue is defined accordingly by the capability of related sectors or issues.

National leadership determines the political capability of a state, while leadership capability is mainly represented by its capacity for reform. Reform is opposite to retrogression and refers to changes in a progressive direction according to changed circumstances; therefore the capacity of reforms is evaluated based on the results of implementation. The capability of a state whose national leadership has continuously carried out prompt reforms will improve more rapidly than that of a state that has implemented few or no reforms. The same applies to different leaderships of the same country, insofar as its national capability will grow faster under a leadership that carries out more reforms than the previous one did, and vice versa. In most cases, the dominant state has weaker motivation than rising states to pursue reforms, because its advanced position engenders pride in its political and social institutions rather than an eager desire to reform them. Carrying out fewer reforms than rising states, however, diminishes the dominant state's competitiveness within a changing environment and eventually leads to its decline.

The leadership capability of different states can never be the same, which explains the law of differential growth in states' national capability. Among all the factors that exert influence on leadership capability, that of the leadership type is often the most direct and important. Upon a change of leadership type, the new leadership has an obvious impact on the growth of national capability. Such a leadership change either accelerates or slows the growth of a state's capability and also brings about changes in relative capability between it and other states. When the disparity change in capability between major states reaches a certain level, the international configuration will shift among unipolar, bipolar, and multipolar shapes. Even establishing moral norms is driven by enlightened self-interests rather than altruism. This mechanism leads to corollary 1: improvements or declines of states' leadership lead to changes in relative capability between states and eventually in the international configuration.

Leadership Type and Strategy Preference

Based on the realist assumption that international society is an anarchical system wherein self-help is the basis on which all states pursue their particular strategic interests, I argue that governmental morality differs from personal and international morality; meanwhile it is universal rather than national. As national leadership rests on the people it rules, governmental morality consists in being responsible for the interests of such people. From the perspective of international politics, governmental morality refers to improving a country's international status, while from the perspective of international community it entails establishing strategic credibility.

According to the sense of governmental responsibility, leadership at the state level can be categorized into four types: inactive, conservative, proactive, and aggressive. This categorization is based on two interacting variables: (1) a leading body's attitude toward the international status quo of its state and (2) its responsible actions with regard to policy mistakes. Inactive and conservative leaderships have no motivation to improve the international status of their states, while proactive and aggressive leaderships have a strong desire to expand their international power. Conservative and proactive leaderships are willing to adjust their policies upon recognizing their mistakes, while inactive and aggressive leaderships are not willing to acknowledge such mistakes, even when the policies concerned dramatically undermine their states' national interests or national capability.

As the type of leadership at state level is determined by its sense of governmental morality, different types of leadership will result in differential growths of national capability. At times when the government of a rising state has a greater sense of responsibility than the dominant state does, such disparity is manifest in the former's implementation of more reforms than the latter, which will gradually reduce the capability disparity between them. If this situation lasts for a number of decades, the rising state's comprehensive capability will catch up with or even surpass that of the dominant state. The rising state will thus become the new dominant state.

Owing to different senses of governmental responsibility, when dealing with the issue of international status, different types of leadership display different strategic preferences. An inactive leadership avoids conflicts or takes no actions to maintain the international power of its state; a conservative leadership prefers to maintain its current status by improving the foreign economic relations; a proactive leadership strives to improve its state's international status by carrying out political reforms and enlarging international support; and an aggressive leadership adopts military approaches to enlarging its international power. The corresponding relationship between leadership types and strategic preferences leads to corollary 2: all states engage in self-help for their own strategic interests in the anarchical international system but adopt different foreign strategies to pursue them.

International Leadership and Norms

Owing to the law of differential growth between different states' capability, the success of rising states will lead to changes in international leading states. Such changes are inevitably accompanied by power redistributions between the dominant state and rising states. Members of the new international leadership will reform the existing international norms in such a way as to ensure optimum durability of their states' leading positions. This mechanism leads to corollary 3: pursuit of self-interest is the primary motivation of state actions as well as the selective force behind the creation of international norms. If the new international leadership is of the same type as the previous one, members of the new leadership will reform the contents of international norms in strict accordance with the shared values between them and their previous leading states. Otherwise, they will reform those norms according to their own values, or in other words, establish a new type of norms.

In general, there are three main approaches for leading states to establish new international norms: example-imitation, support-reinforcement, and punishment-maintenance. The support-reinforcement approach refers to rewarding those states that follow the action principle advocated by leading states, and the punishment-maintenance approach to punishing those that violate this principle. Both approaches function when the policies of leading states cause other states either to gain or lose benefits. Different than both of these, the example-imitation approach is a mechanism whereby other states voluntarily follow the action principle of leading states because they believe that observation of that principle will help them to become as prosperous as the leading state. These three approaches can be applied to the reform of both contents and types of international norms.

According to the two variables of strategic credibility and policy consistency, international leadership can be categorized into four types: humane authority, hegemony, anemocracy, and tyranny. The leadership of a humane authority or of a hegemony has much higher credibility than that of an anemocracy or a tyranny, while the leadership of a humane authority or a tyranny adopts more consistent policies than does that of a hegemony or an anemocracy. In corresponding to types of international leadership, moral norms are those advocated by a humane authority, double-standard norms by a hegemony, coward-bully norms by an anemocracy, and realpolitik norms by a tyranny. When the new international leadership is of a different type than the previous one, it will establish a new type of norms for purposes of maintaining its dominance of the international system. Since there is no guarantee of a change in the type of international leadership toward a better one, the change in the type of international norms is in random directions, rather than in a linear trajectory from realpolitik to morality.

Since the leadership of humane authority guides its foreign policies according to moral principles, its moral actions help it to establish a degree of strategic credibility higher than that of the other three types. Along with improved strategic credibility, humane authority constructs high authority and obtains greater international power. Both power and authority are components of influence but function differently as leadership resources. The former influences other states' behaviors by force, but the latter induces others to follow its ideas voluntarily by virtue of their trust in the leadership. Therefore, moral norms are more helpful than other norms in maintaining a leading state's international leadership for a longer period. Double-standard norms are less effective than moral norms in maintaining a state's international leadership, but more efficient than coward-bully and realpolitik norms. Nevertheless, the morality of leading powers plays a role in maintaining international order on the precondition of their strong national capability. That is to say, the moral conduct of a weak state has a very limited impact on types of international norms.

Component Changes and System Transformation

No dominant state, in the past, present, or future, is capable of avoiding decline or replacement by rising powers. The change in international leadership means power redistribution among major states, but mainly between rising states and the dominant state. The competition between them leads to corollary 4: the zero-sum nature of power brings about a structural contradiction between a rising state and a dominant state, as well as disturbances to the existing international order. Changes in either structural order or normative order lead to conflicts between rising states and dominant states, so causing system instability. Structural order is usually disturbed by power redistribution between major states, and normative order by character changes in international norms. The rivalry between rising states and the dominant state will not be limited to within the domains of material interests but occur also in nonmaterial sectors. When the rising state and the dominant state believe in different ideologies, the rivalry between them will include competition to make their own particular ideologies the mainstream global value. Ideological confrontation is often more fierce than rivalry purely for material interests.

Power redistribution often causes disturbances to international order but does not necessarily bring about system transformation, because international order and international system are two different substances. Although the international norm is the shared component of the international order and the international system, norms define only the specific character of the order or the system and do not make them the same thing. The international order refers to the state of an international system, mainly the situation wherein international actors settle their conflicts peacefully, while the international system refers to a complex society formed by actors interacting according to norms. The order of a system can be both disturbed or resumed without any changes in the type of the three system components—its actors, configuration, and norms. Therefore, the international order is most often disturbed by wars within a given international system, but such international order can also be resumed without system change. The success of a rising state often results in power redistribution as well as a change in order but leads to a system change only in a very few cases.

International power redistribution that causes changes in only one of the three components precludes transformation of the entire system. System transformation refers to the change in the type of a complex whole, namely system change, rather than a change in just one aspect of the system. Therefore, system transformation requires changes in at least two of the three components. In history, states—the major interstate actors—such as city-states, dynasties, monarchies, empires, and nations, have remained the same type for centuries. Because it takes longer for actor types than types of configurations or norms to change, system transformations mostly happen along with simultaneous changes in the type of norms and configurations, rather than a change in actors accompanied by a change in one of the other two components.

International power redistribution differs from the shift of the international geopolitical center. The former refers to the transfer of the leading power from one state or group of states to another, while the latter refers to the geographic change in leading competitors and strategic competition in a given international system. When rising states and dominant states are geographically located on different continents, the transfer of leading power from the latter to the former will bring about the shift of world geopolitical center, but not otherwise. When the two continents have quite different civilizations, the transfer of leadership is often companied by clashes of civilization which often coat the essence of the power rivalry between rising states and dominant states.

A NEW BIPOLAR WORLD

All scientific theories have the function of prediction. Conversely, a theory able to be used for prediction should be a scientific theory. Based on the theory developed in this book, this section will forecast changes in international politics in the coming decade, when China's rise will bring about power redistribution in international politics. All scientific predictions entail a clear timescale; otherwise they cannot be verifiable. For the sake of making the following forecasts testable in the future, the prediction timescale is limited to ten years, namely 2019–2028.

Bipolarization without a Global Leadership

China's rise is highly likely to transfer the American-dominated unipolar configuration of the post–Cold War era into a bipolar one between China and the United States in the coming decade. In comparison with Trump's administration, the Chinese government has a stronger capability in implementing reform plans or making less retrogression. This raises the possibility that China will further reduce its disparity in capability with the United States during Trump's presidency. This possibility may continue even if the American government comes into a new leadership in 2021, because it usually takes longer to resume a country's national capability than to undermine it. Besides China's rise, the other important factor in shaping the bipolar configuration is the huge gap in national capability between other major states and the United States as well as China. At the present, none of the other major states has a comprehensive capability larger than a quarter of the United States' or half of China's. Even if these countries were to be lucky enough to gain national leaderships more capable in reform than those of China and the United States in the coming decade, they have no chance of improving their national capability to China's level within ten years, let alone to America's. In fact, historical probabilities imply that the reform capability of these countries' leaderships is most likely to be the same as that of the United States and China, or even poorer.

The present bipolarization will drive the world center from Europe to East Asia. In a bipolar world, the location of its center entails two conditions: that the geographical region is a core area for strategic competition between the two leading states; and that one of the states is located in that region. In the next ten years, the United States and China will be the only two superpowers. Meanwhile both China and the United States have more strategic interests in East Asia than in any other region, including Europe. China cannot achieve the goal of national rejuvenation unless it becomes the dominant power in East Asia. Likewise, the United States cannot maintain its world-leading status if it loses its dominant influence in this region. Over the coming decade, China-US geopolitical competition will focus on East Asia rather than any other region. Therefore, East Asia will replace Europe as the world center in ten years.

The new bipolar configuration will drive lesser states to choose sides between the United States and China according to given issues, in contrast to what motivated their choices between the United States and the Soviet Union during the Cold War. In the era of globalization, China has established interweaving relations with the rest of world that have disenabled the containment strategy. Faced with the impotence of the containment strategy, the United States no longer has the motivation to aid its allies comprehensively. Meanwhile, China is also reluctant to provide comprehensive aid to its supporters, for concern of avoiding being dragged into war. Responding to these two giants' policy toward their supporters, lesser states' strategies toward the US-China competition will be different from those deployed during the Cold War US-Soviet competition. Instead of siding with one superpower on every issue, they will choose sides according to given interests shared with one of the two superpowers. Some ASEAN states have already adopted a two-track strategy toward China and the United States, whereby they side with China on economic issues and with the United States on security issues. This kind of balancing strategy may become popular among lesser states in the coming bipolar world.

Neither the United States nor China is able to provide a global leadership in the next decade. Global leadership requires leading states to provide security protection for lesser states, either individually or collectively. It is even less possible that China will abandon the nonalignment principle in the next ten years, which means it will not provide security protection for any country, including its neighbors. Although the United States has more than fifty allies, the Trump administration is reluctant to undertake full responsibility to protect them. Meanwhile, the structural conflict between rising states and dominant states means that the United States and China cannot provide the world with a joint leadership, such as "G-2" or

"Chimerica." When the United States and China cannot provide a global leadership, either individually or collectively, we cannot expect that any other international actor, including states and international organizations, has the capability to do so. Without a global leadership, global governance will inevitably become stagnant. In the next decade, therefore, there is a possibility of less progress in cooperation on such issues as climate change, counterterrorism, illegal immigration, and human trafficking.

An Unstable Order but No Cold War

There is minimal danger of a direct war between China and the United States in the coming decade. Nuclear weapons effectively prevented direct war between the United States and the Soviet Union during the Cold War and will play the same role in China-US strategic rivalry. China has not been involved in any large-scale military conflicts since 1989, and the United States has not broken its record of no direct war against a nuclear power since the Cold War. The US government has even constrained from military solutions with regard to North Korean nuclear weapons since the issue first appeared. These facts imply that neither the United States nor China has the courage to engage in a direct war against the other side.

Even a proxy war between China and the United States is unlikely in the next ten years. Differing from Russia's strategic preference, China disvalues the role of proxy war in its rise. Rather, China regards economy as the basis of national capability and thus prefers to enlarge its international influence through economic approaches, such as by establishing the AIIB and advocating the Belt and Road Initiative. As the focus of its strategic preference is on economic influence, therefore, China can hardly be dragged into any proxy war with the United States in the coming decade—something that stands in stark contrast to US-Soviet rivalry during the Cold War.

Keeping the peace between China and the United States may mean no danger of either world war or proxy war between them, but it does not guarantee peace between other states in the coming decade. When leading states are reluctant to become involved in security disputes between other states, especially those in regions distant from where they reside, this will give regional powers an advantage in conflicts with other states within their sphere of influence. They will hence prefer military solutions to diplomatic negotiations when dealing with disputes with their surrounding countries, as seen in the behaviors of Russia, France, India, Turkey, Iran, Saudi Arabia, Israel, Nigeria, Congo, and Egypt. The governments of these states are far more willing than the Chinese government, if not more so than the American leadership, to solve disputes through military solutions. Therefore, the next decade will likely witness intensified security conflicts in the Middle East, Eurasia, South Asia, and Africa.

The bipolarization between the United States and China may exacerbate international polarization in the coming decade, which could lead to more unilateralist actions. Under the conditions of globalization, big companies are able to allocate global resources more efficiently than ordinary companies; thus, those countries with more big companies will have a better chance than other states to rapidly increase their share of global wealth. Both the United States and China have more big companies than any other country in the world, and 132 American enterprises and 115 Chinese appear on the list of the Fortune 500 in 2017.[1] This year, no country's comprehensive national capability can equate to even half of China's, or a quarter of the United States'. Polarization of national capability between superpowers and other states will reduce the significance of other states' support for leading powers. Therefore, the United States and China will become more willing to resolve conflicts through their own capabilities, rather than the collective efforts of their strategic partners. That is to say, international polarization of capability will encourage political unilateralism rather than multilateralism.

Since the United States and China can generally protect their own interests with their own capabilities, they will prefer bilateral diplomacy to multilateral diplomacy in the next decade, which may act as an example for the majority of the international community to follow. In the security domain, making multilateral alliances is the traditional strategy adopted by leading powers amid strategic competition. Neither the Chinese government nor Trump's administration, however, espouses this strategy. Trump's administration is keener on the unilateralist strategy than was George W. Bush's, which weakened America's relations with its traditional allies in the first year of Trump's presidency; and the Chinese government rejects wholesale the idea of making alliances. In the economic field, Trump's administration withdrew from the TPP plan and replaced NAFTA with the US-Mexico-Canada Agreement through bilateral negotiations with Mexico and Canada respectively. China, meanwhile, failed to achieve an FTA with East Asian countries, mainly because of its strategic conflicts with Japan. As long as the United States and China handle conflicts mainly through bilateral diplomacy rather than multilateral approaches, global multilateral institutions will play a lesser role in international affairs. The UN Security Council may consequently experience greater difficulty in achieving agreements between its permanent members in the coming decade.

As long as China continues to reduce economic disparity with the United States in the coming decade, US-China economic rivalry will be intensified. The Trump administration gives top priority to American economic interests, a strategic preference that might be sustained by his successor because most Americans believe that China's challenge to America's international leadership is based on economic rather than on military capability. The US-China trade conflicts that started in 2018 cannot be permanently resolved in the near future and could carry on for a decade. The strategies adopted by China and the United States in their trade conflicts not only connote the new trend of economic nationalism but also imply that economic sanctions could become a popular means for confronting other states in all fields. Their advantages will hence seduce the United States and China into imposing sanctions on other states, a ploy that other major states could well follow to handle conflicts with states weaker than themselves. Therefore, the next decade may witness a less stable international order.

The international system as a whole is nevertheless likely to remain the same for the next decade, albeit with a less stable order. Although the present bipolarization may disturb the international order and is highly likely to shape a bipolar world within the next ten years, it will be difficult for either the United States or China to set up a new type of international norms within this period, let alone change nation-states into a new type of international actor. Therefore, it is possible that the Yalta system will continue through the coming decade without any change of character, just as it did through the Cold War to the post–Cold War period.

Lack of Mainstream Values and Strategic Credibility

There is no ideology able to replace liberalism through establishing a set of new mainstream values to guide the international community over the coming decade. The competition between liberalism and anti-establishmentarianism disenables the United States from resuming its domination of liberalism and from providing a set of new values with global influence. The Chinese government also cannot advance a set of globally influential values abroad until it establishes a popular ideology shared by both the government and the governed at home. Meanwhile, the current bipolarization means that no country or international institution has a capability to set up new global values larger than that of the United States or China. Therefore, it is highly possible that the world will move into an era without mainstream values in the next ten years.

The lack of global mainstream values leaves a vacuum for different ideologies to compete for regional domination or influence on states of a given type. As the United States and China are cognizant that ideological confrontation can easily escalate into cold war, there is scant possibility of any competition between two global influential ideologies such as that during the Cold War. As long as China cautiously avoids ideological competition with the United States, America will not able to turn model disputes into the core of their strategic competition. Instead, the world may see a kaleidoscopic competition between various ideologies in different international forums. The Middle East may be ravaged by the rivalry between Shias and Sunnis; Western countries, mainly European states, may bruise in the battle between liberalism and populism; Latin American countries may fall into intensified conflict over socialism and capitalism; many developing countries may suffer in the struggle between statism and civicism; communist countries may face contention between communism and economic pragmatism; and theocratic states may experience the tension between religion and secularism in the fight for political power.

The recent popularity of one-man decision making in major states will devalue strategic credibility and increase the uncertainty of international politics in the coming decade. The one-man decision-making mechanism operates without carrying out institutional feasibility studies before decisions are made and hence often leads to radical and emotional decisions, including those relating to policy adjustments. When frequent policy adjustments swing in two opposite directions, inconsistency of foreign policy and uncertainty become inevitable. Since the one-man decision-making mechanism in major states is likely to continue in the coming decade, the supreme leaders' personal interests may often overwhelm national interests, including strategic credibility, amid foreign policy making. As leaders' personal interests are mutable, policy driven by personal interests becomes unpredictable. Owing to the prevalent uncertainty of major powers' foreign policy, suspicion and mutual distrust may become a popular phenomenon between states. Along with this situation, major countries may be less cooperative toward each other, instead bent on using a confrontation strategy to deal with disputes. This trend can be illustrated by two events in early 2018, namely, the trade confrontation between the United States and China, and the military confrontation in Syria between Russia and the alliance of the United States, the UK, and France.

When leading powers lack strategic credibility, most states may value their national sovereignty as much as they did during the Cold War, and their sense of global governance may weaken over the next decade. Global governance means distribution of international responsibility to reduce common threats to every country. If leading states are willing to undertake more responsibility in global governance, lesser states will have more confidence in achieving the goal, and thus become amenable to participating in it. Otherwise, they will lose interest in it because global governance is beyond their capability. In the coming bipolar world, neither the United States nor China will be able to undertake global leadership and will be reluctant to shoulder the leading responsibility for global governance. Since neither can improve lesser states' confidence in their responsibility to global governance, the majority of the international community will prefer to handle problems through their own capabilities. In fact, national sovereignty, as of now, is the most reliable means for nation-states to achieve their interests; thus, they may value sovereignty to the extent of refusing to take part in global governance that would be at the cost of their sovereignty. Brexit is a case that shows how much more the UK trusts in its sovereignty than in EU cooperation. America's withdrawal from the Paris Climate Agreement, moreover, could result in nil international cooperation on climate control in the next decade.

Although the post–Cold War liberalist order will be further undermined by lack of a global leadership over the coming decade, the type of double-standard norms is likely to remain unchanged, thus the hegemonic character of the Yalta system will survive accordingly. Trump's administration withdrew from several global regimes, which did undermine their efficiency in maintaining international order but cannot become a suit for other major powers to follow. A state withdraws from an international organization only when it believes that its membership hurts its interests, rather than when it believes that it is simply not beneficial. This means that China, Russia, Japan, Germany, France, and the UK will keep their membership in the present global regimes in the coming decades because membership is not harmful. Thus America's withdrawal from global regimes, even from the UN, World Bank, IMF, and WTO, cannot change the type of basic norms based on the UN Charter in the coming decade.

This book argues that political leadership plays an integral role in international politics but does not contend that global problems can be solved by a single powerful state. Mankind has not transcended the fundamental nature of international relations. World politics is still characterized by the struggle between states for power, prestige, and wealth amid global anarchy. Although globalization has shrunk the globe and established possibilities for the central management of world affairs, mankind has not yet established an international institution capable of this task. When all states are in the same leaky boat without an automatic operating system, one of them should wield the biggest dipper for the security of the boat as a whole. If the leading power does not lead, the other states cannot follow, and the world boat will lose direction. My theory advocates the leadership of humane authority to improve the world, because that type of leadership has managed international affairs better than any other throughout history. Although even this type of leadership cannot guarantee a more desirable world, I nevertheless believe it would offer the best chance of a world more peaceful than it is today.

Ancient Chinese Figures

Bao Si (褒姒, Late Western Zhou Dynasty) was the second wife of King You of the Zhou Dynasty. She was born in the State of Bao, and her family name is Si. King You very much adored Bao Si and made her the new queen after her son Bo Fu was born.

Confucius (孔子, 551–479 BCE) was a teacher, editor, politician, and philosopher in the Spring and Autumn period. He was born in the State of Lu. His family name is Kong, and his given name is Qiu. He was appointed as the minister of judiciary of the State of Lu. After being removed from office, Confucius and his students began to travel around the states, disseminating his philosophy. In the Han Dynasty, Confucius's thoughts were further developed into a system known by the West as Confucianism.

Duke Boyu (鲁公伯御, d. 769 BCE) was the eleventh ruler of the State of Lu and reigned for eleven years. His family name is Ji, and his given name is Kuo. After he was killed by King Xuan of the Zhou Dynasty, his uncle ascended to the crown, as Duke Xiao of Lu.

Duke Huan of Qi (齐桓公, d. 643 BCE) was the ruler of the State of Qi, one of the five hegemonic authorities during the Spring and Autumn period. His family name is Qi, and his given name is Xiaobai. Under his reign, Qi grew into the strongest state in the Chinese interstate system during his time. Duke Huan called four states in an alliance meeting in 679 BCE and became the leader of the first state alliance in Chinese history.

Duke Xi of Qi (齐僖公, d. 698 BCE) was the thirteenth recorded ruler of the State of Qi. His family name is Qi, and his given name is Lufu. He was the father of Duke Huan of Qi, one of the five hegemonic authorities during the Spring and Autumn period. Duke Xi succeeded to the crown in 731 BCE, after his father, Duke Zhuang of Qi, died, and he reigned for thirty-three years.

Emperor Qin Shi Huang (秦始皇, 259–210 BCE) was the founder of the Qin Dynasty and also the first emperor of a unified China. His family name is Ying, and his given name is Zheng. He was born as a prince of the State of Qin and became the king of Qin when he was thirteen. He unified China and brought an end to the Warring States period after he conquered all the other major states.

Emperor Taizong of Tang (唐太宗, 598–649 CE) was the second emperor of the Tang Dynasty of China, ruling from 626 to 649. His family name is Li, and his given name is Shimin. In 630, he sent his general Li Jing against eastern Turks, defeated and captured its Jiali Khan Ashina Duobi, and repelled the Eastern Turks. This made Tang the dominant power in East and Central Asia, and he subsequently took the title of Tengri Qaghan. Emperor Taizong was typically considered to be one of the greatest rulers in China's history, and henceforth, his "Reign of Zhenguan" became regarded as the exemplary model against which all future emperors were measured.

Guanzi (管子, ca. 723–645 BCE), also known as Guan Zhong, was the prime minister and reformer of the State of Qi during the Spring and Autumn period of Chinese history. He was born in the State of Chu. His family name is Guan, and his given name is Yiwu. Recommended by Bao Shuya, he was appointed prime minister by Duke Huan of Qi in 685 BCE. Because of Guan Zhong's reforms and skillful diplomacy, Qi became the most powerful state during his administration.

King Cheng of Zhou (周成王, d. ca. 1021 BCE) was the second king of the Zhou Dynasty and reigned for twenty-one years. His family name is Ji, and his given name is Song. King Cheng was young when he ascended to the throne. His uncle Duke Zhou became the regent and supervised government affairs for several years. With the assistance of Duke Zhou, King Cheng stabilized the Zhou Dynasty's border by defeating several barbarian tribes.

King Huiwen of Qin (秦惠文王, 356–311 BCE), also known as King Hui of Qin, was the ruler of the State of Qin from 338 to 311 BCE during the Warring States period. His family name is Ying, and his given name is Si. During King Hui's reign, Qin grew its military strength rapidly and constantly invaded neighboring states because of its expansionist policy. King Hui ruled Qin for twenty-seven years and died in 311 BCE at the age of forty-six. He was succeeded by his son, King Wu of Qin.

King Huiwen of Zhao (赵惠文王, ca. 309–266 BCE) was the fifth king of the State of Zhao. His family name is Zhao, and his given name is He. He is the second son of King Wu of Zhao. He is famed for his virtue of taking advice. For the interests of Zhao, King Huiwen took the advice of Lin Xiangru, his chief minister, and went to Mian Chi to meet with the king of the State of Qin, disregarding his own safety. During his reign, Zhao enjoyed prosperity in the economy and growth in the military.

King Jie of Xia (夏桀, d. ca. 1600 BCE), also known as Xia Jie, was the seventeenth and also the last ruler of the Xia Dynasty. His family name is Si, and his given name is Gui. He is historically regarded as a tyrant and oppressor. Around 1600 BCE, he was defeated by King Tang of Shang, bringing an end to the Xia Dynasty, which lasted about five hundred years, and beginning the rise to the new Shang Dynasty.

King Kang of Zhou (周康王, d. ca. 1001 BCE) was the third sovereign of the Chinese Zhou Dynasty, and he reigned for twenty-six years. His family name is Ji, and his given name is Zhao. King Kang followed the policy of his father, King Cheng, and expanded the Zhou territory northward and westward. Under his reign, the Zhou Dynasty experienced long-term prosperity.

King Li of Zhou (周厉王, d. ca. 841 BCE) was the tenth king of the Chinese Zhou Dynasty, and his reign is estimated at thirty-seven years. His family name is Ji, and his given name is Hu. King Li was a corrupt and decadent king. To pay for his life of luxury, King Li raised taxes and caused dissatisfaction among his ministers and his people. He therefore instituted a new law that allowed him to punish anyone, mostly by death, who dared to speak against him. King Li's cruel rule soon forced peasants and soldiers into revolt. His rule ended when he was exiled to a place called Zhi near Linfen.

King Mu of Zhou (周穆王, d. ca. 922 BCE) was the fifth king of the Zhou Dynasty, reigning nearly fifty-five years, from ca. 976 BCE to ca. 922 BCE. His family name is Ji, and his given name is Man. King Mu tried to oust invaders in the western part of China and ultimately expand Zhou's influence. During his reign, the Zhou Dynasty was at its peak.

King Nurhachi of Houjin (努尔哈赤, 1559–1626 CE) was the first king of the State of Hou Jin. His family was part of the Aisin Gioro clan. Nurhachi reorganized and united various Jurchen tribes (later known as "Manchu"), and he consolidated the Eight Banners military system and eventually launched attacks on the Ming Dynasty and Joseon Korea. His conquest of the Ming Dynasty's northeastern Liaoning province laid the groundwork for the conquest of the rest of China by his descendants, who founded the Qing Dynasty in 1644.

King Tang of Shang (商汤, ca. 1670–1587 BCE), or Shang Tang, was the first king of the Shang Dynasty. His family name is Zi, and his given name is Lü. He defeated King Jie, a tyrant, and thus ended the Xia Dynasty. King Tang was lauded for his virtues and morals along with other "sage kings."

King Wu of Zhou (周武王, d. 1046 BCE) was the first king of the Zhou Dynasty. His family name is Ji, and his given name is Fa. The chronology of his reign is still in debate, but the most widely accepted theory is that his reign began in 1046 BCE and ended three years later, in 1043 BCE. In 1046 BCE, King Wu ended the Shang Dynasty by defeating the army of King

Zhou of Shang, the last king of the Shang Dynasty, in the Battle of Muye.

King Xuan of Zhou (周宣王, ca. 841–782 BCE) was the eleventh king of the Zhou Dynasty. His family name is Ji, and his given name is Jing. Estimated dates of his reign are ca. 827–782 BCE. He managed to restore royal authority after the Gong He interregnum and contemporarily recovered the Zhou Dynasty from the chaos caused by the cruel policies of his father, King Li of Zhou. His son was the last king of the Western Zhou Dynasty.

King You of Zhou (周幽王, ca. 795–771 BCE) was the twelfth and also the last king of the Western Zhou Dynasty, reigning from 781 to 771 BCE. His family name is Ji, and his given name is Gongsheng. King You was a corrupt and decadent king. He lighted warning beacons for fun and to tease the princes who responded to the beacons. King You ended by being killed in a war launched by the Quanrong nomads.

King Yu of Xia (禹, dates unknown) was a mythological ruler of the Xia Dynasty. His family name is Si, and his given name is Wenming. He is famed for his introduction of flood control and for his upright moral character. He did not appear in inscriptions until vessels dating to the Western Zhou period were found. King Yu and other "sage kings" of ancient China were lauded for their virtues and morals by Confucius and other ancient Chinese thinkers.

King Zhou of Shang (商纣王, ca. 1105–1046 BCE) was the last king of the Shang Dynasty. His family name is Zi, and his given name is Shou. He is historically known as a tyrant. His army was defeated by King Wu of the Zhou Dynasty at the Battle of Muye in 1046 BCE, which ended the five-hundred-year Shang Dynasty. King Zhou was killed in this battle.

Laozi (老子, ca. 571–471 BCE) was an ancient philosopher. His name and birth place have not been ascertained academically. The most widely accepted inference is that his family name is Li and his given name is Er or Dan, and that he was born in the State of Chu. He was known as the reputed author of *Tao*

Te Ching, the founder of philosophical Taoism, and a deity in religious Taoism and other primitive religions in China. Laozi's work has been embraced by various anti-authoritarian movements as well as Chinese legalism. Political theorists influenced by Laozi advocate humility in leadership and a restrained approach to statecraft, either for ethical and pacifist reasons, or for tactical ends.

Lü Buwei (吕不韦, 292–235 BCE) was the prime minister of the State of Qin. His was born in the State of Wei. His family name is Lü, and his given name is Buwei. Under his patronage, *Lüshi Chunqiu,* an encyclopedic Chinese classic text, was compiled around 239 BCE. This book is unique among early texts for its well-organized and comprehensive contents, containing extensive knowledge on numerous subjects such as music and agriculture that are unknown elsewhere.

Mencius (孟子, ca. 372–289 BCE) was born in the State of Zou. His family name is Meng, and his given name is Ke. He served as an official and scholar at the Jixia Academy in the State of Qi from 319 to 312 BCE. He was a philosopher and one of the principal interpreters of Confucianism. He is only secondary to Confucius in this philosophical school.

Mozi (墨子, ca. 468–391 BCE) was born in the State of Song. His family name is Mo, and his given name is Di. He once undertook the position of a minister in Song. Mozi was the founder and the representative figure of the school of Mo. This school was the major competitor of Confucianism in the Warring States period, attracting hundreds of thousands of followers.

Sima Cuo (司马错, the Warring States period) was a well-known general of the State of Qin. He was born in Shaoliang of Qin. His family name is Sima, and his given name is Cuo. He served three kings of Qin, King Huiwen, King Wu, and King Zhaoxiang. Under his command, Qin won three important wars against the State of Shu, the State of Wei, and the State of Chu.

Xi Que (郤缺, d. 597 BCE), also named Xi Chengzi, was the chief general of the State of Jin in Spring and Autumn period. He was born in Ji of the State of Jin. His family name is Xi, and his given name is Que. Recommended by Xu Chen, a government official of Jin, Xi Que was appointed as an official in the military and became a minister as he won the battle against the State of Di. He was promoted to chief general in 601 BCE.

Xunzi (荀子, ca. 313–238 BCE) was a Chinese Confucian philosopher who lived during the Warring States period and contributed to the Hundred Schools of Thought. His family name is Xun, and his given name is Kuang. Xunzi was well respected in the State of Qi; King Xiang of Qi honored him as a teacher and a libation bearer. When Xunzi went south to the State of Chu, Sir Chunshen, the prime minister, gave him a position as magistrate of Lanling. In comparison to the idealist philosophy of Confucius and Mencius, Xunzi argued for the evil nature of human beings and thus emphasized not only the role of morals but also the effects of forces in both governance and diplomacy.

Zhaigong (祭公, Late Western Zhou) was one of the prime advisers of King Mu of the Zhou Dynasty. His family name is Zhai, and his given name is Moufu. He advocated moral politics, and this kept Zhou society stable for a long time. He advised against King Mu's crusade against the tribe of Quanrong and successfully predicted their failure because of this war. Zhaigong Moufu's many suggestions for King Mu were testified by history, which showed his extraordinary foresight and wisdom.

Zhao Xuanzi (赵宣子, ca. 655–601 BCE) was an extraordinary politician and strategist of the State of Jin during the early Spring and Autumn period. His family name is Dun. He served three kings, safeguarding the unity of Jin. During his time, the authority of the royal family of Jin was weakened for the first time, and the family of Zhao possessed the ruling power.

Zheng He (郑和, 1371–1433 CE) was a Chinese mariner, explorer, diplomat, and fleet commander of the Ming Dynasty. His family name is Ma, and his given name is Sanbao. His fleet was the largest and strongest fleet that had the capability of ocean voyage at that time. It navigated on the South China Sea and the

Indian Ocean and visited many places in Southeast Asia, South Asia, western Asia, and East Africa during the period from 1405 to 1433.

Zheng Zijia (郑子家, d. 599 BCE) was a minister of the State of Zheng. His family name is Zheng, and his given name is Zisheng. Zheng was a small state faced with competition between two major powers, the State of Jin and the State of Chu. His story was excerpted from a story named "Zheng Zijia Accused Zhao Xuanzi," which demonstrated how Zheng Zijia used the contradiction between the State of Jin and the State of Chu to reprove Jin's harsh requirements to Zheng.

NOTES

Preface

1. Ronald L. Tammen, Jacek Kugler, Douglas Lemke, Allan C. Stam III, Mark Abdollahian, Carole Alsharabati, Brian Efird, and A.F.K. Organski, *Power Transitions: Strategies for the 21st Century* (New York: Chatham House, 2000), 4–20.

Chapter 1. Morality, Power, and Authority

1. Paul Kennedy, *The Rise and Fall of the Great Powers: Economic Change and Military Conflict from 1500 to 2000* (New York: Random House, 1987), 515.

2. Robert Gilpin, *War and Change in World Politics* (Cambridge: Cambridge University Press, 1986), 156.

3. Richard Ned Lebow, *The Tragic Vision of Politics* (Cambridge: Cambridge University Press, 2003), 361.

4. In 2012, Zhang Feng, Research Fellow at Australian National University, coined the term "moral realism" for an approach that combines the political determinism of Chinese traditional philosophy with the modern realist theory of international relations. See Zhang Feng, "The Tsinghua Approach and the Inception of Chinese Theories of International Relations," *Chinese Journal of International Politics* 5, no. 1 (2012): 95–96.

5. Jannika Brostrom, "Morality and the National Interest: Towards a 'Moral Realist' Research Agenda," *Cambridge Review of International Affairs* 28, no. 4 (2015): 1626–27.

6. See Thompson and Clinton's comments in Hans J. Morgenthau, *Politics among Nations: The Struggle for Power and Peace*, ed. Kenneth W. Thompson and W. David Clinton, 7th ed. (Boston: McGraw-Hill Higher Education, 2005), xxiii.

7. Brostrom, "Morality and the National Interest," 1626.

8. Lebow, *Tragic Vision of Politics*, 16.

9. Morgenthau, *Politics among Nations*, 248.

10. Ibid., 12.

11. Ibid.

12. Ibid., 267.

13. John J. Mearsheimer, "The False Promise of International Institutions," *International Security* 19, no. 3 (1994/1995): 48.

14. "Yan Xuetong Duihua Mearsheimer: Zhongguo Nengfou Heping Jueqi?" [A Dialogue between Yan Xuetong and Mearsheimer: Can China Rise Peacefully?], *iFeng Academia*, September 29, 2013, http://news.ifeng.com/exclusive/lecture /special/yanxuetong/#pageTop.

15. Edward Hallet Carr, *The Twenty Years' Crisis, 1919–1939: An Introduction to the Study of International* Politics (New York: Harper and Row, 1964), 235.

16. Mark R. Amstutz, *International Ethics: Concepts, Theories, and Cases in Global Politics*, 2nd ed. (Lanham, MD: Rowman and Littlefield, 2005), 50.

17. Robert Gilpin, "The Richness of the Tradition of Political Realism," in *Neorealism and Its Critics*, ed. Robert O. Keohane (New York: Columbia University Press, 1986), 319.

18. Morgenthau, *Politics among Nations*, 12.

19. Ibid.

20. Carr, *Twenty Years Crisis'*, 235.

21. Stephen D. Krasner, *Defending the National Interests: Raw Materials Investments and U.S. Foreign Policy* (Princeton, NJ: Princeton University Press, 1978), 35.

22. Brostrom, "Morality and the National Interest," 1632.

23. Ibid., 1626.

24. Lebow, *Tragic Vision of Politics*, 16.

25. Amstutz, *International Ethics*, 10–11.

26. Reinhold Niebuhr, *Moral Man and Immoral Society: A Study in Ethics and Politics* (New York: Charles Scribner's Sons, 1932), 272–74.

27. Max Weber, "Politics as a Vocation," in *From Max Weber: Essays in Sociology*, trans. and ed. H. H. Gerth and C. Wright Mills (New York: Oxford University Press, 1958), 120.

28. Nannerl O. Keohane, *Thinking about Leadership* (Princeton, NJ: Princeton University Press, 2010), 213.

29. David E. Sanger and Jane Perlez, "Trump Hands the Chinese a Gift: The Chance for Global Leadership," *New York Times*, June, 1, 2017, https://www .nytimes.com/2017/06/01/us/politics/climate-accord-trump-china-global -leadership.html; David Frum, "The Death Knell for America's Global Leadership," *Atlantic Daily*, May 31, 2017, https://www.theatlantic.com/international/archive /2017/05/mcmaster-cohn-trump/528609/; Javier C. Hernández, "Turning against Trump: How the Chinese Covered the Climate Pact Exit," *New York Times*, June 4, 2017, https://www.nytimes.com/2017/06/04/world/asia/china-media-climate -trump.html; Joseph E. Stiglitz, "Trump's Rogue America," *Project-Syndicate*, June 2, 2017, https://www.project-syndicate.org/commentary/trump-rogue-america -by-joseph-e—stiglitz-2017-06; G. John Ikenberry, "The Plot against American Foreign Policy: Can the Liberal Order Survive?," *Foreign Affairs* 96, no. 3 (2017): 1–7; Philip Gordon, "A Vision of Trump at War: How the President Could Stumble into Conflict," *Foreign Affairs* 96, no. 3 (2017): 10–19.

30. (1) Care/harm: This foundation is related to our long evolution as mammals with attachment systems and an ability to feel (and dislike) the pain of others. It

underlies the virtues of kindness, gentleness, and nurturance. (2) Fairness/cheating: This foundation is related to the evolutionary process of reciprocal altruism. It generates ideas of justice, rights, and autonomy. (3) Loyalty/betrayal: This foundation is related to our long history as tribal creatures able to form shifting coalitions. It underlies virtues of patriotism and self-sacrifice for the group. It is active anytime people feel that it's "one for all, and all for one." (4) Authority/subversion: This foundation was shaped by our long primate history of hierarchical social interactions. It underlies virtues of leadership and followership, including deference to legitimate authority and respect for traditions. (5) Sanctity/degradation: This foundation was shaped by the psychology of disgust and contamination. It underlies religious notions of striving to live in an elevated, less carnal, nobler way. It underlies the widespread idea that the body is a temple that can be desecrated by immoral activities and contaminants (an idea not unique to religious traditions). Jesse Graham, Jonathan Haidt, Sena Koleva, Matt Motyl, Ravi Iyer, Sean P. Wojcik, and Peter H. Ditto, "Moral Foundations Theory: The Pragmatic Validity of Moral Pluralism," *Experimental Social Psychology* 47 (2012): 55–130, http://ssrn.com/abstract=2184440.

31. Ibid.

32. *Webster's New Collegiate Dictionary* (Massachusetts: G. and C. Merriam, 1977), 902.

33. Gilpin, *War and Change in World Politics*, 13.

34. William Wohlforth, "Unipolar Stability: The Rules of Power Analysis," *Harvard International Review*, Spring 2007, 44–48.

35. Yan Xuetong, *Zhongguo Guojia Liyi Fenxi* [Analysis of Chinese national interests] (Tianjin: Tianjin People's Publishing House, 1996), 47–50.

36. The moral realism theory model's comprehensive strength is the product of resource (R) and political operation (P); thus the formula is CS = R × P. P incorporates both the magnitude and the direction of policy reform, which serves as a measurement of the leadership effectiveness. Therefore, one can further break P down into a product of its components, the direction of reform (α) and amount of reform (β). In this model, β is a magnitude with no direction. α is a vector within the x, y plane, as there are only two directions: right or wrong. When the direction of reform is correct, the formula simplifies to CC = (M + E + C) · β, where $\beta \in (1, + \infty)$. When the direction of reform is incorrect, the formula simplifies to CC = (M + E + C) · β, where $\beta \in (0,1)$.

37. Joseph S. Nye, *The Future of Power* (New York: Public Affairs, 2011), 84.

38. Joseph S. Nye, *The Power to Lead* (Oxford: Oxford University Press, 2008), x.

39. Yan Xuetong, "From Keeping a Low Profile to Striving for Achievement," *Chinese Journal of International Politics* 7, no. 2 (Summer 2014): 166.

40. Alexander Neil, "Japan's Growing Concern over China's Naval Might," BBC News, May 28, 2017, http://www.bbc.com/news/world-asia-39918647.

41. Kiyoshi Takenaka, "Japan Buys Disputed Islands, China Sends Patrol Ships," *Reuters*, September 11, 2012, https://www.reuters.com/article/us-japan

-china/japan-buys-disputed-islands-china-sends-patrol-ships-idUSBRE88A 0GY20120911.

42. "China Ships in Disputed Waters: Japan Coast Guard," Press TV, August 2, 2013, http://www.presstv.ir/detail/2013/08/02/316811/china-ships-in-disputed -waters-japan.

43. David A. Lake, *Hierarchy in International Relations* (Ithaca, NY: Cornell University Press, 2009), 8.

44. Max Weber, *Theory of Social and Economic Organization*, ed. Talcott Parsons (New York: Free Press of Glencoe, 1964), 325–28.

45. Ibid., 328.

46. Angela Dewan, "These Are All the Countries That Are Expelling Russian Diplomats," CNN, March 28, 2018, 11:48 GMT, https://edition.cnn.com/2018/03 /26/europe/full-list-of-russian-diplomats-expelled-over-s-intl/index.html.

47. Julia Jacobo, "Conditions of Ex-Russian Spy, Daughter Improving after They Were Poisoned with Nerve Agent," ABC NEWS, April 6, 2018, 3:59 p.m., http://abcnews.go.com/International/conditions-russian-spy-daughter -improving-poisoned-nerve-agent/story?id=54288681.

48. Marjorie Cohn, "Iraq: A War of Aggression. No WMDs, No Connection to Al Qaeda," *Global Research*, March 19, 2013, http://www.globalresearch.ca/iraq -a-war-of-aggression-no-wmds-no-connection-to-al-qaeda/5327548.

49. "Angry Geithner Once Warned S&P about US Downgrade: Filing," *Business News*, January 22, 2014, http://www.thestar.com.my/Business/Business -News/2014/01/22/Angry-Geithner-Once-Warned-SaP-About-US-Downgrade.

50. Deborah Amos, "Arab Leaders Feel US Abandoned Egypt's Mubarak," NPR, February 9, 2011, http://www.npr.org/2011/02/09/133614346/Egypt-Arab -Leaders.

51. Herb Keinon, "Israeli Critics Open Up on US 'Abandonment' of Mubarak," *Jerusalem Post*, January 31, 2011, http://www.jpost.com/Diplomacy-and-Politics /Israeli-critics-open-up-on-US-abandonment-of-Mubarak.

52. "UN Resolutions Targeting Israel and the Palestinians," If Americans Knew, accessed February 15, 2017, http://ifamericaknew.org/stat/un.html.

53. Takashi Oshima, "US Expresses Disappointment at Abe Visit to Yasukuni Shrine," *Asahi Shimbun*, December 27, 2013, http://ajw.asahi.com/article/behind _news/politics/AJ201312270048.

54. Bill Sweetman, "Japan Increases Defense Spending," *Aviationweek*, December 17, 2013, http://www.aviationweek.com/Article.aspx?id=/article-xml/awx_12 _17_2013_p0-648057.xml.

55. Wang Mingxiu, ed., *Shijie Zhishi Nianjian 1991/1992* [World knowledge yearbook 1991/1992] (Beijing: World Affairs, 1992), 2.

56. Steven Metz, "How America's Enemies Might Assess U.S. Weaknesses— and Act on Them," *World Politics Review*, September 29, 2017, https://www .worldpoliticsreview.com/articles/23264/how-america-s-enemies-might-assess -u-s-weaknesses-and-act-on-them.

57. Nye, *Future of Power*, 83.

58. Xun Kuang, "11: Wang Ba" [Book 11: On sage kings and hegemons], in *Xunzi*

Quanyi [Full translation of *Xunzi*], trans. Jiang Nanhua, Luo Shuqin, and Yang Huanqing (Guiyang: Guizhou People's Publishing House, 1995), 203.

59. Cui Gaowei, ed., *Li Ji* [The book of rites] (Shenyang: Liaoning Education Press, 2000), 1.

60. Quoted in Morgenthau, *Politics among Nations*, 276.

61. Ibid.

62. William R. Castles, "Expressions of American Foreign Policy," *World Affairs* 95, no. 1 (1932), 47–49; Andrew J. Bacevich, "A Moral Foreign Policy? Get Serious," *New Republic*, July 21, 2010, https://newrepublic.com/article/76408/afghanistan-war-obama-bacevich.

Chapter 2. Leadership and Strategic Preferences

1. Lebow, *Tragic Vision of Politics*, xi.

2. Aristotle lists six forms of government depending on who rules and for whom they rule, and he argues for the different social effects of these forms. For an introduction, see Edward Meredith Cope, *An Introduction to Aristotle's Rhetoric: With Analysis Notes and Appendices* (London: Macmillan, 1867), 210–12. For an example of modern Western political writings that stress the role of political rulers, see Fareed Zakaria, *From Wealth to Power—the Unusual Origins of America's World Role* (Princeton, NJ: Princeton University Press, 1998).

3. Robert H. Jackson and Carl G. Rosberg, *Personal Rule in Black Africa: Prince, Autocrat, Prophet, Tyrant* (Berkeley: University of California Press, 1982), 3.

4. Yan Xuetong, "From Keeping a Low Profile to Striving for Achievement," 165–70.

5. Margaret G. Hermann and Joe D. Hagan, "International Decision Making Leadership Matters," *Foreign Policy*, no. 110, special ed. (Spring 1998): 126.

6. Xun Kuang, "11: Wang Ba," 210.

7. Morris Fiorina and Kenneth Shepsle, "Formal Theories of Leadership," in *Leadership and Politics: New Perspectives in Political Science*, ed. Bryan D. Jones (Lawrence: University Press of Kansas, 1989), 36.

8. Alexander Hamilton, James Madison, and John Jay, eds. *The Federalist Papers* (New York: New American Library, 1961), 414.

9. Hermann and Hagan, "International Decision Making," 128.

10. N. Keohane, *Thinking about Leadership*, 53.

11. "Wei Woguo Fazhan Zhengqu Lianghao Zhoubian Huanjing" [Striving for a healthy surrounding environment for our development], *Renmin Ribao* [People's Daily], October 26, 2013, 1.

12. In 2017, China's Xinhua News Agency issued a list of forbidden words, the 120th of which is use of the word "strategy" to describe the B&R plan in international situations. See *Xinhuashe Fabu Xinwen Baodao Jinyongci he Shenyongci* [Xinhua News Agency issuing forbidden and cautiously used phrases in media report], July 2016, 12, https://wenku.baidu.com/view/82319f49e97101f69e3143323968011ca300f793.html.

13. Qi Haixia, "Laozi de Xiaoguo Guamin Sixiang" [Laozi's idea of "small countries few inhabitants"], in *Wangba Tianxia Sixiang Ji Qidi* [Thoughts on world leadership and implications] (Beijing: World Affairs, 2009), 63.

14. Ibid., 65–67.

15. Wu Jing, *Zhenguan Zhengyao* [Important political records of Zhenguan government] (Zhengzhou: Zhongzhou Ancient Book, 2008).

16. "Zhongguo Gongchandang Zhongyang Weiyuanhui Guanyu Jianguo Yilai de Ruogan Lishi Wenti de Jueyi" [The Central Committee of the Chinese Communist Party's resolution on certain historical issues in party history since the founding of the People's Republic of China], in *San Zhong Quanhui Yilai Zhongyao Wenxian Xuanbian (Xia)* [Collection of important documents since the third plenary conference (II)] (Beijing: People's Publishing House, 1982), 808.

17. Kerry Brown, "Trump: The True New Maoist; Mao's True Heir Is Not Xi Jinping, but the New U.S. President," *Diplomat*, January 19, 2017, http://thediplo mat.com/2017/01/trump-the-true-new-maoist/.

18. Gordon, "Vision of Trump at War," 10.

19. Suzanne Mettler, "Democracy on the Brink: Protecting the Republic in Trump's America," *Foreign Affairs* 96, no. 3 (May/June 2017): 121.

20. Sun Xuefeng, "Rethinking East Asian Regional Order and China's Rise," *Japanese Journal of Political Science* 14, no. 1 (2013): 9–30; Sun Xuefeng, *Zhongguo Jueqi Kunjing: Lilun Sikao yu Zhanlue Xuanze* [Dilemma of China's rise: Theoretical thinking and strategic selection] (Beijing: Social Science Academic, 2013), 22–25.

21. Xun Kuang, "5: Fei Xiang" [Book 5: Contra physiognomy], in *Xunzi Quanyi*, 23.

22. "Laolao Bawo Liangan Guanxi Heping Fazhan de Zhuti, Wei Liangan Tongbao Mou Fuzhi, Wei Taihai Diqu Mou Heping" [Firmly adhering to the principle of peace and development in regards to the relationship between the two sides of the Taiwan Strait, while seeking for benefits of people and maintaining peace between the two sides], *Renmin Ribao* [People's Daily], March 5, 2008, 1, http://tw .people.com.cn/GB/26741/117733/index.html.

23. Wang Hongxu, "Xin Zongguo Waijiao de Jiazhi Quxiang yu Zhanlue Xuanze" [The PRC's diplomatic value and strategic preference], *Guoji Guanxi Xueyuan Xuebao* [Journal of the University of International Relations], no. 6 (2011): 11.

24. Xie Xuren, "Fazhan Huli Gongying de Zhong Mei Jingji Hezuo Guanxi" [Developing mutual benefit and win-win economic cooperation between China and America], Ministry of Finance of the People's Republic of China, http://www .mof.gov.cn/zhengwuxinxi/caizhengxinwen/201005/t20100523_319021.html.

25. He Tiantian, "Yin Zhuo: Junshi Jituanhua You Lengzhan Siwei, Jiemeng Bu Fuhe Zhong E Liyi" [Yin Zhuo: The military alliance is a Cold War mentality and does not serve the interests of China and Russia], *iFeng News*, May 19, 2014, http://news.ifeng.com/a/20140519/40363851_0.shtml; "Zhong E Bugao Junshi Tongmeng Yuanyin Fuza, Gangmei Cheng Cengyou Cantong Jiaoxun" [China and Russia reject alliance owing to complex reasons, the Hong Kong media claim that

it is because of historical lessons], *Sohu Junshi* [Sohu Military News], April 22, 2014, http://mil.sohu.com/20140422/n398629853.shtml.

26. Wu Xu, "Zhongguo Ying Fangqi Bujiemeng Zhengce" [China should abandon the nonalignment policy], *Zhongguo Xinwen Zhoukan* [China News Weekly], January 10, 2012, http://opinion.china.com.cn/opinion_14_32214.html; Yan Xuetong, "The Shift of the World Center and Its Impact on the Change of the International System," *East Asia: An International Quarterly* 30, no. 4 (2013), 232.

27. Liu Ruonan and Liu Feng, "Contending Ideas on China's Non-alliance Strategy," *Chinese Journal of International Politics* 10, no. 2 (2017): 156–58.

28. Zhao Pi, "Guanyu Xin Junshi Biange Ruogan Wenti de Zhanlue Sikao" [Strategic thinking on certain military reforms], *Zhanlue Yanjiu* [Strategic Studies], no. 2 (2013): 11; Zhang Xiaotian, "Daguo Quanli Zhuanyi de Bazhong Fangshi yu Woguo de Zhanlue Xuanze" [Eight approaches for power transition between great powers and the strategic choice for China], *Guofang Cankao* [National Defense Reference], nos. 19–20 (2015): 54–57; Ma Debao and Liu Haiqing, "Zhongguo Qiangjun Zhi Lu Juyou Shijie Yiyi" [China's military modernization has world meaning], *Guofang Cankao* [National Defense Reference], no. 21 (2017): 32–34.

29. David Owen and Jonathan Davidson, "Hubris Syndrome: An Acquired Personality Disorder? A Study of US Presidents and UK Prime Ministers over the Last 100 Years," *Brain: A Journal of Neurology*, February 12, 2009, 2.

30. Dacher Keltner, Cameron Anderson, and Deborah H. Gruenfeld, "Power, Approach, and Inhibition" *Psychological Review* 110, no. 2 (2003): 279.

31. Jeremy Hogeveen, Sukhvinder S. Obhi, and Michael Inzlicht, "Power Changes How the Brain Responds to Others," *Journal of Experimental Psychology: General* 143, no. 2 (2014): 759–60.

32. Guan Zhong, "23: Ba Yan" [Book 23: On hegemony], in *Guanzi Yizhu* [Translation of *Guanzi*], trans. Sheng Guangzhi (Changchun: Jilin Literature and History, 1998), 268.

33. Williamson Murray, Macgregor Knox, and Alvin Bernstein, *The Making of Strategy: Rulers, States, and War* (Cambridge: Cambridge University Press, 1994), 1.

34. Xun Kuang, "18: Zheng Lun" [Book 18: Rectifying theses], in *Xunzi Quanyi*, 366.

35. James M. Goldgeier, "The U.S. Decision to Enlarge NATO: How, When, Why, and What Next," *Brookings Review* 17, no. 3 (1999): 18–21.

36. Frum, "The Death Knell for America's Global Leadership."

37. "Merkel: 'Europe's Fate in Its Own Hands,'" Shanghaidaily.com, May 29, 2017, http://www.shanghaidaily.com/world/Merkel-Europes-fate-in-its-own-hands/shdaily.shtml.

38. Xun Kuang, "11: Wang Ba," in *Xunzi Quanyi*, 203.

39. Xun Kuang, "9: Wang Zhi" [Book 9: On the regulations of sage kings], in *Xunzi Quanyi*, 146.

40. Yan Xuetong, "International Leadership and Norm Evolution," *Chinese Journal of International Politics* 4 (2011): 241n244, n245.

41. Guan Zhong, "23: Ba Yan," 268.

42. Yang Bojun, trans., "The Confucian Analects: Book XX Yao Yue," *The Four Books* (Changsha: Hunan, 1992), 255.

43. Yan Xuetong, "International Leadership and Norm Evolution," 245.

44. In 651 BCE, State of Qi (齐) organized a meeting at Kuiqiu with the representatives of the State of Lu (鲁), the State of Song (宋), the State of Zheng (郑), and the State of Wei (魏), and in the presence of a royal representative from Zhou, whose king had the highest judicial authority. The members of this alliance agreed never to attack one another, and to assist one another in the event of being attacked. The duke of Qi thus became the overlord over those weaker states.

45. François de La Rochefoucauld, *Maximes et Reflexions Diverses*, ed. Jean Lafond, 2nd ed. (Paris: Gallimard, 1976), Réflexion 218, 79, cited from Lebow, *Tragic Vision of Politics*, 17.

46. Yang Kuan, *Xi Zhou Shi* [History of West Zhou Dynasty] (Shanghai: Shanghai People's Publishing House, 2003), 850–51.

47. Stiglitz, "Trump's Rogue America."

48. Thomas L. Friedman, "Trump Is a Chinese 'Agent,'" *Gulfnews*, October 28, 2017, http://gulfnews.com/opinion/thinkers/trump-is-a-chinese-agent -1.2003547.

49. Ikenberry, "Plot against American Foreign Policy," 2.

50. Jackson and Rosberg, *Personal Rule in Black Africa*, 80.

51. Yan Xuetong, "International Leadership and Norm Evolution," 244.

52. Yan Xuetong, *Ancient Chinese Thought, Modern Chinese Power* (Princeton, NJ: Princeton University Press, 2011), 43, 47–51, 86–88.

53. Ibid., 50–51, 88–89.

54. Robert Kagan, "The Benevolent Empire," *Foreign Policy*, no. 111 (Summer 1998): 26; Eric Koo Peng Kuan, "The US as Benevolent Hegemon," *Asia Times*, September 23, 2004, http://www.atimes.com/atimes/Front_Page/FI23Aa01 .html.

55. Sheng Guangzhi, "Chapter 17: Bing Fa" [Methods of warfare], in *Guanzi Yizhu* [Interpretation of *Guanzi*] (Changchun: Jilin Literature and History, 1998), 183.

56. Ibid.

57. Jiang Nanhua, Luo Zhuqin, and Yang Hanqing, "Chapter 9: Wang Zhi" [Humane governance], in *Xunzi Quanyi* [Full interpretation of *Xunzi*] (Guiyang: Guizhou People's Publishing House, 1995), 146.

58. Mencius, "Gongsun Chou I," *Mencius*, trans. Wang Changze (Taiyuan: Shanxi Ancient Book, 2003), 45.

59. Shi Yongzhi, "Neisheng Waiwang Xinquan" [A new interpretation of *neisheng waiwang*], *Zhouyi Yanjiu* [Studies on *Zhouyi*], no. 5 (2015): 88–89.

60. Stephen M. Walt, "The Collapse of the Liberal World Order," *Foreign Policy*, June 26, 2016, http://foreignpolicy.com/2016/06/26/the-collapse-of-the -liberal-world-order-european-union-brexit-donald-trump/.

61. Charles W. Kegley and Gregory Raymond, "Networks of Intrigue? Realpolitik, Alliances and International Security" in *Reconstructing Realpolitik*, ed. Frank

Whelon Wayman and Paul Francis Diehl (Ann Arbor: University of Michigan Press, 1994), 185–98.

Chapter 3. Corollaries of International Change

1. Morgenthau, *Politics among Nations*, 4.

2. Guan Zhong, "Ba Yan 23," 270.

3. Richard Wike, Bruce Stokes, Jacob Poushter, and Janell Fetterolf, *U.S. Image Suffers as Publics around World Question Trump's Leadership* (Washington, DC: Pew Research Center, June 26, 2017), 3.

4. Peter Baker, "Souring World Views of Trump Open Doors for China and Russia," *New York Times*, January 18, 2018, http://www.wral.com/souring-world-views-of-trump-open-doors-for-china-and-russia/17268302/.

5. Yan Xuetong and Yang Yuan, *Guoji Guanxi Fenxi* [The analysis of international relations] (Beijing: Peking University Press, 2013), 44–45.

6. Hong Liangji, *Chunqiu Zuo Zhuan Gu* [Explanation of the chronicle of Zuo] (Beijing: Chinese Book, 1987), 367.

7. Barry Buzan and Richard Little, *International Systems in World History: Remaking the Study of International Relations* (Oxford: Oxford University Press, 2000), 239.

8. The five hegemons refers to the powerful rulers of Chinese states of the Spring and Autumn period of Chinese history (770 to 476 BCE). The hegemons mobilized the remnants of the Zhou Empire, according to shared mutual political and martial interests. The five hegemons were Duke Huan of Qi (齐桓公), Duke Wen of Jin (晋文公), King Zhuang of Chu (楚庄王), King Helü of Wu (吴王阖闾), and King Goujian of Yue (越王勾践).

9. "Brexit Impact on China Market Limited: Economists," *Xinhua News*, June 24, 2016, http://news.xinhuanet.com/english/2016-06/24/c_135464355.htm.

10. Gideon Rose, "Neoclassical Realism and Theories of Foreign Policy," *World Politics* 51, no. 1 (1998): 144–72.

11. Amstutz, *International Ethics*, 49.

12. Kenneth N. Waltz, *Theory of International Politics* (Reading: Addison-Wesley, 1983), 97.

13. Sun Xuefeng, "Rethinking East Asian Regional Order and China's Rise."

14. Shepard B. Clough, *The Rise and Fall of Civilization* (New York: Columbia University Press, 1970), 263.

15. Gilpin, *War and Change in World Politics*, 187.

16. John J. Mearsheimer, *The Tragedy of Great Power Politics* (New York: W. W. Norton, 2001), 21.

17. Graham Allison, *Destined for War: Can America and China Escape Thucydides's Trap?* (Boston: Houghton Mifflin Harcourt, 2017).

18. "Zhong E Lianhe Shengming: Shuangfang Bu Juyou Jiemeng Xingzhi, Bu Zhendui Disanguo" (China-Russia joint statement: bilateral relations are not alliances against third parties), *Wangyi*, June 26, 2016, 08:44:09, http://money.163.com/16/0626/08/BQFNAG3800253B0H_all.html.

19. Michael Beckley, "The Myth of Entangling Alliances: Reassessing the Security Risks of U.S. Defense Pacts," *International Security* 39, no. 4 (Spring 2015): 47.

20. Amstutz, *International Ethics*, 48.

21. Xiangming Fang and Phaedra S. Corso, "Child Maltreatment, Youth Violence, and Intimate Partner Violence Developmental Relationships," *American Journal of Preventative Medicine* 33, no. 4 (2007): 281.

22. Xun Kuang, "23: Xing E" [Book 23: Evil nature of man], in *Xunzi Quanyi*, 489.

23. Alexander Wendt, *Social Theory of International Politics* (Cambridge: Cambridge University Press, 1999), 233–38.

24. James E. Dougherty and Robert L. Pfaltzgraff Jr., *Contending Theories of International Relations: A Comprehensive Survey* (New York: Addison Wesley Longman, 2001), 64.

25. Yan Xuetong, "International Leadership and Norm Evolution," 241–43.

26. James M. Lindsay, Maurice R. Greenberg, James M. Goldgeier, "By Focusing Now, Clinton Can Renegotiate ABM Treaty," *Los Angeles Times*, April 2, 2000, http://www.cfr.org/world/focusing-now-clinton-can-renegotiate-abm-treaty/p6347.

27. White House, "U.S. Withdrawal from the ABM Treaty: President Bush's Remarks and US Diplomatic Notes," Arms Control Association, https://www.armscontrol.org/act/2002_01-02/docjanfeb02; "US Lifts India and Pakistan Sanctions," BBC News, September 23, 2001, http://news.bbc.co.uk/2/hi/americas/1558860.stm.

28. Jim VandeHei and Dafna Linzer, "U.S., India Reach Deal on Nuclear Co-operation," *Washington Post*, March 3, 2006, http://www.washingtonpost.com/wp-dyn/content/article/2006/03/02/AR2006030200183.html.

29. Amstutz, *International Ethics*, 49.

30. Wang Shengzu, ed. *Guoji Guanxi Shi (1871–1918)* [History of international relations (1871–1918)] (Beijing: World Affairs, 1995), 359–61.

31. Michael Fullilove, "Do We Really Want China to Be a Responsible Stakeholder in Global Affairs," Brookings, December 3, 2010, https://www.brookings.edu/opinions/do-we-really-want-china-to-be-a-responsible-stakeholder-in-global-affairs/.

32. Yan Xuetong, "Wuxu Tixi Zhong de Guoji Zhixu" [International order in anarchic systems], *Guoji Zhengzhi Kexue* [Quarterly Journal of International Politics] 1, no. 1 (2016): 13.

33. George Bush, "Address before a Joint Session of the Congress on the State of the Union," American Presidency of Project, January 29, 1991, http://www.presidency.ucsb.edu/ws/?pid=19253.

34. Gilpin, *War and Change in World Politics*, 26 and 111.

35. Hedley Bull, *The Anarchical Society: A Study of Order in World Politics*, 3rd ed. (Beijing: Palgrave Macmillan, 2002), 8 and 9.

36. Evelyn Goh, *The Struggle for Order: Hegemony, Hierarchy and Transition in Post–Cold War East Asia* (Oxford: Oxford University Press, 2013), 16.

37. Article 2, chapter I, "Purposes and Principles," Charter of the United Nations, http://www.un.org/en/sections/un-charter/chapter-i/index.html.

38. Yan Xuetong, "Shift of the World Center," 228–30.

Chapter 4. Power Redistribution and World Center

1. Øystein Tunsjø, *The Return of Bipolarity in World Politics: China, the United States, and Geostructural Realism* (New York: Columbia University Press, 2018), 181.

2. Susan E. Reid, "Who Will Beat Whom? Soviet Popular Reception of the American National Exhibition in Moscow, 1959," *Russian and East European Studies* 9, no. 4 (2008): 885–904.

3. Paul Krugman, "The Myth of Asia's Miracle," *Foreign Affairs* 73, no. 6 (1994): 62–78.

4. Nye, *Future of Power*, 202.

5. Robert Kagan, *The World America Made* (New York: Alfred A. Knopf, 2012), 131.

6. Nuno P. Monterio, *Theory of Unipolar Politics* (New York: Cambridge University Press, 2014), 4.

7. Lake, *Hierarchy in International Relations*, 181–82.

8. "American Federal Budget Deficit Persists for a Fourth Year, Breaks $1 Trillion," *United Morning Paper* (Singapore), last modified July 29, 2012, http://www.zaobao.com/gj/gj120729_001.shtml.

9. "American Republican Party Proposes to Achieve a Balanced Budget within Ten Years," *Southern Daily*, March 14, 2013, A09.

10. Edward J. McCaffery, "Trump's Massive Tax Cut—for the Rich," CNN, September 28, 2017, http://edition.cnn.com/2017/09/27/opinions/trump-tax-plan-opinion-mccaffery/index.html.

11. Fareed Zakaria, "The Debt Deal's Failure," *Time*, August 19, 2013, 14.

12. The Office of the Press Secretary of the White House, "Remarks by National Security Advisor Susan Rice on the 2015 National Security Strategy," White House, February 6, 2015, http://www.whitehouse.gov/the-press-office/2015/02/06/remarks-national-security-advisor-susan-rice-2015-national-security-stra.

13. "Remarks by President Trump on His Trip to Asia," Office of the Press Secretary of the White House, November 15, 2017, https://www.whitehouse.gov/the-press-office/2017/11/15/remarks-president-trump-his-trip-asia.

14. Bi Yuanfang, "Qu Xing: Zhong E Buneng Jiemeng, Fouze Hui Baofa Xin Lengzhan" [Qu Xing: China and Russia should not make alliance, otherwise a new cold war will occur], December 6, 2014, http://world.huanqiu.com/exclusive/2014-12/5229619.html; Richard A. Bitzinger, "Warring Ideas: Yan Xuetong's Awful Concept of a Chinese Military Alliance," *Asia Times*, February 16, 2016, http://www.atimes.com/article/warring-ideas-yan-xuetongs-awful-concept-of-a-chinese-military-alliance/.

15. Allison, *Destined for War*, 28.

16. "Duke Cheng—the 12th Year," *Zuo Zhuan* [Zuo's Commentary], trans. Hu Zhihui (Changsha: Hunan People's Publishing House, 1996), 607–8.

17. *Shijie Zhishi Nianjian 1989/90* [World affairs yearbook 1989/90] (Beijing: World Affairs, 1990), 714.

18. Ibid.

19. Thomas C. Schelling, *The Strategy of Conflict* (Cambridge, MA: Harvard University Press, 1960), 257–66.

20. James Warren, "Obama Tones Down Talk of Military Aid for Ukraine, but Won't Rule It Out Either," *New York Daily News*, February 9, 2015, 2:06 p.m., http://www.nydailynews.com/news/politics/obama-tones-talk-military-aid -ukraine-article-1.2108681.

21. Michael Eisenscher, "Donald Trump, Congress, and War with North Korea," *Counter Punch*, November 21, 2017, https://www.counterpunch.org/2017 /11/21/donald-trump-congress-and-war-with-north-korea/.

22. Yan Xuetong, "The Instability of China-US Relations," *Chinese Journal of International Politics* 3, no. 3 (Autumn 2010): 280–85.

23. White House, *National Security Strategy of the United States of America* (Washington, DC: White House, December 2017), http://www.dtic.mil/dtic/tr /fulltext/u2/1043812.pdf.

24. Yan Xuetong and Qi Haixia, "Football Game Rather Than Boxing Match: China-US Intensifying Rivalry Does Not Amount to Cold War," *Chinese Journal of International Politics* 5, no. 2 (2012): 124–27.

25. Waltz, *Theory of International Politics*, 138–43.

26. Mearsheimer, *Tragedy of Great Power Politics* (updated ed., New York: W. W. Norton, 2014), chapter 10.

27. Robert O. Keohane and Joseph S. Nye, *Power and Interdependence: World Politics in Transition* (Boston: Little, Brown, 1977), 13.

28. "Will an Integrated ASEAN Region Challenge China?" Knowledge@wharton, January 15, 2014, http://knowledge.wharton.upenn.edu/article/will-an -integrated-asean-region-challenge-china/.

29. Megan Slack, "Our Dependence on Foreign Oil Is Declining," *White House Blog*, March 1, 2012, 9:30 a.m. EST, http://www.whitehouse.gov/blog/2012/03 /01/our-dependence-foreign-oil-declining.

30. "A Bao Wenzhang: 2011, Shijie Chuzai Shizi Lukou" [An article in an Argentinian newspaper: The world is at the crossroads 2011], Xinhunew.com, January 22, 2011, http://news.xinhuanet.com/world/2011-01/22/c_121009347 .htm.

31. Xiong Xin and Li Muzi, "Quanqiu Jingji Juece Quanli Zhongxin Zhuanyi Buke Bimian" [The shift of the global economic power is inevitable], Hexun Net, September 8, 2010, http://news.hexun.com/2010-09-08/124834325.html.

32. Quoted in Tang Weijie, "Zhongguo Waizhang Bu Rentong Shijie Quanli Zhongxin Dongyilun" [Chinese foreign minister disagrees on the opinion of eastward-shift of the world power center], *China News*, July 31, 2010, http://www .chinanews.com/gn/2010/07-31/2438006.shtml.

33. Halford John Mackinder, *Democratic Ideals and Reality* (London: National Defense University, 1942), 106.

34. For relevant arguments, see Tanja A. Börzel and Frank Schimmelfennig,

"Coming Together or Drifting Apart? The EU's Political Integration Capacity in Eastern Europe," *Journal of European Public Policy* 24, no. 2 (2017): 278–96.

35. Lefton S. Stavrianos, *The World since 1500: A Global History* (London: Prentice-Hall, 1966), 457.

36. Quoted in Fang Lianqing, Wang Bingyuan, and Liu Jinzhi, *Guoji Guanxi Shi (Zhanhou Juan)* [History of postwar international relations] (Beijing: Peking University Press, 2006), 47.

37. Lord Green, "As the US Falters and Europe Declines, Look East to See the Future," *South China Morning Post,* November 23, 2017, http://m.scmp.com/comment/insight-opinion/article/2121297/america-falters-and-europe-declines-look-east-see-future.

38. "Government Expenditure on Defense," *Eurostat,* March 2018, http://ec.europa.eu/eurostat/statistics-explained/index.php/Government_expenditure_on_defence.

39. Chen Yan, "Jinnian Junfei Zengjia 7.6%" [The defense budget of this year increases 7.6%], *Sina News,* March 3, 2016, http://news.sina.com.cn/c/nd/2016-03-05/doc-ifxqaffy3628549.shtml.

40. Kirk Spitzer, "Japan Approves Record-High Budget, Focusing on Defense, Economic Recovery," *USA Today,* March 29, 2016, https://www.usatoday.com/story/news/world/2016/03/29/japan-government-defense-budget-economic-recovery/82376314/.

41. "South Korea—Government Defense Expenditure," Countryeconomy.com, https://countryeconomy.com/government/expenditure/defence/south-korea.

42. White House, *National Security Strategy of the United States of America* (Washington, DC: White House, December 2017), http://www.dtic.mil/dtic/tr/fulltext/u2/1043812.pdf, 25, 46.

43. Robert S. Ross and Øystein Tunsjø, "U.S.-China Relations: From Unipolar Hedging toward Bipolar Balancing," in *Strategic Adjustment and the Rise of China: Power and Politics in East Asia* (Ithaca, NY: Cornell University Press, 2017), 59.

44. White House, *National Security Strategy of the United States of America,* 46.

45. Ibid., 65.

46. Nicola Di Cosmo, *Ancient China and Its Enemies: The Rise of Nomadic Power in East Asian History* (Cambridge: Cambridge University Press, 2002).

47. Theories about power transition and hegemony cycles have reached the same conclusion. See A. F. K. Organski, *World Politics* (New York: Alfred A. Knopf, 1958); George Modelski and William R. Thompson, "Long Cycles and Global War," in *Handbook of War Studies,* ed. Manus I. Midlarsky (Boston: Unwin Hyman, 1989), 23–54; Gilpin, *War and Change in World Politics,* 15.

48. Aaron Blake, "Trump's Menacing United Nations Speech, Annotated," *Washington Post,* September 19, 2017. https://www.washingtonpost.com/news/the-fix/wp/2017/09/19/trumps-menacing-united-nations-speech-annotated/?utm_term=.3d65e546ccf8.

49. Joseph S. Nye, *Bound to Lead: The Changing Nature of American Power* (New York: Basic Books, 1990), 34.

50. Martin Jacques, *When China Rules the World*, 2nd ed. (London: Penguin Books, 2009), 539.

51. Mark Leonard, *What Does China Think?* (London: Fourth Estate, 2008).

52. Chung-in Moon, *Zhongguo Jueqi Da Zhanlue: Yu Zhongguo Zhishi Jingying de Shenceng Duihua* [Grand Strategies of China's Rising: In-Depth Dialogue with Leading Chinese Intellectuals], trans. Li Chunfu from Korean version (Beijing: World Affairs, 2011).

Chapter 5. Leadership and International Norms

1. Richard C. Snyder, H. W. Bruck, and Burton Sapin, "Decision-Making as an Approach to the Study of International Politics," in *Foreign Policy Decision-Making*, ed. Richard Snyder, H. W. Bruck, and Burton Sapin, rev. ed., 21–152. (New York: Palgrave Macmillan, 2002), 119.

2. Dougherty and Pfaltzgraff, *Contending Theories of International Relations*, 559.

3. The type "in-order-to motives" refers to initiating a policy to realize a goal. Lyndon Baines Johnson initiated the Vietnam War in order to prevent Southeast Asian states from falling into communist hands, and George W. Bush initiated the Iraq War in order to expand American domination of the Middle East.

4. Martha Finnemore and Kathryn Sikkink, "International Norms Dynamics and Political Change," *International Organization* 52, no. 4 (1998): 887–917.

5. Ibid., 891 and 896–97.

6. G. John Ikenberry and Charles A. Kupchan, "Socialization and Hegemonic Power," *International Organization* 44, no. 3 (1990): 290.

7. Ibid., 290–92.

8. Amy Gurowitz, "Mobilizing International Norms: Domestic Actors, Immigrants, and the Japanese State," *World Politics* 51, no. 3 (1999): 413–45.

9. Ikenberry and Kupchan, "Socialization and Hegemonic Power," 290.

10. Stephen Krasner, "Structural Causes and Regime Consequences: Regimes as Intervening Variables," in *International Regimes*, ed. Stephen Krasner (Ithaca, NY: Cornell University Press, 1983), 2.

11. Some scholars regard "behavioral norms" as a belief in nonviolent cooperation. I deem it improper to exclude all violent interactions between states from the concept of the "behavioral norms." From a historical perspective, military cooperation between states might also correspond to international norms. That is why there is a distinction between just and unjust wars.

12. Xun Kuang, "9: Wang Zhi," in *Xunzi Quanyi*, 146.

13. An Guozheng, Guo Chongli, and Yang Zhenwu, eds., *Shijie Zhishi Da Cidian* [Dictionary of world knowledge] (Beijing: World Affairs, 1998), 1542.

14. Dai De, ed. "Da Dai Li Ji: Yong Bing" [The elder Dai's record of rites: Employing troops], in *Zhongguo Xianqin Guojiajian Zhengzhi Sixiang Xuandu* [Pre-Qin Chinese thoughts on foreign relations], ed. Yan Xuetong and Xu Jin (Shanghai: Fudan University Press, 2008), 236.

15. Laura Smith-Spark and Barbara Starr, "US Investigates Possible Russia Role in Syria Chemical Attack," CNN, http://edition.cnn.com/2017/04/07/world/syria-military-strikes-donald-trump-russia/.

16. An Guozheng, Guo Chongli, and Yang Zhenwu, *Shijie zhishi Zhishi Da Cidian*, 728.

17. Buzan and Little, *International Systems in World History*, 190–240.

18. Wendt, *Social Theory of International Politics*, 268.

19. Gilpin, *War and Change in World Politics*, 34.

20. Hong Liangji, *Chunqiu Zuo Zhuan Gu*, 386.

21. Chen Weihua, "UN Puts New Sanctions on North Korea," *China Daily*, March 3, 2016, http://usa.chinadaily.com.cn/epaper/2016-03/03/content_23722823.htm.

22. Li Tiecheng, *Lianheguo de Licheng* [The history of the United Nations] (Beijing: Beijing Language and Culture University Press, 1993), 647.

23. *Shijie Zhishi Nianjian 1991/92* (World affairs yearbook 1991/92) (Beijing: World Affairs, 1992), 1–4.

24. Li Weiqi, *Guo Yu Zhanguo Ce* [History of the State of Lu and stratagems of warring states] (Changsha: Yuelu History, 1988), 12n122.

25. Ibid., 180.

26. Ibid.

27. Hong Liangji, *Chunqiu Zuo Zhuan Gu*, 191.

28. Xun Kuang, "11: Wang Ba," in *Xunzi Quanyi*, 203.

29. Lin Pinshi, *Lüshi Chunqiu Jin Zhu Jin Yi* [Current interpretation and translation of Springs and Autumns of Master Lüh] (Taibei: Taiwan Commercial Book, 2005), 174.

30. University of Taiwan Three Troops, *Zhongguo Lidai Zhanzheng Shi* [Chinese war history] (Beijing: China CITIC, 2012), 31. Although it is debatable whether the Xia was a tribe or a state, there has been no challenge to the memory of the wars between King Yu of Xia and the three Miao tribes located in the West of China.

31. Zhou Caizhu and Qi Ruirui, *Mozi Quanyi* [Full translation of *Mozi*] (Guiyang: Guizhou People's, 1995), 149.

32. Li Weiqi, *Guo Yu Zhanguo Ce*, 49.

33. Working Group on the Assessment of Strategic Environment of Russia, "Eluosi Qiangshi Jueqi Shuping" [On Russia's forceful rise], *Xiandai Guoji Guanxi* [Contemporary International Relations], no. 2 (2009): 19–24.

34. Zhu Feng, "E Ge Chongtu de Guoji Zhengzhi Jiedu" [An Interpretation of the Russia-Georgia conflict from the perspective of international politics], *Xiandai Guoji Guanxi* [Contemporary International Relations], no. 11 (2008): 6–12.

35. An Guozheng, Guo Chongli, and Yang Zhenwu, *Shijie Zhishi Da Cidian*, 227.

36. Wendt, *Social Theory of International Politics*, 249–50.

37. Ibid., 257–58.

38. Ibid., 250–51.

39. University of Taiwan Three Troops, *Zhongguo Lidai Zhanzheng Shi*, 42n62.

40. An Guozheng, Guo Chongli, and Yang Zhenwu, *Shijie Zhishi Da Cidian*, 155n637.

41. Robert J. Art, *Meiguo Da Zhanlue* [A Grand Strategy for America], trans. Guo Shuyong (Beijing: Peking University Press, 2005), 88–94.

Chapter 6. International Mainstream Values

1. Arthur M. Schlesinger, *The Coming of the New Deal: 1933–1935, the Age of Roosevelt* (New York: Houghton Mifflin, 2003), 186–88.

2. Jamie Peck, "Remaking Laissez-Faire," *Progress in Human Geography* 32, no. 1 (2008): 3–43.

3. Susanne Soederberg, "From Neoliberalism to Social Liberalism: Situating the National Solidarity Program within Mexico's Passive Revolutions," *Latin American Perspectives* 28, no. 3 (2008): 104–23. See also Herbert Kitschelt, "Formation of Party Cleavages in Post-Communist Democracies: Theoretical Propositions," *Party Politics* 1, no. 4 (1995): 447–72.

4. Clause 2, article 1 of chapter I: "Purposes and Principles of the UN Charter," http://www.un.org/en/sections/un-charter/chapter-i/index.html, retrieved on September 11, 2017.

5. Francis Fukuyama, "The End of History?," *National Interest*, no. 16 (1989): 4.

6. Jeffrey Tucker, "Trumpism: The Ideology," *Beautiful Anarchy*, July 14, 2015, https://tucker.liberty.me/trumpism-the-ideology/.

7. Tony Blair, "Is Democracy Dead? Tony Blair: For True Democracy, the Right to Vote Is Not Enough," *New York Times*, December 4, 2014, www.nytimes.com/2014/12/04/opinion/tony-blair-is-democracy-dead.html; Francis Fukuyama, "The Decay of American Political Institutions," *American Interest*, December 8, 2013, https://www.the-american-interest.com/2013/12/08/the-decay-of-american-political-institutions/.

8. Yoni Appelbaum, "Is the American Idea Doomed?," *Atlantic*, November 2017, https://www.theatlantic.com/magazine/archive/2017/11/is-the-american-idea-over/540651/.

9. Catherine Rampell, "Trump's Good Political Timing: Younger Americans Are Shunning Democracy," *Washington Post*, August 15, 2016, https://www.washingtonpost.com/opinions/donald-trumps-good-political-timing/2016/08/15/21a0e264-6301-11e6-96c0-37533479f3f5_story.html?utm_term=.b45d52ca32bd.

10. Appelbaum, "Is the American Idea Doomed?"

11. Neil Howe, "Are Millennials Giving Up on Democracy?," *Forbes*, October 31, 2017, https://www.forbes.com/sites/neilhowe/2017/10/31/are-millennials-giving-up-on-democracy/#759224152be1.

12. Ibid.

13. Keith A. Spencer, "A Wrestler Called "The Progressive Liberal" Is Riling Appalachian Crowds, but the Sport Is a Mirror for Politics throughout America,'

Salon, June 30, 2017, https://www.salon.com/2017/06/29/the-progressive-liberal
-wrestler/; Randall Smith, "Liberal Progressivism's Presumption," *For Public and
Tradition*, July 5, 2017, http://angelqueen.org/2017/07/05/liberal-progressivisms
-presumption/; Justin Campbell, "Liberal or Progressive? You Can't Be Both,"
Spectator, September 20, 2017, https://www.spectator.com.au/2017/09/liberal
-or-progressive/.

14. Howe, "Are Millennials Giving Up On Democracy?"

15. Mark L. Haas and David W. Lesch, "Uprising in the Arab World: Tyranny,
Anarchy, and (Perhaps) Democracy," in *The Arab Spring: The Hope and Reality of
the Uprisings*, ed. Mark L. Haas and David W. Lesch (Boulder, CO: Westview,
2017), 1–10.

16. Seung-Whan Choi and Patrick James, "Are US Foreign Policy Tools Effective in Proving Human Rights Conditions?," *Chinese Journal of International Politics*
10, no. 3 (Autumn 2017): 350.

17. Appelbaum, "Is the American Idea Doomed?"

18. Peter Harris, "China in British Politics: Western Unexceptionalism in the
Shadow of China's Rise," *Chinese Journal of International Politics* 10, no. 3 (Autumn
2017): 242.

19. Christian Reus-Smit, "Cultural Diversity and International Order," *International Organization* 71, no. 4 (Fall 2017): 881.

20. Kevin Rudd, "The West Isn't Ready for the Rise of China," *New Statesman*,
July 11, 2012, https://www.newstatesman.com/politics/international-politics
/2012/07/kevin-rudd-west-isnt-ready-rise-china.

21. Xi Jinping, "Juesheng Quanmian Jiancheng Xiaokang Shehui, Duoqu Xin
Shidai Zhongguo Tese Shehuizhuyi Weida Shengli" [Secure a decisive victory in
building a moderately prosperous society in all respects and strive for the great
success of socialism with Chinese characteristics for a new era], *Renmin Ribao*
[People's Daily], October 28, 2017, 2.

22. Hou Lulu, "Fazhan de Zhongguo Jiang Wei Shijie Dailai Gengduo Jiyu"
[Developed China will bring about more opportunities to the world], *Renmin
Ribao* [People's Daily], February 2, 2018, 3.

23. Xi Jinping, "Juesheng Quanmian Jiancheng Xiaokang Shehui, Duoqu Xin
Shidai Zhongguo Tese Shehuizhuyi Weida Shengli," 4.

24. Hu Jintao, "Zai Zhonggong Shiliujie Sizhongquanhui Shang de Gongzuo
Baogao" [Report on the fourth plenary session of the Sixteenth Party Congress]
(Beijing: Central Committee Archive, 2006), 247.

25. Robert Kuttner, "Taking Bannon's Economic Nationalism Seriously,"
American Prospect, August 21, 2017, http://prospect.org/article/taking-bannons
-economic-nationalism-seriously.

26. For instance, both Barack Obama and Donald Trump criticized NATO's
free riders, notwithstanding their many differences in political opinions. For relevant news, see Mark Landler, "Obama Criticizes the 'Free Riders' among America's Allies," *New York Times*, March 10, 2016, https://www.nytimes.com/2016/03
/10/world/middleeast/obama-criticizes-the-free-riders-among-americas

-allies.html; see also Glenn Kessler, "Trump's Claim That the U.S. Pays the 'Lion's Share' for NATO," *Washington Post*, March 30, 2016, https://www.washingtonpost .com/news/fact-checker/wp/2016/03/30/trumps-claim-that-the-u-s-pays-the -lions-share-for-nato/?utm_term=.a3b3e3e5c2c8.

27. Yan Xuetong, "From Keeping a Low Profile to Striving for Achievement," 165–70.

28. Cheng Xiangyang, Zhang Xinmin, Jiang Qing, and Baixue, "Wangdao yu Xianjin Zhongguo zhi Waijiao: Gaizao Wushi Wangdao Waijiao Guweijinyong" [The principle of humane authority and China's diplomacy today: Reforming pragmatic humane authority diplomacy by making the past serve the present], Ifeng. com, April 15, 2011, http://culture.ifeng.com/huodong/special/wangdaoluntan /shendu/detail_2011_04/15/5769768_0.shtml; Sun Ru, "Tuijin 'Wangdao' Waijiao Zhengdang Qishi" [It is time to adopt humane authority diplomacy), *Huanqiu Shibao* [Global Times], April 1, 2013, http://opinion.huanqiu.com/opinion_world /2013-01/3486363.html.

29. The State Council Information Office of the People's Republic of China, *Zhongguo de Heping Fazhan* [China's peaceful development] (Beijing: People's Publishing House, 2011), 24.

30. Qian Tong, "Xi Jinping Zai Zhoubian Waijiao Gongzuo Zuotanhui Shang Fabiao Zhongyao Jianghua" [Xi Jinping delivers an important speech at the Conference on Diplomatic Work toward Surrounding Countries], *Renmin Ribao* [People's Daily], October 26, 2013, 1.

31. Xi Jinping, "Juesheng Quanmian Jiancheng Xiaokang Shehui, Duoqu Xin Shidai Zhongguo Tese Shehuizhuyi Weida Shengli," 5.

32. Wang Yi, "Exploring the Path of Major-Country Diplomacy with Chinese Characteristics," *Foreign Affairs Journal*, no. 10 (Autumn 2013): 14.

33. C. Fred Bergsten, "A Partnership of Equals: How Washington Should Respond to China's Economic Challenge," *Foreign Affairs*, July/August 2008, https:// www.foreignaffairs.com/articles/asia/2008-06-01/partnership-equals; Niall Ferguson, "Not Two Countries, but One: Chimerica," *Telegraph*, March 4, 2007, 12:01 a.m. GMT, https://www.telegraph.co.uk/comment/personal-view/3638174/Not -two-countries-but-one-Chimerica.html.

34. Appelbaum, "Is the American Idea Doomed?"

35. Payman Yazdani, "Prof. Baker: US Withdrawal from International Treaties, Opportunity for China, Iran," MEHR News Agency, October 25, 2017, 10:36 a.m., https://en.mehrnews.com/news/128939/US-withdrawal-from-intl-treaties -opportunity-for-China-Iran.

36. Xi Jinping, "Juesheng Quanmian Jiancheng Xiaokang Shehui, Duoqu Xin Shidai Zhongguo Tese Shehuizhuyi Weida Shengli," 3.

37. Ibid., 4.

38. Tan Yihua, "Wang Qishan Canjia Dang de Shijiuda Hunansheng Daibiaotuan Taolun" [Wang Qishan attending the discussion of Hunan delegation of the Nineteenth Party Congress], ifeng news, Sichuan News Net, October 19, 2017, http://news.ifeng.com/a/20171019/52708819_0.shtml.

39. Zhonghua Renmin Gongheguo Xianfa (Constitution of the People's Re-

public of China), People.com, March 22, 2018, http://sz.people.com.cn/n2/2018 /0322/c202846-31369478.html.

40. *Summary of the 2018 National Defense Strategy of the United States of America: Shaping the American Military's Competitive Edge* (Washington, DC: Department of Defense, 2018), 9, https://www.defense.gov/Portals/1/Documents/pubs /2018-National-Defense-Strategy-Summary.pdf.

41. Xi Jinpin, "Xieshou Jianshe Gengjia Meihao de Shijie: Zai Zhongguo Gongchandang yu Shijie Zhengdang Gaoceng Duihuahui Shang de Zhuzhi Jianghua" (Joining hands to establish a better world: Speech at CPC in Dialogue with World Political Parties High-Level Meeting), Central Government of the PRC, http://www.gov.cn/xinwen/2017-12/01/content_5243852.htm.

42. Kishore Mahbubani, "How Strongmen Coopted Democracy," *New York Times*, September 13, 2017, https://www.nytimes.com/2017/09/13/opinion /strongman-world-democracy.html?mcubz=0&_r=1.

43. Keren Yarhi-Milo, "After Credibility: American Foreign Policy in the Trump Era," *Foreign Affairs*, January/February 2018, 68–69.

44. Jackie Wattles and Jethro Mullen, "Trump Threatens China with New $100 Billion Tariff Plan," CNNMoney, April 6, 2018, 8:01 a.m., http://money.cnn.com /2018/04/05/news/trump-tariff-china-trade-war/index.html; Jethro Mullen, "China's Xi Jinping Says Tariffs on Car Imports Will Be Cut This Year," CNNMoney, April 10, 2018: 4:28 a.m., http://money.cnn.com/2018/04/09/news/economy /china-xi-jinping-economy-trade/index.html.

45. "24 Agreements Signed between India and China during PM Modi's Visit," NDTV.com, May 15, 2015, 10:34, https://www.ndtv.com/cheat-sheet/24 -agreements-signed-between-india-and-china-during-pm-modis-visit-763246.

46. Steve George and Anish Gawande, "China and India in War of Words over Bhutan Border Dispute," CNN, August 25, 2017, https://edition.cnn.com/2017 /07/03/asia/bhutan-india-border-dispute/index.html.

47. Joe McDonald, "China Retaliates against Proposed US Tariffs by Targeting $50B in American Soybeans, Other Goods," NBCDFW.com, April 4, 2018, 3:57 a.m., https://www.nbcdfw.com/news/national-international/China-Vows-Same -Strength-Measures-Against-US-Tariffs-478730033.html.

48. Efe Tanay, "What's behind Turkey's Sudden Rapprochement with Russia?," Russia Direct, August 10, 2016, http://www.russia-direct.org/opinion/whats -behind-turkeys-sudden-rapprochement-russia.

49. Sandy Fitzgerald, "North Korea Media Mocks Pence for Not Interacting with Delegation," *Newsmax*, February 17, 2018, 1:02 p.m., https://www.newsmax .com/newsfront/north-korea-vice-president-mike-pence-olympics-kim-yo-jong /2018/02/17/id/843971/.

50. "North Korea Canceled Planned Meeting with US Vice President, Mike Pence," *Telegraph*, February 21, 2018, 1:38 a.m., https://www.telegraph.co.uk /news/2018/02/21/north-korea-canceled-planned-meeting-us-vice-president -mike/.

51. "Bisai Shuide Heanniu Da, Shijie Benbugai Zheyang" [Competing for whose nuclear weapon is larger, the world should not be like that], *Huanqiu Shibao*

[Global Times], January 4, 2018, 1:01 a.m., http://opinion.huanqiu.com/editorial /2018-01/11495595.html.

52. "Chuancheng Youyi Shi Zhongchao Gongtong Shouyi de Da Zhanlue" [Inheriting China-DPRK friendships is a grand strategy benefiting to both sides], *Huanqiu Shibao* [Global Times], March 28, 2018, 11:45 a.m., http://opinion .huanqiu.com/editorial/2018-03/11704002.html.

53. Zhang Qiaosu, "Xi Jinping Tong Jin Zhengen Juxing Huitan" [Xin Jinping and Kim Jong-un having a meeting], www.news.cn, January 3, 2018, http://www .xinhuanet.com/world/2018-03/28/c_1122600292.htm; Harry J. Kazianis, "The North Korea–China Summit: Did Kim Ask Xi for Help with His Trump Meeting? Here's What May Have Happened," Foxnews, March 28, 2018, http://www .foxnews.com/opinion/2018/03/28/north-korea-china-summit-did-kim-ask-xi -for-help-with-his-trump-meeting-here-s-what-may-have-happened.html.

54. Christopher Scoll, "N Korean Media Coverage of Kim's Trip to Beijing, in English," *Asia Times*, March 31, 2018 4:43 a.m., http://www.atimes.com/article /n-korean-media-coverage-kims-trip-beijing-english/.

55. Nicole Gaouette and Elizabeth Joseph, "UN Adopts Tough New Sanctions on North Korea," CNN, updated 13:27 GMT, December 24, 2017, https://edition .cnn.com/2017/12/22/politics/un-us-north-korea-resolution/index.html; "Russian Tankers Have Smuggled Oil to North Korea, a Breach of U.N. Sanctions," NBC News, December 30, 2017, 5:53 a.m., https://www.nbcnews.com/news/world/ russian-tankers-have-smuggled-oil-north-korea-breach-u-n-n833531.

56. Reus-Smit, "Cultural Diversity and International Order," 855.

57. John Rawls, *A Theory of Justice* (Cambridge, MA: Belknap Press of Harvard University Press, 1971), 3, 7, and 8.

58. Reinhold Niebuhr, *The Nature and Destiny of Man: A Christian Interpretation; Human Nature* (Louisville: Westminster John Knox, 1996), 268.

59. For the detailed definition, see John E. Roemer, *Equality of Opportunity* (Cambridge, MA: Harvard University Press, 2000), 25–27.

60. Rosan Smits et al., "Revolution and Its Discontents: State, Factions and Violence in the New Libya," Conflict Research Unit, Clingendael Institute, September 2013, 40–55, https://www.clingendael.org/sites/default/files/pdfs/Libya %20-%20Revolution%20and%20its%20discontents.pdf.

61. Yao Tianchong and Yu Tianying, "'Gongtong Dan Youqubie Zeren' Chuyi" [Essay on the principle of common but different responsibility], *Shehui Kexue Jikan* [Social Science Journal], no. 1 (2011): 99–101, http://wenku.baidu.com/view /75135a8dd0d233d4b14e6989.html. Clause 3, article 4 of the UN Framework Convention on Climate Change states, "The developed country Parties and other developed Parties included in Annex II shall provide new and additional financial resources to meet the agreed full costs incurred by developing country Parties in complying with their obligations under Article 12, paragraph 1. They shall also provide such financial resources, including the transfer of technology needed by the developing country Parties to meet the agreed full incremental costs of implementing measures that are covered by paragraph 1 of this Article and that are agreed between a developing country Party and the international entity or entities referred to in Article 11, in accordance with that Article. The implementation of

these commitments shall take into account the need for adequacy and predictability in the flow of funds and the importance of appropriate burden sharing among the developed country Parties." https://unfccc.int/resource/docs/convkp/conveng.pdf.

62. See United Nations Framework Convention on Climate Change (1992), https://unfccc.int/resource/docs/convkp/conveng.pdf.

63. An Guozheng, Guo Chongli, and Yang Zhenwu, *Shijie Zhishi Da Cidian*, 953.

64. Graham Smith and Corinne Wales, "Citizens' Juries and Deliberative Democracy," *Political Studies* 48 (2000): 52.

65. Adam Przeworski and Fernando Limongi, "Modernization: Theories and Facts," *World Politics* 49 (1997): 155–83.

66. Peter Taylor, "Iraq War: The Greatest Intelligence Failure in Living Memory," *Telegraph*, March 18, 2013, http://www.telegraph.co.uk/news/worldnews/middleeast/iraq/9937516/Iraq-war-the-greatest-intelligence-failure-in-living-memory.html.

67. Rawls, *Theory of Justice*, 86.

68. Ibid., 85.

69. Han Xiaoming and Qing Mu, "Meimei: Xuliya Zhanzheng Daozhi le 21 Shiji Zui Yanzhong de Rendao Zainan" [American media says, the war in Syria is the largest humanitarian disaster in the 21st century], April 6, 2017, http://world.huanqiu.com/exclusive/2017-04/10430595.html.

70. Wang Changze, trans., "*Gaozi I.*" *Mencius* (Taiyuan: Shanxi Ancient Book, 2003), 183.

71. Graham Allison, "China vs. America: Managing the Next Clash of Civilizations," *Foreign Affairs*, September/October 2017, 84.

72. Francis Njubi Nesbitt, *Race for Sanctions: African Americans against Apartheid, 1946–1994* (Bloomington: Indiana University Press, 2004), 149.

73. Rawls, *Theory of Justice*, 60–61.

74. "Official Development Assistance," Organization for Economic Cooperation and Development (OECD), August 2016, http://www.un.org/esa/ffd/wp-content/uploads/2016/01/ODA_OECD-FfDO_IATF-Issue-Brief.pdf.

75. See Steve Paulson et al., "The Moral Animal: Virtue, Vice, and Human Nature," *Annals of the New York Academy of Sciences*, 2016, 52, http://onlinelibrary.wiley.com/doi/10.1111/nyas.13067/epdf.

76. Charles Horton Cooley, *Human Nature and the Social Order* (New Brunswick, NJ: Transaction, 2009), 422–23.

77. "Book XVI: Ji Shi, 'The Confucian Analects,'" *Zhonghua San Jing* [Three Chinese classical books], ed. Yao Youzhi and Yan Qiying (Hangzhou: Shanghai Culture, 2014), 46.

78. Cheng Keqin, "*Musilin de Wuzhi* Fengbo de Beihou" [Behind *Innocence of Muslims*], *Guangming Ribao* [Guangming Daily], September 22, 2012, http://epaper.gmw.cn/gmrb/html/2012-09/22/nw.D110000gmrb_20120922_5-08.htm?div=-1.

79. Lin Fengmin, "*Chali Zhoukan* Shijian Jiqi Youyin" [The event of *Charlie Hebdo* and its cause], *Xuexi Shibao* [Learning Times], January 12, 2015, A2.

80. Xun Kuang, "5: Fei Xiang," in *Xunzi Quanyi*, 73.

81. Allison, "China vs. America," 81.

82. Ibid.

83. White House, *National Security Strategy of the United States of America*, 25.

Chapter 7. Transformation of the International System

1. Yang Chengxu, "Zhongguo Yu Guoji Tixi" [China and the international system], in *Shijie Dashi Yu Zhongguo Heping Fazhan* [The world trend and China's peaceful development], ed. Xu Dunxin (Beijing: World Affairs, 2006), 54–55.

2. Zhao Guangcheng and Fu Ruihong, "Guoji Tixi de Jiegouxing Bianhua Xilun" [Analysis of structural changes in international system], *Xiandai Guoji Guanxi* [Contemporary International Relations], no. 8 (2011): 32.

3. Buzan and Little, *International System in World History*, 37–47.

4. Waltz, *Theory of International Politics*, 40.

5. Robert A. Mundell and Alexander K. Swoboda, eds., *Monetary Problems of the International Economy* (Chicago: University of Chicago Press, 1969), 343.

6. Stanley Hoffmann, "International Systems and International Law," in *The State of War—Essays on the Theory and Practice of International Politics*, ed. Stanley Hoffmann (New York: Praeger, 1965), 88–122.

7. David Kang, *East Asia before the West: Five Centuries of Trade and Tribute* (New York: Columbia University Press, 2010), 81.

8. Lin Limin, "G20 Jueqi Shi Guoji Tixi Zhuanxing de Qidian" [The rise of G20 is the starting point of the transformation of international systems], *Xiandai Guoji Guanxi* [Contemporary International Relations], no. 11, 2009, 36–38; Liu Ming, Huang Renwei, and Gu Yongxing, "Zhuanxing Zhong de Guoji Tixi: Zhongguo Yu Ge Zhuyao Liliang de Guanxi" [The international system in transformation: The relations between China and other major powers], *Guoji Wenti Yanjiu* [International Studies], no. 4 (2008): 19; Qin Yaqing, "Guoji Tixi Zhuanxing Ji Zhongguo Zhanlue Jiyuqi de Yanxu" [The transformation of international systems and the continuation of the period of China's strategic opportunities], *Xiandai Guoji Guanxi* [Contemporary International Relations], no. 4 (2009), 36.

9. He Yao, "Dangdai Guoji Tixi yu Zhongguo de Zhanlue Xuanze" [The Contemporary international systems and China's strategic choices], in *Guoji Huanjing Yu Zhongguo de Heping Fazhan* [International environment and China's peaceful development], ed. Institute of the World Economy and Politics of the Academy of Social Sciences of Shanghai (Beijing: Current Affairs, 2006), 3n6, n7; Tang Yongsheng and Li Dongwei, "Guoji Tixi Bianqian yu Zhongguo Guojia Anquan Chouhua" [Changes in international system and China's national security strategy], *Shijie Jingji yu Zhengzhi* [World Economy and Politics], no. 12 (2014): 29.

10. Gilpin, *War and Change in World Politics*, 40.

11. He categorizes the control structure of an international system into three forms: a single powerful state in control, bipolar structure, and balance of power among three or more states. Ibid., 29.

12. Ibid., 41–42.

13. Ibid., 41.

14. It would be a misunderstanding to assume that all states are of the same type in a given interstate/international system. For example, in the Huaxia area of East Asia during the Spring and Autumn period, as a royal state, the Zhou Dynasty coexisted with many vassal states, such as the states of Qin, Chu, Qi, Jin, Han, Lu, Zhao, Wei, and so on. In Europe, the Holy Roman Empire (962 to approximately 1806 CE) once existed simultaneously alongside various kingdoms, such as the Prussian Kingdom, the Kingdom of Bavaria, the Saxon Kingdom, the Dukedom of Wurttemberg, the Grand-Duchy of Baden, the Hessian Emirate, the Principality of Anhalt, the Elector of Mainz, and the Liberty of Bremen. At present, the United States is a national state while Saudi Arabia is monarchy, and the Vatican is a papal state.

15. Torbjorn Knutsen, *Guoji Guanxi Lilun Shi Daolun* [History of International Relations Theory], trans. Yu Wanli and He Zongqiang (Tianjin: Tianjin People's Publishing House, 2005), 139.

16. Stavrianos, *World since 1500*, 322n431, n457, n472.

17. Yang Kuan, *Zhanguo Shi* [History of warring states] (Shanghai: Shanghai People's Publishing House, 2003), 2.

18. Liu Debin, ed., *Guoji Guanxi Shi* [The history of the international relations] (Beijing: Higher Education, 2003), 26n27, n45; Hugo Krabbe, *Jindai Guojia Guannian* [Modern Concepts of the State], trans. Wang Jian (Beijing: Commercial, 1957), 1–24.

19. Liu Debin, *Guoji Guanxi Shi*, 24–25.

20. Ibid., 89.

21. Guan Zhong, "23: Ba Yan," 268.

22. Lebow, *Tragic Vision of Politics*, 311.

23. Wang Shengzu, ed. *Guoji Guanxi Shi 1871–1918* (History of international relations 1871–1918) (Beijing: World Affairs, 1995), 438–43.

24. Wang Shengzu, ed., *Guoji Guanxi Shi 1917–1929* [History of international relations 1917–1929] (Beijing: World Affairs, 1995), 118.

25. Li Keqiang, "Zhengfu Gongzuo Baogao" [Report on the work of the government], in *Shibada Yilai Zhongyao Wenxian Xuanbian (Shang)* [Selection of important documents since the Eighteenth Party Congress, vol. 1] (Beijing: Central Document, 2014), 856. In Chinese government documents, "*guoji tixi*" (international system) and "*guoji zhixu*" (international order) are used either alternatively or simultaneously because they are misunderstood as conveying the same meaning.

Chapter 8. Historical Cases of System Transformation

1. Yang Kuan, Xi Zhou Shi, 871.

2. He Maochun, *Zhongguo Waijiao Tongshi* [A general history of Chinese diplomacy] (Beijing: Social Science Academic, 1996), 13–14.

3. The five service system consists of a set of interstate norms whereby the Zhou King's capital city was at the center and its core and periphery extended a

good distance. The five-hundred-*li* area surrounding the capital city was called the *dian* ordinance, where various grains were planted, and which served as the king's supplier of provisions. The next encircling five-hundred-li area, called the *hou* ordinance, mainly provided the king with labor and territorial protection. Around that was the twenty-five-hundred-li area called the *bin* ordinance, which contained the feudal lord states that made up China proper. Within this area, every five hundred li (1 li = .5 km) constituted one *qi*, the order comprising the *hou qi*, *dian qi*, *nan qi*, *cai qi*, and *wei qi*. These were mostly responsible for cultural education and military support. The next area was made up of the *yao* ordinance and the *huang* ordinance, each covering a one-thousand-li area, but their distance from the center is unclear. The *yao* ordinance was an order divided into two areas: the man ordinance and the *yi* ordinance, each covering five hundred li, governed under a similar political order but with reduced taxation, and the *huang* ordinance order was similarly divided into the *zhen* ordinance and the *fan* ordinance, each also covering five hundred li, governed by fundamental political systems and norms, and where the population mobility was high. There are nevertheless different explanations academically of the five service system; see also Ye Zicheng, *Chunqiu Shiqi de Zhongguo Waijiao Sixiang* [Chinese ideas and thoughts of diplomacy during the Spring-Autumn period] (Hong Kong: Hong Kong Social Science, 2003), 28; Yang Kuan, Xi Zhou Shi, 453; and the Shanghai Normal University Ancient Materials Research Team, *Guo Yu* [The chronicles of the State of Lu] (Shanghai: Shanghai International, 1978), 4.

4. Shanghai Normal University Ancient Materials Research Team, *Guo Yu*, 1–3.

5. There were military conflicts between the feudal vassals among themselves and between the feudal vassals and tribes during the leadership of King Wu and King Cheng, but they were much fewer than those that broke out after the accession of King Zhao. See He Maochun, *Zhongguo Waijiao Tongshi*, 23.

6. Ibid.

7. Yang Kuan, *Xi Zhou Shi*, 453.

8. Ibid.

9. Ibid., 840–41, 849.

10. Huang Yongtang, *Guo Yu Quanyi* [Full translation of *Guo Yu*] (Guiyuang: Guizhou People's Publishing House, 2009), 20; Yang Kuan, Xi Zhou Shi, 842.

11. Yang Kuan, Xi Zhou Shi, 850.

12. Gu Derong and Zhu Shunlong: *Chunqiu Shi* [History of the Spring and Autumn period] (Shanghai: Shanghai People's Publishing House, 2001), 41–42; Yang Kuan, Xi Zhou Shi, 851.

13. Gu Derong and Zhu Shunlong, *Chunqiu Shi*, 21; Yang Kuan, Xizhou Shi, 2.

14. Kalevi J. Holsti, *International Politics: A Framework for Analysis* (Englewood Cliffs, NJ: Prentice Hall, 1995), 33.

15. Hong Liangji, *Chunqiu Zuo Zhuan Gu*, 285.

16. Gu Derong and Zhu Shunlong, *Chunqiu Shi*, 85.

17. Yang Kuan, *Xi Zhou Shi*, 2.

18. Ibid., 278–83.

19. Ibid., 303.

20. Ibid., 719.

21. Ibid., 457–58.

22. Stavrianos, *World since 1500*, 322n431, n457, n472.

23. From 1902 to 1911, Britain's military expenses reached a peak, those of the next largest military powers of Russia, Germany and France each constituting only two-thirds to three-fourths of it, and those of Austria-Hungary and Italy less than half. After the United States won the Spanish-American War in 1898 and Japan won the Russo-Japanese War in 1905, the power of both increased greatly but could by no means compare with that of England. See Wang Shengzu, ed., *Guoji Guanxi Shi 1871–1918* [History of international relations 1871–1918] (Beijing: World Affairs, 1995), 357–58.

24. Ibid., 329.

25. Ibid., 334.

26. Ibid., 410.

27. Ibid., 402–3.

28. The Spanish-American War resulted in Spain ceding Cuba, Puerto Rico, the West Indies, Guam, and the Philippines to the United States. The Anglo-Boer War resulted in the Boer Republics losing their independence and agreeing to come under the sovereignty of the British Crown; the British Empire established the Union of South Africa by bringing together the Cape, Natal, Transvaal, and the Orange Free State. The Russo-Japanese War saw Russia give its leasehold rights to Port Arthur and the southern part of Sakhalin Island and nearby islands to Japan and caused it to recognize Korea as part of the Japanese sphere of interest. In 1910, Japan went on to officially annex Korea. The Italo-Turkish War resulted in Turkey recognizing Tripolitania and Cyrenaica as Italian possessions. After the First Balkan War, the Ottoman Empire gave up all its land on the European continent that ran west of a line drawn from the Aegean Sea to the Black Sea (with the exception of Albania) and the Island of Crete to Montenegro, Serbia, Bulgaria, and Greece. After the Second Balkan War, Greece and Serbia split Macedonia, the Ottomans regained Adrianople, and Bulgaria lost the land that it had won in the First Balkan War and also some of its own territory. The eight Allied powers invasion of China saw Russia's occupation of China's three northeastern provinces, and the obtaining of Russian, Italian, British, and Austro-Hungarian concessions in Tianjin. After the second Moroccan crisis, the French army occupied Algerian territory. After the Agadir incident, France handed over 27,500 square kilometers of its possessions in the Congo to Germany, while Germany ceded a piece of land east of Lake Chad to France. Following the Russian invasion of Mongolia, Russia occupied Chinese territory in Tannu Uriankhai. See Wang Shengzu, ed., *Guoji Guanxi Shi 1871–1918*, 274–394.

29. The 1922 Covenant of Naval Arms Limitation between the United States, England, France, Italy, and Japan stipulated that the ratio of their navies would be 5 to 5 to 3 to 1.75 to 1.75. See Wang Shengzu, *Guoji Guanxi Shi 1871–1918*, 118.

30. Ibid., 90–91.

31. Ibid., 84–91.

32. An Guozheng, Guo Chongli, and Yang Zhenwu, *Shijie Zhishi Da Cidian*, 549.

33. Wang Shengzu, ed., *Guoji Guanxi Shi 1929–1939* [History of international relations 1929–1939] (Beijing: World Affairs, 1995), 59–62, 83–86, 148–49, 184–87, 277–380; Wang Shengzu, ed., *Guoji Guanxi Shi 1939–1945* [The history of international relations 1939–1945] (Beijing: World Affairs, 1995), 4–5.

34. An Guozheng, Guo Chongli, and Yang Zhenwu, *Shijie Zhishi Da Cidian*, 984.

35. Wang Shengzu, ed., *Guoji Guanxi Shi 1949–1959* [History of international relations 1949–1959] (Beijing: World Affairs, 1995), 309–10; Wang Shengzu, *Guoji Guanxi Shi 1960–1969* [History of international relations 1960–1969] (Beijing: World Affairs, 1995), 105–7.

36. Xun Kuang, "11: Wang Ba," in *Xunzi Quanyi*, 206.

37. *Shijie Zhishi Nianjian 1991/92*, 846.

38. "UK, US Reject Catalonia's Independence from Spain," *Rediffnews*, October 27, 2017, http://news.rediff.com/commentary/2017/oct/27/uk-us-reject-catalonias-independence-from-spain/f0f76bb3f0ce01d42fd00e5503091738; "Europe Rejects Catalonia's Independence," En.Hberler.com, October 27, 2017, https://en.haberler.com/update-europe-rejects-catalonia-s-independence-1123115/.

39. Stockholm International Peace Research Institute, *SIPRI Nianjian: Junbei Caijun he Guoji Anquan* [SIPRI Yearbook 2003: Armaments, Disarmament and National Security], trans. China Association for Arms Control and Disarmament (Beijing: World Affairs, 2004), 127–30. The definition of a large military conflict is a military conflict in which at least one thousand armed people are killed; see ibid., 140.

40. Yuen Foong Khong, "The American Tributary System," *Chinese Journal of International Politics* 6, no. 1 (Spring 2013), 6.

Chapter 9. Conclusion

1. "2017 Nian Caifu Shijie 500 Qiang Paihangbang" [Fortune 500 Ranking of 2017], *Fortune China*, July 20, 2017, http://www.fortunechina.com/fortune500/c/2017-07/20/content_286785.htm.

SELECTED BIBLIOGRAPHY

Allison, Graham. "China vs. America: Managing the Next Clash of Civilizations." *Foreign Affairs*, September/October 2017, 80–89.

———. *Destined for War: Can America and China Escape Thucydides's Trap?* Boston: Houghton Mifflin Harcourt, 2017.

Amstutz, Mark R. *International Ethics: Concepts, Theories, and Cases in Global Politics*. 2nd ed. Lanham, MD: Rowman and Littlefield, 2005.

An Guozheng, Guo Chongli, and Yang Zhenwu, eds. *Shijie Zhishi Da Cidian* [Dictionary of world knowledge]. Beijing: World Affairs, 1998.

Appelbaum, Yoni. "Is the American Idea Doomed?" *Atlantic*, November 2017. https://www.theatlantic.com/magazine/archive/2017/11/is-the-american-idea-over/540651/.

Art, Robert J. *Meiguo Da Zhanlue* [A grand strategy for America]. Trans. Guo Shuyong. Beijing: Peking University Press, 2005.

Baker, Peter. "Souring World Views of Trump Open Doors for China and Russia." *New York Times*, January 18, 2018. http://www.wral.com/souring-world-views-of-trump-open-doors-for-china-and-russia/17268302/.

Beckley, Michael. "The Myth of Entangling Alliances: Reassessing the Security Risks of U.S. Defense Pacts." *International Security* 39, no. 4 (Spring 2015): 7–48.

Bergsten, C. Fred. "A Partnership of Equals: How Washington Should Respond to China's Economic Challenge." *Foreign Affairs*, July/August 2008. https://www.foreignaffairs.com/articles/asia/2008-06-01/partnership-equals.

"Bisai Shuide Heanniu Da, Shijie Benbugai Zheyang" [Competing for whose nuclear weapon is larger, the world should not be like that]. *Huanqiu Shibao* [Global Times], January 4, 2018. http://opinion.huanqiu.com/editorial/2018-01/11495595.html.

Börzel, Tanja A., and Frank Schimmelfennig. "Coming Together or Drifting Apart? The EU's Political Integration Capacity in Eastern Europe." *Journal of European Public Policy* 24, no. 2 (2017): 278–96.

Brostrom, Jannika. "Morality and the National Interest: Toward a 'Moral Realist' Research Agenda." *Cambridge Review of International Affairs* 28, no. 4 (2015): 1624–39.

Bull, Hedley. *The Anarchical Society: A Study of Order in World Politics*. 3rd ed. Beijing: Palgrave Macmillan, 2002.

Buzan, Barry, and Richard Little. *International Systems in World History: Remaking the Study of International Relations*. Oxford: Oxford University Press, 2000.

Carr, Edward Hallett. *The Twenty Years' Crisis, 1919–1939: An Introduction to the Study of International Politics*. New York: Harper and Row, 1964.

Choi, Seung-Whan, and Patrick James. "Are US Foreign Policy Tools Effective in Proving Human Rights Conditions?" *Chinese Journal of International Politics* 10, no. 3 (Autumn 2017): 331–56.

Cooley, Charles Horton. *Human Nature and the Social Order*. New Brunswick, NJ: Transaction, 2009.

Castles, William R. "Expressions of American Foreign Policy." *World Affairs* 95, no. 1 (1932): 47–49.

"Chuancheng Youyi Shi Zhongchao Gongtong Shouyi de Da Zhanlue" [Inheriting China-DPRK friendships is a grand strategy benefiting to both sides]. Huanqiu Shibao [Global Times], March 28, 2018. http://opinion.huanqiu.com/editorial /2018-03/11704002.html.

Clough, Shepard B. *The Rise and Fall of Civilization*. New York: Columbia University Press, 1970.

Cope, Edward Meredith. An Introduction to Aristotle's Rhetoric: With Analysis Notes and Appendices. London: Macmillan, 1867.

Cosmo, Nicola Di. *Ancient China and Its Enemies: The Rise of Nomadic Power in East Asian History*. Cambridge: Cambridge University Press, 2002.

Cui Gaowei, ed. *Li Ji* [The book of rites]. Shenyang: Liaoning Education, 2000.

Dai De, ed. "Da Dai Li Ji: Yong Bing" [The elder Dai's record of rites: Employing troops]. In *Zhongguo Xianqin Guojiajian Zhengzhi Sixiang Xuandu* [Pre-Qin Chinese thoughts on foreign relations], ed. Yan Xuetong and Xu Jin, 235–37. Shanghai: Fudan University Press, 2008.

De La Rochefoucauld, François. *Maximes et Reflexions Diverses*, ed. Jean Lafond, 2nd ed. Paris: Gallimard, 1976.

Dougherty, James E., and Robert L. Pfaltzgraff Jr. *Contending Theories of International Relations: A Comprehensive Survey*. New York: Addison Wesley Longman, 2001.

Fang Lianqing, Wang Bingyuan, and Liu Jinzhi. *Guoji Guanxi Shi (Zhanhou Juan)* [History of postwar international relations]. Beijing: Peking University Press, 2006.

Fang, Xiangming and Phaedra S. Corso. "Child Maltreatment, Youth Violence, and Intimate Partner Violence Developmental Relationships." *American Journal of Preventative Medicine* 33, no. 4 (2007): 281–90.

Ferguson, Niall. "Not Two Countries, but One: Chimerica." *Telegraph*, March 4. https://www.telegraph.co.uk/comment/personal-view/3638174/Not-two -countries-but-one-Chimerica.html.

Finnemore, Martha. "Constructing Norms of Humanitarian Intervention." In *The Culture of National Security: Norms and Identity in World Politics*, ed. Peter J. Katzenstein, 153–85. New York: Columbia University Press, 1996.

Finnemore, Martha, and Kathryn Sikkink. "International Norms Dynamics and Political Change." *International Organization* 52, no. 4 (1998): 887–917.

Fiorina, Morris, and Kenneth Shepsle. "Formal Theories of Leadership." In *Leadership and Politics: New Perspectives in Political Science*, ed. Bryan D. Jones, 17–40. Lawrence: University Press of Kansas, 1989.

Fitzgerald, Sandy. "North Korea Media Mocks Pence for Not Interacting with Delegation." *Newsmax*, February 17, 2018. https://www.newsmax.com/newsfront/north-korea-vice-president-mike-pence-olympics-kim-yo-jong/2018/02/17/id/843971/.

Fukuyama, Francis. "The End of History?" *National Interest*, no. 16 (1989): 3–18.

George, Steve, and Anish Gawande. "China and India in War of Words over Bhutan Border Dispute." CNN, August 25, 2017. https://edition.cnn.com/2017/07/03/asia/bhutan-india-border-dispute/index.html.

Gilpin, Robert. "The Richness of the Tradition of Political Realism." In *Neorealism and Its Critics*, ed. Robert O. Keohane, 301–21. New York: Columbia University Press, 1986.

———. *War and Change in World Politics*. Cambridge: Cambridge University Press, 1986.

Goh, Evelyn. *The Struggle for Order: Hegemony, Hierarchy and Transition in Post–Cold War East Asia*. Oxford: Oxford University Press, 2013.

Goldgeier, James M. "The U.S. Decision to Enlarge NATO: How, When, Why, and What Next." *Brookings Review* 17, no. 3 (1999): 18–21.

Gordon, Philip. "A Vision of Trump at War: How the President Could Stumble into Conflict." *Foreign Affairs* 96, no. 3 (2017): 10–19.

Graham, Jesse, Jonathan Haidt, Sena Koleva, Matt Motyl, Ravi Lyer, Sean P. Wojcik, and Peter H. Ditto. "Moral Foundations Theory: The Pragmatic Validity of Moral Pluralism." *Experimental Social Psychology* 47 (2012): 55–130. http://ssrn.com/abstract=2184440.

Gu Derong and Zhu Shunlong. *Chunqiu Shi* [History of the Spring and Autumn period]. Shanghai: Shanghai People's Publishing House, 2001.

Guan Zhong. "23: Ba Yan" [Book 23: On hegemony]. In *Guanzi Yizhu* [Translation of *Guanzi*], trans. Sheng Guangzhi, 268–81. Changchun: Jilin Literature and History, 1998.

Gurowitz, Amy. "Mobilizing International Norms: Domestic Actors, Immigrants, and the Japanese State." *World Politics* 51, no. 3 (1999): 413–45.

Haas, Mark L. and David W. Lesch, "Uprising in the Arab World: Tyranny, Anarchy, and (Perhaps) Democracy." In *The Arab Spring: The Hope and Reality of the Uprisings*, ed. Mark L. Haas and David W. Lesch. Boulder, CO: Westview. 2017.

Hamilton, Alexander, James Madison, and John Jay, eds. *The Federalist Papers*. New York: New American Library, 1961.

Harris, Peter. "China in British Politics: Western Unexceptionalism in the Shadow of China's Rise." *Chinese Journal of International Politics* 10, no. 3 (Autumn 2017): 241–67.

He Maochun. *Zhongguo Waijiao Tongshi* [A general history of Chinese diplomacy]. Beijing: Social Science Academic, 1996.

He Yao. "Dangdai Guoji Tixi Yu Zhongguo de Zhanlue Xuanze" [The contemporary international systems and China's strategic choices]. In *Guoji Huanjing Yu Zhongguo de Heping Fazhan* [International environment and China's peaceful development], ed. Institute of the World Economy and Politics of the Academy of Social Sciences of Shanghai, 3–22. Beijing: Current Affairs, 2006.

Hermann, Margaret G., and Joe D. Hagan. "International Decision Making Leadership Matters." *Foreign Policy*, no. 110, special ed. (Spring 1998): 110–28.

Hoffmann, Stanley. "International Systems and International Law." In *The State of War—Essays on the Theory and Practice of International Politics*, ed. Stanley Hoffmann, 88–122. New York: Praeger, 1965.

Hogeveen, Jeremy, Sukhvinder S. Obhi, and Michael Inzlicht. "Power Changes How the Brain Responds to Others." *Journal of Experimental Psychology: General* 143, no. 2 (2014): 755–62.

Holsti, Kalevi J. *International Politics: A Framework for Analysis*. Englewood Cliffs, NJ: Prentice Hall, 1995.

Hong Liangji. *Chunqiu Zuo Zhuan Gu* [Explanation of the chronicle of Zuo]. Beijing: Chinese Book, 1987.

Hou Lulu. "Fazhan de Zhongguo Jiang Wei Shijie Dailai Gengduo Jiyu" [Developed China will bring about more opportunities to the world] *Renmin Ribao* [People's Daily], February 2, 2018, 3.

Huang Yongtang. *Guo Yu Quanyi* [Full translation of *Guo Yu*]. Guiyuang: Guizhou People's Publishing House, 2009.

Ikenberry, G. John. "The Plot against American Foreign Policy: Can the Liberal Order Survive?" *Foreign Affairs* 96, no. 3 (2017): 1–7.

Ikenberry, G. John, and Charles A. Kupchan. "Socialization and Hegemonic Power." *International Organization* 44, no. 3 (1990): 283–315.

Jackson, Robert H., and Carl G. Rosberg. *Personal Rule in Black Africa: Prince, Autocrat, Prophet, Tyrant*. Berkeley: University of California Press, 1982.

Jacques, Martin. *When China Rules the World*, 2nd ed. London: Penguin Books, 2009.

Jepperson, Ronald L., Alexander Wendt, and Peter J. Katzenstein. "Norms, Identity, and Culture in National Security." In *The Culture of National Security: Norms and Identity in World Politics*, ed. Peter J. Katzenstein, 33–78. New York: Columbia University Press, 1996.

Kagan, Donald. *Pericles of Athens: The Birth of Democracy*. New York: Free Press, 1991.

Kagan, Robert. "The Benevolent Empire." *Foreign Policy*, no. 111 (Summer 1998): 24–35.

———. *The World America Made*. New York: Alfred A. Knopf, 2012.

Kang, David. *East Asia before the West: Five Centuries of Trade and Tribute*. New York: Columbia University Press, 2010.

Kazianis, Harry J. "The North Korea–China Summit: Did Kim Ask Xi for Help with His Trump Meeting? Here's What May Have Happened." Foxnews, March 28, 2018. http://www.foxnews.com/opinion/2018/03/28/north-korea-china -summit-did-kim-ask-xi-for-help-with-his-trump-meeting-here-s-what-may -have-happened.html.

Kegley, Charles W., and Gregory Raymond. "Networks of Intrigue? Realpolitik, Alliances and International Security." In *Reconstructing Realpolitik*, ed. Frank Whelon Wayman and Paul Francis Diehl, 185–98. Ann Arbor: University of Michigan Press, 1994.

Keltner, Dacher, Cameron Anderson, and Deborah H. Gruenfeld. "Power, Approach, and Inhibition." *Psychological Review* 110, no. 2 (2003): 265–84.

Kennedy, Paul. *The Rise and Fall of the Great Powers: Economic Change and Military Conflict from 1500 to 2000*. New York: Random House, 1987.

Keohane, Nannerl O. *Thinking about Leadership*. Princeton, NJ: Princeton University Press, 2010.

Keohane, Robert O., and Joseph S. Nye. *Power and Interdependence: World Politics in Transition*. Boston: Little, Brown, 1977.

Khong, Yuen Foong. "The American Tributary System." *Chinese Journal of International Politics* 6, no. 1 (Spring 2013): 1–48.

Kitschelt, Herbert. "Formation of Party Cleavages in Post-Communist Democracies: Theoretical Propositions." *Party Politics* 1, no. 4 (1995): 447–72.

Knutsen, Torbjorn. *Guoji Guanxi Lilun Shi Daolun* [History of international relations theory]. Trans. Yu Wanli and He Zongqiang. Tianjin: Tianjin People's Publishing House, 2005.

Krabbe, Hugo. *Jindai Guojia Guannian* [Modern concepts of the state]. Trans. Wang Jian. Beijing: Commercial, 1957.

Krasner, D. Stephen. *Defending the National Interests: Raw Materials Investments and U.S. Foreign Policy*. Princeton, NJ: Princeton University Press, 1978.

———. "Structural Causes and Regime Consequences: Regimes as Intervening Variables." In *International Regimes*, ed. Stephen Krasner, 1–22. Ithaca, NY: Cornell University Press, 1983.

Krugman, Paul. "The Myth of Asia's Miracle." *Foreign Affairs* 73, no. 6 (1994): 62–78.

Kuan, Eric Koo Peng. "The US as Benevolent Hegemon." *Asia Times*, September 23, 2004. http://www.atimes.com/atimes/Front_Page/FI23Aa01.html.

Lake, David A. *Hierarchy in International Relations*. Ithaca, NY: Cornell University Press, 2009.

Layman, C. Stephen. "God and the Moral Order." *Faith and Philosophy* 19, no. 3 (2002): 304–16.

Lebow, Richard Ned. *The Tragic Vision of Politics*. Cambridge: Cambridge University Press, 2003.

Leonard, Mark. *What Does China Think?* London: Fourth Estate, 2008.

Li Keqiang. "Zhengfu Gongzuo Baogao" [Report on the work of the government]. In *Shibada Yilai Zhongyao Wenxian Xuanbian (Shang)* [Selection of important documents since the Eighteenth Party Congress, vol. 1]. Beijing: Central Document, 2014.

Li Tiecheng. *Lianheguo de Licheng* [The history of the United Nations]. Beijing: Beijing Language and Culture University Press, 1993.

Li Weiqi. *Guo Yu Zhanguo Ce* [History of the State of Lu and stratagems of warring states]. Changsha: Yuelu History, 1988.

Lin Limin. "G20 Jueqi Shi Guoji Tixi Zhuanxing de Qidian" [The rise of G20 is the starting point of the transformation of international systems]. *Xiandai Guoji Guanxi* [Contemporary International Relations], no. 11 (2009): 36–38.

Lin Pinshi. *Lüshi Chunqiu Jin Zhu Jin Yi* [Current interpretation and translation of Springs and Autumns of Master Lüh]. Taibei: Taiwan Commercial Book, 2005.

Liu Debin, ed. *Guoji Guanxi Shi* [The history of international relations]. Beijing: Higher Education, 2003.

Liu Ming, Huang Renwei, and Gu Yongxing. "Zhuanxing Zhong de Guoji Tixi: Zhongguo Yu Ge Zhuyao Liliang de Guanxi" [The international system in transformation: The relations between China and other major powers]. *Gouji Wenti Yanjiu* [International Studies], no. 4 (2008): 18–25.

Mackinder, Halford John. *Democratic Ideals and Reality*. London: National Defense University, 1942.

Mahbubani, Kishore. "How Strongmen Coopted Democracy." *New York Times*, September 13, 2017. https://www.nytimes.com/2017/09/13/opinion/strongman-world-democracy.html?mcubz=0&_r=1.

McDonald, Joe. "China Retaliates against Proposed US Tariffs by Targeting $50B in American Soybeans, Other Goods." NBCDFW.com, April 4, 2018. https://www.nbcdfw.com/news/national-international/China-Vows-Same-Strength-Measures-Against-US-Tariffs-478730033.html.

Mearsheimer, John J. "The False Promise of International Institutions." *International Security* 19, no. 3 (1994/1995): 5–49.

———. *The Tragedy of Great Power Politics*. New York: W. W. Norton, 2001; updated ed., New York: W. W. Norton, 2014.

Mencius. "Gongsun Chou I." In *Mencius*, trans. Wang Changze. Taiyuan: Shanxi Ancient Book, 2003.

Mettler, Suzanne. "Democracy on the Brink: Protecting the Republic in Trump's America." *Foreign Affairs* 96, no. 3 (May/June 2017): 121–26.

Modelski, George, and William R. Thompson. "Long Cycles and Global War." In *Handbook of War Studies*, ed. Manus I. Midlarsky, 23–54. Boston: Unwin Hyman, 1989.

Monterio, Nuno P. *Theory of Unipolar Politics*. New York: Cambridge University Press, 2014.

Moon, Chung-in. *Zhongguo Jueqi Da Zhanlue: Yu Zhongguo Zhishi Jingying de Shenceng Duihua* [Grand strategies of China's rising: In-depth dialogue with leading Chinese intellectuals]. Trans. Li Chunfu. Beijing: World Affairs, 2011.

Morgenthau, Hans J. *Politics among Nations: The Struggle for Power and Peace*, ed. Kenneth W. Thompson and W. David Clinton, 7th ed. Boston: McGraw-Hill Higher Education, 2005.

Mundell, Robert A., and Alexander K. Swoboda, eds. *Monetary Problems of the International Economy*. Chicago: University of Chicago Press, 1969.

Murray, Williamson, Macgregor Knox, and Alvin Bernstein. *The Making of Strategy: Rulers, States, and War*. Cambridge: Cambridge University Press, 1994.

Nesbitt, Francis Njubi. *Race for Sanctions: African Americans against Apartheid, 1946–1994*. Bloomington: Indiana University Press, 2004.

Niebuhr, Reinhold. *Moral Man and Immoral Society: A Study in Ethics and Politics.* New York: Charles Scribner's Sons, 1932.

———. *The Nature and Destiny of Man: A Christian Interpretation; Human Nature.* Louisville: Westminster John Knox, 1996.

"North Korea Canceled Planned Meeting with US Vice President, Mike Pence." *Telegraph*, February 21, 2018. https://www.telegraph.co.uk/news/2018/02/21/north-korea-canceled-planned-meeting-us-vice-president-mike/.

Nye, Joseph S. *Bound to Lead: The Changing Nature of American Power.* New York: Basic Books, 1990.

———. *The Future of Power.* New York: Public Affairs, 2011.

———. *The Power to Lead.* Oxford: Oxford University Press, 2008.

Organski, A.F.K. *World Politics.* New York: Alfred A. Knopf, 1958.

Owen, David, and Jonathan Davidson. "Hubris Syndrome: An Acquired Personality Disorder? A Study of US Presidents and UK Prime Ministers over the Last 100 Years." *Brain: A Journal of Neurology*, February 12, 2009, 1–11.

Paulson, Steve, et al., "The Moral Animal: Virtue, Vice, and Human Nature." *Annals of the New York Academy of Sciences*, 2016, 39–56. http://onlinelibrary.wiley.com/doi/10.1111/nyas.13067/epdf.

Peck, Jamie. "Remaking Laissez-Faire." *Progress in Human Geography* 32, no. 1 (2008): 3–43.

Przeworski, Adam, and Fernandao Limongi. "Modernization: Theories and Facts." *World Politics* 49 (1997): 155–83.

Qi Haixia. "Laozi de Xiaoguo Guamin Sixiang" [Laozi's political idea of "small countries few inhabitants"]. In *Wangba Tianxia Sixiang Ji Qidi* [Thoughts of world leadership and implications], 48–68. Beijing: Shijie Zhishi Chubanshe [World Affairs], 2009.

Qin Yaqing. "Guoji Tixi Zhuanxing Ji Zhongguo Zhanlue Jiyuqi de Yanxu" [The transformation of international systems and the continuation of the period of China's strategic opportunities]. *Xiandai Guoji Guanxi* [Contemporary International Relations], no. 4 (2009): 35–37.

Rawls, John. *A Theory of Justice.* Cambridge, MA: Belknap Press of Harvard University Press, 1971.

Reid, Susan E. "Who Will Beat Whom? Soviet Popular Reception of the American National Exhibition in Moscow, 1959." *Russian and East European Studies* 9, no. 4 (2008): 885–904.

Reus-Smit, Christian. "Cultural Diversity and International Order." *International Organization* 71, no. 4 (Fall 2017): 851–85.

Roemer, John E. *Equality of Opportunity.* Cambridge, MA: Harvard University Press, 2000.

Rose, Gideon. "Neoclassical Realism and Theories of Foreign Policy." *World Politics* 51, no. 1 (1998): 144–72.

Ross, Robert S., and Øystein Tunsjø. "U.S.-China Relations: From Unipolar Hedging toward Bipolar Balancing." In *Strategic Adjustment and the Rise of China: Power and Politics in East Asia.* Ithaca, NY: Cornell University Press, 2017.

"Russian Tankers Have Smuggled Oil to North Korea, a Breach of U.N. Sanctions."

NBC News, December 30, 2017. https://www.nbcnews.com/news/world/russian-tankers-have-smuggled-oil-north-korea-breach-u-n-n833531.

Schelling, Thomas C. *The Strategy of Conflict*. Cambridge, MA: Harvard University Press, 1960.

Schlesinger, Arthur M. *The Coming of the New Deal: 1933–1935, the Age of Roosevelt*. New York: Houghton Mifflin, 2003.

Scoll, Christopher. "N Korean Media Coverage of Kim's Trip to Beijing, in English." *Asia Times*, March 31. http://www.atimes.com/article/n-korean-media-coverage-kims-trip-beijing-english/.

Shanghai Normal University Ancient Materials Research Team. *Guo Yu* [The Chronicles of the State of Lu]. Shanghai: Shanghai International, 1978.

Sheng Guangzhi. "Chapter 17: Bing Fa" [Methods of warfare]. In *Guanzi Yizhu* [Interpretation of Guanzi]. Changchun: Jilin Literature and History, 1998.

Shi Yongzhi. "Neisheng Waiwang Xinquan" [A new interpretation of *neisheng waiwang*]. *Zhouyi Yanjiu* [Studies on *Zhouyi*], no. 5 (2015): 88–89.

Shijie Zhishi Nianjian 1989/90 [World affairs yearbook 1989/90]. Beijing: World Affairs, 1990.

Shijie Zhishi Nianjian 1991/92 [World affairs yearbook 1991/92]. Beijing: World Affairs, 1992.

Smith, Graham, and Corinne Wales. "Citizens' Juries and Deliberative Democracy." *Political Studies* 48 (2000): 51–65.

Snyder, Richard C., H. W. Bruck, and Burton Sapin. "Decision-Making as an Approach to the Study of International Politics." In *Foreign Policy Decision-Making*, ed. Richard C. Snyder, H. W. Bruck, and Burton Sapin, rev. ed., 21–152. New York: Palgrave Macmillan, 2002.

Soederberg, Susanne. "From Neoliberalism to Social Liberalism: Situating the National Solidarity Program within Mexico's Passive Revolutions." *Latin American Perspectives* 28, no. 3 (2008): 104–23.

Stavrianos, Lefton S. *The World since 1500: A Global History*. London: Prentice-Hall, 1966.

Stockholm International Peace Research Institute. *SIPRI Yearbook 2003: Armaments, Disarmament and National Security*. Trans. China Association for Arms Control and Disarmament. Beijing: World Affairs, 2004.

Summary of the 2018 National Defense Strategy of the United States of America: Shaping the American Military's Competitive Edge. Washington, DC: Department of Defense, 2018. https://www.defense.gov/Portals/1/Documents/pubs/2018-National-Defense-Strategy-Summary.pdf.

Sun Xuefeng. "Rethinking East Asian Regional Order and China's Rise." *Japanese Journal of Political Science* 14, no. 1 (2013): 9–30.

———. *Zhongguo Jueqi Kunjing: Lilun Sikao yu Zhanlue Xuanze* [Dilemma of China's rise: Theoretical thinking and strategic selection]. Beijing: Social Science Academic, 2013.

Swan, Jonathan. "How Trumpworld Is Winging a Trade War." *Axios*, April 9, 2018. https://www.axios.com/winging-a-trade-war-donald-trump-d5a36398-22e8-4428-8a53-54095e04d759.html.

Tan Yihua. "Wang Qishan Canjia Dang de Shijiuda Hunansheng Daibiaotuan

Taolun" [Wang Qishan attending the discussion of Hunan delegation of the Nineteenth Party Congress]. Sichuan News Net, October 19, 2017. http://news .ifeng.com/a/20171019/52708819_0.shtml.

Tanay, Efe. "What's behind Turkey's Sudden Rapprochement with Russia?" Russia Direct, August 10, 2016. http://www.russia-direct.org/opinion/whats-behind -turkeys-sudden-rapprochement-russia.

Tang Yongsheng and Li Dongwei. "Guoji Tixi Bianqian Yu Zhongguo Guojia An-quan Zhanlue Chouhua" [Changes in international system and China's national security strategy]. *Shijie Jingji Yu Zhengzhi* [World Economy and Politics], no. 12 (2014): 27–36 and 155.

Tunsjø, Øystein, *The Return of Bipolarity in World Politics: China, the United States, and Geostructural Realism.* New York: Columbia University Press, 2018.

University of Taiwan Three Troops. *Zhongguo Lidai Zhanzheng Shi* [Chinese war history]. Beijing: China CITIC, 2012.

Walt, Stephen M. "The Collapse of the Liberal World Order." *Foreign Policy*, June 26, 2016. http://foreignpolicy.com/2016/06/26/the-collapse-of-the-liberal -world-order-european-union-brexit-donald-trump/.

Waltz, Kenneth N. *Theory of International Politics.* Reading: Addison-Wesley, 1983.

Wang Changze, trans. "*Gaozi I.*" *Mencius.* Taiyuan: Shanxi Ancient Book, 2003.

Wang Hongxu. "Xin Zhongguo Waijiao de Jiazhi Quxiang yu Zhanlue Xuanze" [The PRC's diplomatic value and strategic preference]. *Guoji Guanxi Xueyuan Xuebao* [Journal of the University of International Relations], no. 6 (2011): 9–16.

Wang Mingxiu, ed. *Shijie Zhishi Nianjian 1991/1992* [World knowledge yearbook 1991/1992]. Beijing: World Affairs, 1992.

Wang Shengzu, ed. *Guoji Guanxi Shi 1871–1918.* [History of international relations 1871–1918]. Beijing: World Affairs, 1995.

———. *Guoji Guanxi Shi 1917–1929* [History of international relations 1917–1929]. Beijing: World Affairs, 1995.

———. *Guoji Guanxi Shi 1929–1939* [History of international relations 1929–1939]. Beijing: World Affairs, 1995.

———. *Guoji Guanxi Shi 1939–1945* [History of international relations 1939–1945]. Beijing: World Affairs, 1995.

———. *Guoji Guanxi Shi 1949–1959* [History of international relations 1949–1959]. Beijing: World Affairs, 1995.

———. *Guoji Guanxi Shi 1960–1969* [History of international relations 1960– 1969]. Beijing: World Affairs, 1995.

Wang Yi. "Exploring the Path of Major-Country Diplomacy with Chinese Char-acteristics." *Foreign Affairs Journal*, no. 10 (Autumn 2013): 10–23.

Wattles, Jackie, and Jethro Mullen. "Trump Threatens China with New $100 Bil-lion Tariff Plan." CNNMoney, April 6, 2018. http://money.cnn.com/2018/04 /05/news/trump-tariff-china-trade-war/index.html.

Weber, Max. "Politics as a Vocation." In *From Max Weber: Essays in Sociology*, trans. and ed. H. H. Gerth and C. Wright Mills, 77–128. New York: Oxford University Press, 1958.

Weber, Max. *Theory of Social and Economic Organization*. Ed. Talcott Parsons. New York: Free Press of Glencoe, 1964.

Wendt, Alexander. *Social Theory of International Politics*. Cambridge: Cambridge University Press, 1999.

White House. *National Security Strategy of the United States of America*. Washington, DC: White House, December 2017. http://www.dtic.mil/dtic/tr/fulltext /u2/1043812.pdf.

Wike, Richard, et al. *U.S. Image Suffers as Publics around World Question Trump's Leadership*. Washington, DC: Pew Research Center, June 26, 2017.

Wohlforth, William. "Unipolar Stability: The Rules of Power Analysis." *Harvard International Review*, Spring 2007, 44–48.

Working Group on the Assessment of Strategic Environment of Russia. "Eluosi Qiangshi Jueqi Shuping" [On Russia's forceful rise]. *Xiandai Guoji Guanxi* [Contemporary International Relations], no. 2 (2009): 19–24.

Wu Jing. *Zhenguan Zhengyao* [Important political records of Zhenguan government]. Zhengzhou: Zhongzhou Ancient Book, 2008.

Xi Jinping. "Juesheng Quanmian Jiancheng Xiaokang Shehui, Duoqu Xin Shidai Zhongguo Tese Shehuizhuyi Weida Shengli" [Secure a decisive victory in building a moderately prosperous society in all respects and strive for the great success of socialism with Chinese characteristics for a new era]. *Renmin Ribao* [People's Daily], October 28, 2017, 1–5.

———. "Xieshou Jianshe Gengjia Meihao de Shijie: Zai Zhongguo Gongchandang yu Shijie Zhengdang Gaoceng Duihuahui Shang de Zhuzhi Jianghua" [Joining hands to establish a better world: Speech at CPC in dialogue with world political parties high-level meeting)]. Central Government of the PRC, 2017.

Xun Kuang. *Xunzi Quanyi* [Full translation of *Xunzi*]. Trans. Jiang Nanhua, Luo Shuqin, and Yang Huanqing. Guiyang: Guizhou People's Publishing House, 1995.

Yan Xuetong. *Zhongguo Guojia Liyi Fenxi* [Analysis of Chinese national interests]. Tianjin: Tianjin People's Publishing House, 1996.

———. *Ancient Chinese Thought, Modern Chinese Power*. Princeton, NJ: Princeton University Press, 2011.

———. "From Keeping a Low Profile to Striving for Achievement." *Chinese Journal of International Politics* 7, no. 2 (Summer 2014): 153–84.

———. "The Instability of China-US Relations." *Chinese Journal of International Politics* 3, no. 3 (Autumn 2010): 263–92.

———. "International Leadership and Norm Evolution." *Chinese Journal of International Politics* 4 (2011): 233–64.

———. "Wuxu Tixi Zhong de Guoji Zhixu" [International order in anarchic systems]. *Guoji Zhengzhi Kexue* [Quarterly Journal of International Politics] 1, no. 1 (2016): 1–32.

———. "The Shift of the World Center and Its Impact on the Change of the International System." *East Asia: An International Quarterly* 30, no. 4 (2013): 217–35.

Yan Xuetong and Qi Haixia. "Football Game Rather Than Boxing Match: China-US

Intensifying Rivalry Does Not Amount to Cold War." *Chinese Journal of International Politics* 5, no. 2 (2012): 105–27.

Yan Xuetong and Yang Yuan. *Gouji Guanxi Fenxi* [The analysis of international relations]. Beijing: Peking University Press, 2013.

Yang Chengxu. "Zhongguo Yu Guoji Tixi" [China and the international system]. In *Shijie Dashi Yu Zhongguo Heping Fazhan* [The world trend and China's peaceful development], ed. Xu Dunxin, 54–60. Beijing: World Affairs, 2006.

Yang Kuan. *Xizhou Shi* [History of West Zhou Dynasty]. Shanghai: Shanghai Publishing House, 2003.

———. *Zhanguo Shi* [History of warring states]. Shanghai: Shanghai Publishing House, 2003.

Yao Tianchong and Yu Tianying. "'Gongtong Dan Youqubie Zeren' Chuyi" [Essay on the principle of common but different responsibility]. *Shehui Kexue Jikan* [Social Science Journal], no. 1 (2011). http://wenku.baidu.com/view/75135a8dd0d233d4b14e6989.html.

Yarhi-Milo, Keren. "After Credibility: American Foreign Policy in the Trump Era." *Foreign Affairs*, January/February 2018, 68–69.

Yazdani, Payman. "Prof. Baker: US Withdrawal from International Treaties, Opportunity for China, Iran." MEHR News Agency, October 25, 2017. https://en.mehrnews.com/news/128939/US-withdrawal-from-intl-treaties-opportunity-for-China-Iran.

Ye Zicheng. *Chunqiu Shiqi de Zhongguo Waijiao Sixiang* [Chinese ideas and thoughts of diplomacy during the Spring-Autumn period]. Hong Kong: Hong Kong Social Science, 2003.

Yuen Foong Khong. "The American Tributary System." *Chinese Journal of International Politics* 6, no. 1 (Spring 2013): 1–47.

Zakaria, Fareed. *From Wealth to Power—the Unusual Origins of America's World Role*. Princeton, NJ: Princeton University Press, 1998.

Zhang Feng. "The Tsinghua Approach and the Inception of Chinese Theories of International Relations." *Chinese Journal of International Politics* 5, no. 1 (2012): 73–103.

Zhao Guangcheng and Fu Ruihong. "Guoji Tixi de Jieguoxing Bianhua Xilun" [Analysis on structural changes in international system]. *Xiandai Guoji Guanxi* [Contemporary International Relations], no. 8 (2011): 32–38.

Zhao Pi. "Guanyu Xin Junshi Biange Ruogan Wenti de Zhanlue Sikao" [Strategic thinking on certain military reforms]. *Zhanlue Yanjiu* [Strategic Studies], no. 2 (2013): 9–19.

Zhonghua Renmin Gongheguo Xianfa (Constitution of the People's Republic of China). People.com, March 22, 2018. http://sz.people.com.cn/n2/2018/0322/c202846-31369478.html.

Zhu Feng. "E Ge Chongtu de Guoji Zhengzhi Jiedu" [An interpretation of the Russia-Georgia conflict from the perspective of international politics]. *Xiandai Guoji Guanxi* [Contemporary International Relations], no. 11 (2008): 6–12.

Zhou Caizhu and Qi Ruirui. *Mozi Quanyi* [Full translation of *Mozi*]. Guiyang: Guizhou People's Publishing House, 1995.

INDEX

Abe, Shinzo 20, 86, 140
Abkhazia 119
Abyssinia (Ethiopia) 184
Adams, John Quincy 23
Adrianople 239n28
Aegean Sea 239n28
Afghanistan War 186, 187
Africa 26, 95, 147, 186, 201
    East Africa 214
    South Africa 60, 149, 186
Africa, the Caribbean, and the Pacific (ACP)
    147
Agadir Crisis 183
aggressive leadership 30, 32, 36, 47, 52, 102,
    193–194
Albania 239n28
Allison, Graham 64, 149, 152
Amstutz, Mark R. 5
anarchical system 3, 51, 62, 64, 66, 74, 79,
    82, 105, 118, 148, 192, 194
anemocracy xiv, 40, 43–46, 48, 52, 108, 117,
    121, 123, 176, 178, 195
annexation 20, 77, 89, 115, 121, 159, 161–64,
    170, 180, 182, 185
Anti-Ballistic Missile Treaty (ABM) 71
anti-establishmentarianism 50, 101, 129, 137,
    153, 203
Anti-France Coalition 159, 160, 164
Appelbaum, Yoni 129, 137
Arab Spring 18, 130
ASEAN 91, 97, 199
Asia 93, 98, 131, 186, 202
Asia-Pacific 41, 98
Australia 60, 61, 130, 131
Austria 169, 182
Austria-Hungary 239n23

ba (霸 hegemon) 49
badao (霸道 principle of hegemony) 48
Balkan War 183, 239n28

Bao Si 46, 207
Bay of Pigs 186
Belgrade 98
benevolence 48–49, 58, 134, 145–46, 149,
    154
Bergsten, C. Fred 137
bipolar 57–59, 82, 87–88, 94, 96–97, 99,
    102–3, 139, 153, 156, 158–59, 161, 163–65,
    168–71, 178, 184, 188, 198–99, 203, 205,
    236n11
bipolarization 81–87, 93–103, 136, 143, 145,
    153, 156, 172, 188, 198, 201, 203
Black Sea 239n28
Boer War 183, 239n28
Brazil 60
Brexit 60, 129, 205
BRICS 93
Britain (UK) 18–19, 38, 59–60, 95, 99, 129,
    169–70, 181–83, 187, 204–5, 239nn23 and
    28
Brostrom, Jannika 3, 6
Brown, Kerry 32
Bulgaria 239n28
Bull, Hedley, 75
Bush, George H. W. 37, 74, 85
Bush, George W 15, 18, 37, 71, 85, 90, 105,
    121, 202, 228n3
Buzan, Barry 157

Caliphate Empire 163
Cambodia 186
Canada 18, 61, 95
Cape 239n28
Carr, Edward, 5–6
charismatic authority 17
Charlie Hebdo 151
cheng (诚 crediility) 135
Chimerica 137, 200
China-Vietnam War 186
China's Peaceful Development 134

Chinese traditional values 50, 135–36, 138, 145, 154
  benevolence 48–49, 58, 134, 145–46, 149, 154
  righteousness 134, 145–146, 149–150, 154
  rites 23, 117, 145, 151–152, 154, 228n11
Churchill, Winston 42, 95
CIA 142
city-states 87, 159–60, 163, 197
civicism 139, 204
civility 151–154
classical realism 3–4, 6, 23, 68
Clausewitz, Carl Von 3
Clinton, Bill 37, 41, 71, 85, 90, 121–22
Clinton, W. David 3
communism 101, 127, 129, 139, 204
comprehensive capability 13–15, 24, 26–27, 31, 33–34, 40–41, 47, 51, 56–57, 59–60, 78, 82, 85–86, 98, 131, 133, 191, 193, 198
Confucianism 127, 134, 146, 149, 207, 212
Confucius 22, 101, 110, 151, 207, 211–213
Congo 201, 239n28
conservative leadership 31, 34–35, 47, 193
Convention of Washington Naval Arms Limitation 183, 239n29
Convention on the Prohibition of the Development, Production, Stockpiling and Use of Chemical Weapons and on Their Destruction (CWC) 110
Corollary 1 56, 79, 81–82, 192
Corollary 2 61–62, 64, 79, 82, 100, 194
Corollary 3 67, 79, 104, 194
Corollary 4 72, 79, 126, 137, 196
Crimea 89
Crimean War 95
Cuba 91, 111, 115, 239n28
cultural capacity 57
Cultural Revolution 32
Cyrenaica 239n28
Czechoslovakia 184, 186

Daoism 30, 52, 149
  Tao Te Ching 34, 212
democratic peace 187
Deng Xiaoping 27, 101, 133
di (帝 emperor) 49
Diaoyu/Senkaku Islands 15, 91, 170
differential growth 12, 55–56, 165, 192, 193–94
direct war 88–90, 100, 102, 200
Doklam area 142
dong shi xiao pin (东施效颦 an ugly girl imitates a beauty's frown) 144

Dougherty, James E. 105
Duke Huan of Qi 45, 207–08, 223n8
Duke Wen of Jin 223n8

East Asia 48, 96–99, 156–57, 198–99, 237n14
economic capability 41
economic determinism 31, 34, 52
economic pragmatism 133, 136, 139, 204
Egypt 18, 63, 201
Eight Allied Powers Invasion of China 239
Eighteenth Party Congress 134
El-Sadat, Anwar 38
Emperor Taizong of the Tang Dynasty 31, 208
enfeoffment 159, 163
Erdogan, Recep Tayyip 87, 140, 142
Eritrea-Ethiopian War 187
ethical foundation 10
  authority/subversion 10, 217n30
  care/harm 10, 216n30
  fairness/cheating 10, 217n30
  loyalty/betrayal 10, 217n30
  sanctity/degradation 10, 217n30
Eurasia 14, 97, 201
Europe 20, 64, 93–99, 101, 127–29, 153, 156–57, 159–60, 162, 198–99, 237n14
  Eastern Europe 93–94
  European Community (EC) 147
  European Union (EU) 16, 18, 94, 97, 144, 187, 205
  Western Europe 128, 169
example-imitation 113–14, 120, 124, 144, 194
external inducement 106–7

fairness 10, 145–47, 149–50, 154, 217n30
fascism 127, 129
fen fa you wei (奋发有为 striving for achievement) 134
Ferguson, Niall 137
feudalism 162
Finnemore, Martha 105
Fiorina, Morris 27
five service norms 174–75, 182
  Dian, Hou, Bin (宾), *Yao* (要), and *Huang* (荒) 156, 174–76, 237–238n3
  Hou (侯), *Dia* (甸), *Nan* (男), *Cai* (采), and *Wei* (卫) 175
five service system 156, 237–38, 237n3
four Asian tigers 98
France 1, 19, 59–60, 95, 99, 164, 169–70, 182–83, 201, 204–05, 239nn23, 28 and 29
Friedman, Thomas 46
FTA 202

G-2 137, 200
G20 93
Gallup 57
Geneva Convention 10, 115
Genghis Khan of the Mongol Empire 32
Georgia 119, 187
Germany 19, 44, 60, 64, 93, 97, 99, 169, 182,
    184, 205, 239n23 and 28
        East Germany 94
        West Germany 63, 94
Gilpin, Robert 2, 5, 12, 63, 75, 113, 158,
    215–17
Global Fortune 500 201
global governance 144, 153, 200, 204–5
global leadership 9, 98, 199–200, 205
Global Times 143
globalization 52, 90–92, 100, 102, 150, 199,
    201, 206
glorious isolation 181
Gordon, Philip 32
Graham, Jesse 10
Grand Strategies of China's Rise 101
Greece 54, 87, 239n28
Guam 239n28
Guanzi (Guan Zhong) 39, 43, 49, 54, 56, 168,
    208
Gulf War 21, 115, 186–87

Hagan, Joe 27–28
Han Dynasty 99, 207
Hapsburg Dynasty 160, 181
hard power 13–14
hegemonic leadership 44–45, 119–20, 169
hegemony xiv, 2, 14, 25, 27, 40, 43, 48–49,
    52, 64, 77, 89, 108, 119, 121, 123, 174, 176,
    195
        benevolent hegemon 49
Hermann, Margaret 27–28
Hitler, Adolf 27, 47, 95
Hobbesian culture 120–21
Hoffman, Stanley 157
Hogeveen, Jeremy 38
Hohenzollern Dynasty 176, 197
Hong Kong 97–98, 187
Hu Jintao 132
Hu Yaobang 133
Huang (皇 great ruler) 49
Huaxia (China, Chinese) 159, 237n14
Huhai (Emperor of the Qin Dynasty) 168
hui (惠 beneficence) 135
humane authority xiv, 40, 43–45, 47–53, 66,
    108–09, 111, 118–19, 121, 123, 127, 134, 136,
    174, 176, 178, 195, 206

humanitarian intervention 123
Hun 99
Hungary 169, 186, 239n23
Hussein, Saddam 18, 20–21

Ikenberry, G. John 46, 106–7, 114
imperial system 163
imperialist leadership 169
inactive leadership 30, 33–34, 47, 193
India 19, 54, 60, 63, 71, 87, 99, 105, 114, 140,
    141–42, 163, 186, 201
inherited traits 68
Innocence of Muslims 151
institutional arrangement 76
internalization 106–7, 112–14, 123–24
international authority 17–19, 21–24, 40, 42,
    47, 51
        interstate authority 179
international configuration xiv, 54–55, 57–
    59, 74, 77–79, 82, 97, 102, 156, 158, 161,
    164–69, 171–72, 181, 184, 188, 191–92
international institution 76, 148, 203, 206
international order 6, 17, 42–45, 48, 55, 62–
    80, 104, 126–27, 131, 151–55, 171–72, 184,
    188, 195–96, 202–5
international power transition xiv, 78
international society 29, 75, 77–78, 80, 108–
    9, 111, 114, 124, 148, 153, 192
international system change 156
        component change 156, 158–59, 163–
        65, 171, 196
        interaction change 158
        system transformation (system change)
        71, 155–56, 158–66, 170–74, 177, 184,
        188, 196–97
Iran 71, 120, 138, 141, 186 201
Iraq 18, 21, 115, 148, 186–87
Islamic fundamentalism 129, 153,
Island of Crete 239n28
Israel 20, 38, 186, 201
Israeli invasion of Lebanon 187
Italo-Turkish War 183, 239n28
Italy 63–64, 169–70, 182–84, 239n23

Jackson, Robert H. 26, 46
Jacques, Martin 101
Japan 15–16, 20, 44, 60, 63–64, 83, 86, 91,
    97–99, 140, 169–70, 183–84, 202, 205,
    239n23
Jigong Moufu 175
Jinghao Conference 174
Johnson, Lyndon B. 105
jueqi (崛起 rise) 34

Jurchen Empire 161
justice 3–4, 6, 9, 22, 43, 66, 118, 145–46,
    148–50, 154, 164, 217, 234n, 235n

Kagan, Robert 84
Kalevi Holsti 177
Kang, David 157
Kantian culture 120
keeping a low profile 27, 133–35
Keltner, Dacher 38
Kennan, George 3
Kennedy, Paul 1
Keohane, Nannerl 9, 28
Keohane, Robert O. 91
Khong, Yuen Foong 188
Kim Jong Un 143
Kim Yo Jong 143
King Cheng of Zhou Dynasty 175, 209
King Goujian of Yue 223n8
King Helü of Wu 223n8
King Hui of Qin 209
King Huiwen of Qin 209, 213
King Huiwen of Zhao 117, 209
King Jie of the Xia Dynasty 121, 209–10
King Kang of Zhou Dynasty 175, 209–10
King Li of Zhou Dynasty 176, 210–11
King Mu of Zhou Dynasty 175–76, 210, 213
King Nan of Zhou Dynasty 180
King Tang of Shang Dynasty 174–75, 209–
    10
King Wu of Zhou Dynasty 174–75, 211–12
King Xuan of Zhou Dynasty 176, 182, 207,
    211
King You of Zhou Dynasty 46, 176–78, 207,
    211
King Yu of the Xia Dynasty 54, 118, 211
King Zhao of Zhou Dynasty 175, 238n5
King Zhou of Shang Dynasty 121, 211–12
King Zhuang of Chu 223n8
Korean War 186
Krasner, Stephen D. 108
Kuiqiu Alliance 178–79, 222n44
Kupchan, Charles A. 106–7, 114
Kuwait 20, 115
Kyoto Protocol 147

La Rochefoucauld, François de 45
Lake, David A. 16, 84
Laozi 34, 101, 212
Latin America 115, 128, 139, 186, 204
leading by example 22, 70, 114, 124, 134
League of Nations 121, 169–70, 183
    Covenant of the League of Nations 183

Lebow, Richard Ned 2, 3, 6, 168
Leonard, Mark 101
li wen lai xue (礼闻来学 come to learn rites)
    23
Liang Qichao 101
liberalist values xv, 31, 50, 101, 127–40, 145–
    47, 150, 153, 203–4
Libya 118, 146, 187
Little, Richard 157
Lockean culture 120–21
Lomé Convention 147
Lüshi Chunqiu (spring and autumn of Master
    Lü) 118, 212

Macedonia 239n28
Mackinder, Halford John 93
magisterium 159, 162
Mahbubani, Kishore 140
mainstream values xv, 76, 126, 136, 153, 203
Manchu 99, 210
Mao Zedong 32, 38, 63, 101
Mar-a-Lago 143
Marshall Plan 185
Marxism 31, 132, 134, 138
Mearsheimer, John 5, 64
Mencius 49, 126, 149, 212–13
Merkel, Angela 42
Metz, Steven 21
Middle Ages 159, 162
Middle East 18, 98, 131, 139, 153, 156, 201,
    204
military capability 15, 63, 66, 99–100, 180,
    202
millennials 51, 130, 153
Ming Dynasty 99, 210, 214
McCaffery, Edward J. 84
Modi, Narendra 87, 140–41
Monarch 163
Monterio, Nuno P. 84
Montenegro 239n28
Moon, Chung-in 101
moral realism xiv 2, 5–8, 78, 215n4, 217n36
morality
    governmental morality 8–10, 24, 26,
        192–93
    individual morality 24
    national morality 9, 24
    private morality 8, 24
    public morality 8, 24
    universal morality, 5, 9–10, 23
Morgenthau, Hans J. 3–5, 11–12, 54
Moroccan Crisis 183, 239n28
Moscow Protocol 183

motivation 7, 30, 67, 79, 104, 114, 191–94, 199
  because-of motives 105
  in-order-to motives 105
Mount Li 177
Moism 149
Mozi 119, 212
Mubarak, Mohammed Hosni 18
Mughal Empire 60, 163
multipolar 57, 159, 161, 163–65, 177, 179–81,
  184, 192
Mundell, Robert 157
Murray, Williamson 39
Muslim states 163
Myanmar 187

NAFTA 137, 202
Natal 239n28
nation-states 158–60, 162–63, 165, 171, 181,
  185, 203, 205
National Defense Strategy 139
national interests 6, 8–9, 12–15, 26, 61, 66–
  68, 106, 109, 142, 193, 204
National Missile Defense system (NMD) 71
national rejuvenation 15, 36, 199
National Security Strategy 99
nationalism 127, 129, 133, 153
Niebuhr, Reinhold 3, 8
Nineteenth Party Congress 132, 135, 138
Nixon, Richard 38
Nonaligned Movement 65
nonalignment principle 35, 41, 65, 87, 199
nonalliance 221
noninterference and nonannexation 159,
  163
normative persuasion 106–7, 114
North Atlantic Treaty Organization (NATO)
  10, 41–42, 58, 94–95, 119, 122, 185, 187,
North Korea (DPRK) 71, 89, 91, 110, 114,
  143–44, 200
Nurhachi of Later Jin 32, 210
nurtured traits 68
Nye, Joseph S 13–14, 22, 217–18, 225.

Obama, Barack 18, 37, 41, 57, 69, 84–86, 89–
  90, 98–99, 121–122
Oceania 61
offensive strategies 64
Olympic Games 73, 143, 147
one-man decision-making 140–42, 145, 153,
  204
opening-up principle 132,
operational capability 24
Orange Free State 239n28

Oslo Accords 38
Ottoman Empire 59, 163, 169, 181 239n28
Owen, David 38

Paine, Thomas 23
Pakistan 186
Palestine 20, 38
punishment-maintenance 113, 115, 120, 124,
  194
Paris Climate Agreement 46, 137, 205
Pence, Mike 143
Persian Empire 160, 163, 181
Persian Gulf War 115, 186–87
Pew Research Center 57
Pfaltzgraff, Robert, L.105
Philippines 239n28
pluralists 3
Poland 184
polarization 150, 201
political capability 13, 26, 40, 56, 94, 191
political determinism 31, 52, 215n4
political leadership xiv, 2, 4, 11, 13, 16, 24–29,
  32, 37, 51, 55–56, 61, 63, 66, 79, 82, 85,
  134, 165–66, 172, 174, 190–91, 206
populism 101, 129, 139, 153, 204
Port Arthur 239n28
Portugal 1, 182
post-Caliphate Times 159, 161
post-Cold War 14, 57, 59, 91, 96, 103, 123,
  127–28, 156, 158, 184, 187–89, 198, 203,
  205
power redistribution 55, 73, 81, 93, 97, 99,
  102–103, 158, 161, 163, 170, 191, 196–97
proactive leadership 30–31, 35, 47, 193
protectionism 144, 153, 202
proxy war 64, 89, 100, 185–86, 200
Puerto Rico 239n28
Putin, Vladimir Vladimirovich 38, 86, 94,
  119, 140
Pyeongchang 143

Qin (亲 closeness) 135
Qin Dynasty 37, 159, 161, 168, 174, 180, 208
Qing Dynasty 188, 210
quanli (权力 power) 16
Quanrong (tribe) 175–77, 211, 213
quanwei (权威 authority) 16

Rabin, Yitzhak 38
rational authority 17
Rawls, John 145, 148, 150
Reagan, Ronald Wilson 85, 88
reform capability 198

ren (仁 benevolence) 134
ren yi qun fen (人以群分 human beings grouped by types) 28
Rice, Susan 85
righteousness 134, 145–46, 149–50, 154
rising state's dilemma 33, 52, 73
rites 23, 117, 145, 150–52, 154
Roman Empire 59, 159, 162, 237n14
Romanoff Dynasty 160, 181
Rong (容 inclusiveness) 135
Roosevelt, Franklin 27, 44, 127, 181
Rosberg, Carl G. 26, 46
royal state 159, 163, 174, 180, 237n14
Rudd, Kevin 131
Russia 14, 18–19, 38, 41, 57, 60, 65, 86, 95, 97–99, 119, 140, 142, 144, 182–83, 201, 204–5, 239nn23 and 28

Safavid Empire163
Sakhalin Island 239n28
Saudi Arabia 60, 111, 130, 187, 201
Schelling, Thomas C. 88
secularism 129, 139, 204
self-help 62, 79, 82, 192, 194
separatist movements 115, 187
Serbia 239n28
Shang Dynasty 121, 174, 209, 210, 211, 212
Shepard, Clough 63
Shepsle, Kenneth 27
Shias 139, 204
Sikkink, Kathryn 105, 228
Sima Cuo 213
Singapore 98, 140
Singer, David 157
Sino-Indian War 186
smart power 14
Snyder, Richard C 105
social Darwinism 32, 52, 109
socialization 107, 123–24
soft power xiii, 13–14, 22, 101, 131
solidarists 3
Somalia War 187
son of heaven 162, 180,
Song Dynasty 99, 161
South Africa 60, 149, 186, 239n28
South Asia 60, 201, 214
South China Sea 214
South Korea 20, 97–98, 101, 143
South Ossetia 119
sovereignty 15, 20, 76, 144, 153, 158–62, 162, 170–71, 183, 204–5, 239n28
Soviet Union (USSR) 14, 56, 58–60, 64–65, 74, 77, 83, 88–91, 94–95, 98–99, 101–102, 119–20, 122–23, 127, 168–69, 185–86, 199–200
Spanish-American War 183, 239nn23 and 28
Spring and Autumn period 45, 58–59, 114, 117–18, 121, 159, 161–63, 174, 177–80, 185, 207–8, 213–14, 223n8, 237n14, 238n3
Stalin, Joseph 27, 42
Standard & Poor's Financial Services LLC 18
State of Chu 59, 87, 178, 185, 208, 212–14
State of Han 180, 237n14
State of Jin 58–59, 87, 99, 114, 185, 210, 213–14, 223n8
State of Lu 119, 176, 207, 222n44, 238n3
State of Qi 45, 59, 116–17, 163, 178–80, 207–8, 213, 222n44
State of Qin 116–17, 163, 180, 208–9, 212–13
State of Song 212, 222n44
State of Wei 180, 212–13, 222n44
State of Wu 59
State of Xu 179
State of Yue 59
State of Zhao 117, 209
State of Zheng 114, 214, 222n44
statism 139, 204
Stettin in the Baltic 95
Stiglitz, Joseph E 46.
Stockholm Conference 147
strategic credibility 9, 17–24, 29, 40–44, 47, 49, 65–66, 70–71, 74, 110, 117, 119, 134, 136, 140, 144, 153, 185, 193, 195, 204
strategic preference xiv, 6–7, 25–26, 33, 36–37, 39, 47, 52, 61–65, 68–69, 79, 100, 104, 193–194, 200, 202
    avoiding conflicts 34, 36, 52, 193
    enlarging international support 36, 52, 194
    imposing economic impacts 34, 36, 52
    military expansion 36, 52, 184
    striving for achievement 27, 134–135
    structural contradiction 72–73, 79, 126, 137, 196
Sun Xuefeng xv, 33
Sunnis 139, 204
support-reinforcement 113–115, 120, 124, 194
Swoboda, Alexander 157
Syria 110, 118, 130, 148, 187, 204

Taiwan 33, 97–98, 187
Tang Dynasty 31, 208
tao guang yang hui (韬光养晦 keeping a low profile) 133
Thompson, Kenneth W. 3
Thucydides 3

Thucydides's trap 64
traditional authority 17
Transatlantic Trade and Investment Partnership (TTIP) 69
Trans-Pacific Partnership Agreement (TPP) 69, 202
Transvaal 239n28
Treaty for the Renunciation of War 183
Treaty of Versailles 183
Treaty on the Non-Proliferation of Nuclear Weapons (NPT) 105, 114, 129
tributary system 76, 156–57, 180, 188
Trieste in the Adriatic 95
Tripolitania 239n28
Trump, Donald xiii, 9, 14, 18, 25, 32, 37, 41–42, 46, 57, 69, 84, 86, 89–90, 98–99, 110, 121–22, 129, 133, 136–37, 139–41, 143, 152, 171, 198–99, 202, 205
Turkey 87, 140, 201, 239n28
types of international norms 79, 109, 112, 116, 120, 123, 195
    coward-bully 109–10, 117, 122–23, 174, 177–79, 195
    double-standard 45, 109, 111, 115, 117, 119–23, 176, 178–79, 184–89, 195, 205
    moral norms 47, 109–110, 116–18, 192, 195
    realpolitik 46, 52, 66, 109–11, 114–23, 142, 165, 174, 176–77, 179, 181–86, 188, 195
tyrannical leadership 46–47, 116
tyranny xiv, 40, 43–48, 52, 77, 108, 121, 123, 174, 176, 195

Ukraine 89
ultra-leftism 36
UNESCO 137
Union of South Africa 239n28
unipolar 57–9, 82, 84, 94, 96–7, 99, 103, 156, 158–59, 161, 163, 165, 168–69, 171, 174, 177–78, 180, 184, 188, 192, 198
United Nations (UN) 10, 12, 18, 20, 76, 115, 128, 149, 169–70, 171, 202, 205
    UN Charter 115, 128, 171, 205
    UN Security Council 12, 76, 169, 202
US Congress 89, 148, 183, 187

vassal 159, 162–63, 174–80, 237n14, 238n3
Versailles-Washington System 157, 159–60, 162–63, 184
Vienna System 156, 159–60, 162, 164
Vietnam-Cambodia War 186

Waltz, Kenneth 4, 62, 91, 157
Wang (王 humane authority) 49, 134
Wang Qishan 138
Wang Yi 135
wangdao (王道 principle of humane authority) 48
War in Afghanistan 187
War in Georgia 187
War in Kosovo 187
War in Syria 187
Warring States 116–17, 121, 159, 161–62, 174, 177, 179–80, 183, 188, 208–9, 213
Warsaw Pact 122
Weber, Max 9, 17
wei (伪 nurtured traits) 68
Wendt, Alexander 68, 112–13, 120–21, 157
West Indies 239n28
Westphalia System 156, 159, 164
Westphalia Treaty 160–61
Wilhelm II (Emperor of Germany) 182
Wilson, Woodrow 23, 183
Winter Olympic Games 143
World Health Organization 8
world-island 93
World Trade Organization (WTO) 10, 69, 205
World War I 23, 64, 91, 93, 121–22, 157, 160, 169–70, 181–84
World War II 19–20, 23, 27, 42, 44, 47, 64, 77, 89, 93, 95–96, 98, 107, 114, 121–23, 128–29, 157, 160, 163, 169–71, 181, 184, 188
wu wei er zhi (无为而治 laissez-faire) 30, 127

xing (性 inherited traits) 68
xing mie guo (兴灭国 revival of a states) 44
xiong cai da lue (雄才大略 great talent and bold vision) 49
Xunzi (Xun Kuang) 22, 25, 27, 33, 39, 43, 49, 68, 109, 118, 151, 155, 186, 213

Yalta System 157, 159–60, 163, 170–72, 184, 188, 203, 205
Yang Chengxu 156
Yang Jiechi 93
Yarhi-Milo, Keren 141
Yeltsin, Boris Nikolayevich 119
Yemen 118, 130, 187
yi (义 righteousness) 134
yi jing cu zheng (以经促政 improving political relations through economic cooperation) 34
Ying Zheng (Emperor of the Qin) 32, 180

yishen zuoze (以身作则 leading by example)
  22
Yu Qing 117
Yuan Dynasty 161
Yugoslavia 186

Zeng Guopan 101
zero-sum 72, 79, 126, 137, 196

Zhao Xuanzi 114, 214
Zheng He 208, 214
Zheng Zijia 114, 214
Zhou Dynasty 46, 174–77, 179–80, 182, 207,
  209–13
    Western Zhou Dynasty 44, 159, 163,
      174, 177–79, 188, 207, 211
Zuo Zhuan (the chronicle of Zuo) 117

A NOTE ON THE TYPE

This book has been composed in Adobe Text and Gotham. Adobe Text, designed by Robert Slimbach for Adobe, bridges the gap between fifteenth- and sixteenth-century calligraphic and eighteenth-century Modern styles. Gotham, inspired by New York street signs, was designed by Tobias Frere-Jones for Hoefler & Co.